MY COUNTRY IS THE WORLD

GARRY DAVIS

Independence is my happiness and I view things as they are, without regard to place or person; my country is the world . . .
—THOMAS PAINE: *The Rights of Man*

TO YOU

© 1961 by Garry Davis

All rights reserved. This book, or parts thereof, must not be reproduced in any form without permission.

First Printing, 1961
G.P. Putnam's Sons, N.Y., N.Y.
Library of Congress Catalog Number: 61-8341
Longmans, Green & Co., Toronto
McDonald's, London

Second Printing, 1984
Juniper Ledge Publishing Co., Sorrento, ME
L.C.: 84-082393

ACKNOWLEDGMENTS

I wish to express my grateful acknowledgment and thanks to friends throughout the world, many of whom not only encouraged me to write this book but offered practical provision during its various work phases. Especially I want to thank my seven voluntary secretaries since 1950 when this book was begun: Mr. Shanti Krishnan, Miss Ruth Allanbrook, Miss Esther Peter, Miss Audrey Peters, Miss Gloria Sandler, Miss Sylvia Burnell and Miss Muriel Tredwell. Finally, to my friend and editor, William Honan, without whose ruthless, yet perceptive blue pencil the mass of accumulated material over the years might still be lying in numerous cartons in the basement, go my deep respects and grateful thanks.

G.D.

LIST OF PLATES

Certificate showing loss of U.S. Nationality	*following page*		32
The Author on U.N. territory, Paris, 1948	,,	,,	32
The World Citizen Identity Card	,,	,,	48
The Author in front of Buckingham Palace	,,	,,	48
Samples from the World Passport	,,	,,	72
British "official" identity document	,,	,,	128
Letter from Ecuadorean Ambassador to Washington	,,	,,	128
The Author taking the Oath of Allegiance to World Government	,,	,,	144
The Author at Amsterdam Airport	,,	,,	144
On release from jail in Hanover	,,	,,	176
The Author camping on Capri	,,	,,	176
The World Credit	,,	,,	192

PROLOGUE

A young man, a United States citizen, once asked my advice about a problem.

"I want to travel to Bulgaria," he said.

"What stops you?" I asked.

In reply he handed me his passport, on one page of which was affixed a rubber stamp stating that the passport was restricted for travel to Bulgaria along with several other nations.

"How does this prevent you from travelling to Bulgaria?" I asked.

"They won't let me!" he exclaimed. "That damn restriction! See for yourself."

"Yes, I see," I said, "but if you really want to go to Bulgaria, come back in three days with your passport, and I'll fix it."

On the third day, he and his passport were back. Before he could protest, I produced a rubber stamp and quickly stamped the restricted page directly beneath the restriction.

"Hey, what the hell are you doing?" he exploded. "That's illegal. You can't do that."

"Here, read it," I said, handing it back. He did so, stood for a moment perplexed, then burst into laughter.

"Of course, of course," he said. "Don't know why I didn't see it. Thanks a million." The next time I heard from him was six months later after he had returned from Bulgaria.

The stamp I had affixed on his passport read: *The above restriction is hereby removed.*

You might say that this book is merely an enlargement on the same theme.

I think this is what Henry Thoreau had in mind when he wrote that if *"one* HONEST man ... ceasing to hold slaves, were actually to withdraw from this copartnership, and be locked up in the county jail thereby, it would be the abolition of slavery in America."

I think this is what the Continental Congress in Philadelphia, on July 4, 1776, meant by the words, "When, in the course of human events, it becomes necessary for one people to dissolve the political bands which have connected them with another..." I think also that this is what Article X of the United States Constitution means when it says: "The powers not delegated to the United States by the Constitution, nor prohibited by it to the States, are reserved to the States respectively, *or to the people.*" (My italics.)

I think this is what Jesus Christ meant when he said: "The Truth shall set you free."

The above restriction is hereby removed.

To my way of thinking, if those six words spell revolt, I cannot but call myself a revolutionary.

Homo sapiens, man calls himself. *Sapiens:* knowing: the perception of truth. But one of the tragedies of our times is that modern man—as man of ages past—doesn't know himself. He has even lost confidence in his own, innate capacity. He restricts himself. And only then does he yearn to be free.

Man's deadliest, self-imposed, restrictive device is nationalism.

You and I may be fellow humans, but we are not fellow nationalists. I am a fellow who wilfully withdrew from the co-partnership of citizen and national state and declared himself a world citizen. With a nod to Thoreau's discernment, I have, for my trouble, hung my hat in eleven county jails in as many countries plus two ships' brigs. If spending time in county-jails-of-the-world, however, would further the understanding of one world and one mankind, I would gladly forfeit my freedom again this very day. For it is my considered opinion that this understanding alone is the *sine qua non* of world peace. You are about to join me in my adventures as an unrestricted, wilfully denationalised citizen in the mid-twentieth century razor-edge world between nations It is a lonely, bizarre world, untrod by human feet, unthought by human mind. But in it, tenuous, fragile yet fulfilling, resides world peace. We, this world and I, became friends and lovers. Thus was I able to experience this noble ideal as personal, immediate, actual, and if this book has any uniqueness, it is in this relationship.

How did it all begin and what originally motivated me? To be honest I don't know all the answers, and doubtless I never will. Some will call me a natural-born rebel. Others will see in me an incorrigibly naïve idealist, childish in his acceptance of the principle that man is fundamentally reasonable, good and peaceful. And still others, as will be seen, have described me in far less complimentary terms.

In writing about some of it, I discovered—I confess somewhat to my regret—that a book is not a life; an autobiography is not a mirror. It is rather like a kaleidoscope, bits of coloured glass which, when held up to the light of scrutiny, form patterns of behaviour. After twisting the box this way and that, you recognize the shape and colour of the particular bits. But while the bits, the appearances, can be seen and understood, the whole remains elusive and ever changing. I think this is the way with a man's autobiography.

Then, the first person singular was often uncomfortable and restricting in itself. Which came first, the "I," the eye, or the why? One wants naturally to be liked and appreciated, especially if one has suffered misinterpretation in the past. On the other hand, if that were all, a book wouldn't be worth the writing, much less the reading. Now that all the words are in place, I think what I really sought was for you, through me, to be able to re-examine your own loyalties, to think about you *and* the world, you *in* the world, your world, my world, *our* world. Yet the last thing I wanted to write was a sermon or an essay. I hope I haven't.

If you have any restrictions artificially imposed on your own free intelligence, I want this book to be the rubber stamp which reads: *The above restriction is hereby removed.*

And so, my fellow citizen of this world and brother man, whoever you are and wherever you may be, in honesty and confidence, I commend myself, my ideas and my few experiences, insofar as poor words can convey them, to your earnest discernment. It is an act of faith.

I was "born" a World Citizen on May 25, 1948. My "conception," however, took place almost seventeen years ago over Peenemünde...

I

The sky was suddenly dark. A burst of flak opened in slow motion in front of us like a black rose from hell. Unavoidably we churned into its very heart, fragmentation smacking the fuselage of our B-17 with a sickening patter.

Instinctively, my left hand shoved the throttle forward as my right hand hauled the heavy wheel back and to starboard. Old, battle-worn Calamity Jane roared out of formation. Lindy, my pilot, grabbed the wheel as my eyes darted over the instrument panel.

I pressed the intercom button. "Number Three engine gone and Two going. Oil temperature on all engines rising ... fast. Superchargers out. Losing altitude about ... 700 per minute."

Rocky, our engineer, tapped my shoulder. He pointed out the window. I winced, then found my voice. "Left main tank hit! Spraying gas! Number Two on fire!"

"Feather Two. Feather Three," Lindy's voice ripped in my ears. My fingers got busy. The oxygen mask seemed to be pressing my face like a cast.

"How's gas?" called Lindy frantically as he began re-trimming the ship.

"About 800 gallons without the left main. Not enough for the North Sea and just barely enough for a beeline ... on the deck."

"Means straight through the goddam Ruhr."

"Right."

"Navigator to pilot."

"Come in, Mac."

"If things get too hot, there's Sweden 'cross the bay."

"Yeah, I know."

We all knew the co-ordinates to Sweden.

It was August, 1944. We were flying at 29,000 feet and our oil demolitions had just hit Peenemünde, Dr. Wernher von Braun's heavy-water experimental station, and Lord knows what else. Our group had gone in fourth and Jerry's reception party was in full swing.

I looked ahead. Our group was pulling away. We were losing altitude rapidly. Jerry had just developed some new, fast jets which were certain to smell us out over the Ruhr; that is, if ground flak didn't get us first. Escape into neutral Sweden was the only rational choice, but even that was hazardous in our condition.

"Emergency procedure and prepare for crash landing," called Lindy, as he swung old Calamity Jane out over the Baltic Sea, nursing his way toward Sweden.

I sat back in my seat wearily. Landing in a neutral country meant we would be interned and, according to the Geneva Convention, restricted from combat missions even if we should escape. The war would be over for us. In one sense, I didn't want that to happen. I hadn't settled my score yet with Jerry. When Bud, my brother, was killed at Salerno, his old tub of a destroyer blown to Kingdom Come in the early hours of the invasion, I prayed for a chance to exact revenge.

But in another sense, I was glad to be heading for Sweden—or at least glad to have been forced into that predicament. Perhaps my "score" never could be settled. Perhaps dropping incendiary bombs on soldiers and civilians alike was not the way to settle it. Ever since my first mission over Brandenburg, I had felt pangs of conscience, and, underneath all the grief, emotionalism and propaganda-nourished hatred, I had begun to question the morality of punishing the German people with our superior fire power. How many bombs had I dropped? How many men, women and children had I murdered? Wasn't there another way, I kept asking myself.

An hour later, after putting .45 slugs through our new-fangled radar units, we were being escorted by a group of bumble-bee-like Swedish fighters down to a neutral field.

I had done my last killing.

Some three months after the Peenemünde raid, my mother happened to be making a bond-raising broadcast with Paul Muni at the Broadway Theatre. Her script read that she had lost one son at Salerno, another was stationed at West Point, and a third was interned in a neutral country.

Marjorie, my youngest sister, sped down the aisle of the

crowded theatre five minutes before air time. "Mother! Mother!" she called as she spied her in the first row, talking with friends.

"Well, what is it, dear?"

"Mother, listen," Marge said breathlessly. "If you had one wish in the world, just one wish, what would you wish for?"

Mother turned pale and choked. "For Garry to be here."

Marge turned to Dad and me coming down the aisle. Mother gave a gasp and came rushing up to embrace me. All eyes turned to us, and I brushed back the tears with embarrassment. I was home at last, sporting an "Escapee Boot" on the breast pocket of my uniform.

That night we had a homecoming celebration at Lindy's restaurant on Broadway. Everything I had always known and loved was there that November night: the glitter, the lights, good food, well-dressed show people, gaiety and frivolity.

"Garry hasn't changed a bit..."

"Same old clown..."

"I always said it'd take more than a war to change him..."

But of course I had changed. And being back on Broadway in a famous theatrical restaurant brought the contrast into focus. As the son of Meyer Davis, one of the country's most successful band leaders, show business had seemed a natural vocation for me. At home, my brothers and I were always mixing with theatrical celebrities, entertaining and spoofing them. After graduating from Episcopal Academy in Overbrook, where I was more renowned for my portrayal of Dick Deadeye than my scholarship, I had studied acting at the Carnegie Institute of Technology. My first Broadway "break" came in 1940 when, as Danny Kaye's understudy in *Let's Face It*, I took over the night Danny came down with laryngitis. There were fan letters, a Columbia screen test offer, and feelers for the lead in a comedy planned for the next season. My stage career had seemed assured, except for the fact that a few weeks later I was classified 1-A and drafted.

Now, here I was in Lindy's, trying to recapture the past.

"Why don't you go on *We, The People*, Garry?" someone asked. "You know, Returning War Hero."

"Great," I said.

"You must have had some thrilling experiences."

"Yes, I suppose I have," I replied, and then under the twinkling lights I found myself telling how a B-17 blew up on our wing over Brandenburg from a direct hit in the main tank, a great red flame devouring the cockpit as the bombardier and navigator scurried around like trapped rats in the forward blister looking for a way out that didn't exist. There was an embarrassed silence. What's the matter with me? I asked myself. That's not a joke! Someone ordered another round of drinks. The light conversation picked up, but *We, The People* somehow didn't get mentioned again. I tried to get back into the spirit of frivolity but caught myself thinking of this being our first family reunion without my brother Bud.

The war did not last long after that November evening. Like most veterans I locked away my memories of it and began picking up the threads of my interrupted career. My first post-war show was the Ray Bolger revue, *Three To Make Ready*, where, after several months, I won featured billing as a comedian. Off-stage, however, I was a sober clown indeed. The defensive shell I had built around my own involvement with the war was steadily chipped away by the bristling headlines of the post-war years. Berlin became the focal point of the Cold War. There was trouble brewing in Korea, Trieste, Israel, Jordan, Algeria, Kashmir, Malaya, and Kenya. Moreover, the United Nations seemed to have been stillborn, a glorified *Kaffeeklatsch* incapable of solving major problems. The world I had fought to restore to health, and for which my brother had died, was, only a few short years later, already festering with new sores.

I felt personally responsible. Why, exactly, I cannot say. Perhaps it was because I was a professional entertainer, because the contrast between making people laugh and forget and the necessity of urging them to sit up and take notice of the world around them was unavoidable and, to me, deeply mocking. Or perhaps it was what I had seen of the war—no more than many of my comrades to be sure, but sufficient to make me feel that I was obligated to communicate the horrors I had seen. Or indeed, it may have been the loss of Bud and at least a dozen other close friends whose corpses had briefly decorated barbed-wire entanglements in Italy, France, the Pacific Islands. Now, already, they were almost forgotten except for their names, which collected dust in brass relief on the honour rolls of small-town post offices and public parks.

These were *my* friends, *my* generation, *my* flesh and blood. No one else, it seemed, really understood: not even the widows who wept silently at night; nor the mothers whose hair had turned bone white; no one *really* understood except those of us who had been out there with them and heard them laugh the night before *it* happened, heard them jeer obscenities and unpatriotic slogans that might have started a Congressional investigation, and then seen them die the next morning with sighs of relief that the goddam thing had finally come to an end; no one who counted really understood and no one who knew the truth about the war knew how to tell it. There was only me. It came down to that. And yet even I did not know what to do about it. The only thing that was clear in my mind was that I, Garry Davis, was in some way personally responsible for the march of nations toward World War Three. I was not immune because I was in show business, a "nonstrategic" profession. I was not immune because I had "done my patriotic duty". U-235 was no respecter of veterans or actors. The world itself and every city and town and hamlet in it was now on the front line. According to the best brains on the planet, World War Three was really to be the war to end wars. Communist or capitalist, black or white, king or pauper, sage or fool, man, woman, or child, there would be no innocent bystanders in World War Three. And yet, somehow I felt I was only standing by during the awful preparations. It was intolerable to me.

During the fall of 1947 I looked hard, both at myself and at the world about me. Neither sight was reassuring. My very ignorance appalled me. I was stunned at my inability to get reasonable answers to the burning questions of the day. I was disgusted, even horrified, with the superficiality of conversation with my family and friends. What they said was not so much insincere as it was two-dimensional and empty, like arguing where to place the new television set when the house was on fire. In the face of questions of sheer survival, we all seemed to be babbling at each other like fools.

My family and friends in turn became worried about me. Had the "wit" run dry? Was Garry turning serious?

In my new silence, a curious phrase beat faintly inside my mind, a phrase which seemed to echo from nation to nation and in the minds of men around the globe. "One world or none," wrote Wendell Willkie; "One world or none," reaffirmed

Bertrand Russell and Albert Schweitzer; "One world or none," repeated Gandhi and Einstein. And in this, for the first time, I saw the provincialism of my own thinking. It was nation-centric. Rather than "one world or none," the concept of "my country, right or wrong" had dominated my discussions and dinner-table talk. I began to see a beacon through the gloom.

In January 1948, I read Cord Meyer's *Peace or Anarchy*, which proposed to express the idea of "one world or none" by means of a world federation as an alternative to warring nations. At first, I thought this was the cure for our diseased world and I was greatly excited. Of course all nations should join a world federation, I reasoned, just as our individual sovereign states had joined together to form the federal United States! Almost immediately, I volunteered to work for the United World Federalists. I attended meetings, hammered out policy statements, distributed literature, and organized chapters on New York's West Side. But I never joined the U.W.F. Something was missing. World tension was mounting too rapidly and the World Federalists seemed to be moving too slowly. The one world— my world—was about to be blown up any day. I wanted a crusade, not a meeting. I wanted total commitment, not a membership card and a lapel button.

Underneath my impatience and anxiety was a sentence from a book by Emery Reves, *The Anatomy of Peace*, which was "required reading" for all federalists. Reves had written: "We must clarify principles and arrive at axiomatic definitions as to what causes war and what creates peace in human society."

Somehow, I wasn't convinced that the federalists had faced this challenge squarely. To be sure, I would argue with my federalist friends, if the nation-states would relinquish enough of their sovereignty and in a short enough time, war might be narrowly averted. But the roots of war, or the axiomatic definitions as Reves had put it, seemed to me to be inherent in the nation-state itself. And how could nations federate or unite, I argued, if by definition they exist only by being separate and distinct from one another? To eliminate war, I concluded, one would first have to eliminate nations. True federation would accomplish this, but no nation was willing to dissolve itself.

I felt, therefore, that the federation of nations was impossible and that if anything was going to be federated, it would be people, the very people who made up nations. Thus, it seemed to me that the World Federalists were talking when they should have been acting—urging when they should have been personally declaring themselves. The Madisons, Monroes and Jeffersons of this country, I reasoned, had not merely urged a central government for all citizens of the separate states. There had been a point at which America's founding fathers had *declared* it and literally described themselves as "Americans" and not just Virginians or Pennsylvanians. There was a point at which they ceased to be mere proponents of an idea and became practitioners of it. This, the World Federalists were not willing to do. And it was through their default—a default, I felt, as much of moral courage as political sagacity—that I began to see my rôle, my obligation to grasp an idea from the air of advocacy and plant it in the ground of action. I would bring about world government, I reasoned, precisely as all other governments had been brought into being: simply by declaring myself an actual citizen of that government and then behaving like one.

But how?

How did one *practise* "one world" in a broken world? How could one *be* of all humanity and at the same time of a single nation? Weren't the two mutually incompatible? Didn't loyalty to an inclusive humanity preclude loyalty to the exclusive state? Or could one have a dual loyalty as if in two concentric circles, one within the other?

I was not able to answer any of these questions until one day I picked up *The New York Times* and read about Henry Noel, a young Harvard graduate who had renounced his United States citizenship in July 1947 and had begun working as a labourer in Kassel, Germany, rebuilding a bombed-out church. I stared at the newspaper in wonderment. Here was a bold, dramatic and logical protest against the exclusive character of the state. But it was more. It was an affirmation of the fundamental sovereignty of the individual upon which all government rests. Henry Noel, in wilfully casting himself loose from the nation, was now on humanity's side. Here then was the key to action *and* total commitment. In order to become a citizen of the entire world, to declare my prime allegiance to mankind, I would first have to renounce my United States nationality. I would secede from the old and declare the new.

2

I chose Paris. In answer to my inquiry, the Attorney-General of the United States had informed me that a citizen must be on foreign soil in order to renounce his citizenship legally.

Accordingly, May 19, 1948, found me at Place de la Concorde patiently seated under the big roof of the United States Embassy waiting my turn to see Miss Agnes Schneider, the pro-consul assigned to handle passport difficulties for voyaging U.S. citizens. Miss Schneider had been in the consular business for thirty-five years and had seen many Americans in trouble, mostly because they had unwittingly lost their passports.

Miss Schneider beckoned to me and I approached.

"And now, Mr. Davis, how can I help you?"

"I wish to renounce my U.S. nationality."

"You want... but Mr. Davis, we're here to protect Americans... and you're an American citizen."

"I wish to renounce that," I said, "and claim world citizenship."

She was looking at me wide-eyed, her hands spread across her desk.

"Well!" she said as she got up. "Just a moment, Mr. Davis." She disappeared into an inner chamber and returned, beckoning for me to join her. We went into a large private office where sat a middle-aged man in a grey suit, his expression carefully prepared like a frieze.

"Well now, Mr. Davis," he began cosily, "Miss Schneider here tells me you want to renounce your citizenship."

"I do."

"Why?"

"If you'll pardon me, sir," I said, "but isn't this irrelevant? My reasons are of no concern to you as a consular officer. As I understand it, you are here to serve U.S. citizens. Well, I'm a U.S. citizen with a passport to prove it. I wish to be served."

His eyes clouded over. "Well now, Mr. Davis," he started, leaning forward, "I think I can understand how you feel, world conditions and all, eh?" He looked at me sharply. "You're a veteran, aren't you?"

"Yes sir."

"Aaaaaaahhh," he intoned like an opera singer. "Well, suppose we think it over, and I'm sure matters will be satisfactorily straightened out."

"What matters, sir?" I asked.

"Come back Thursday, Davis," he said brusquely. "We'll have to get instructions from Washington."

I left, piqued. It was a stall. On Thursday, May 25, when I returned, I was again ushered into the private office. The Consul was there and greeted me with: "Changed your mind?"

"Of course not. What's the decision from Washington?"

"Oh, we didn't call Washington. Just wanted to give you a little time to cool off."

"That's what I thought," I said, feeling my blood rise. "If I am not given the Oath of Renunciation in the next five minutes, I will report you to Washington myself for neglect of duty. Furthermore, I will give a story to the press that you have refused to abide by the provisions of the Nationality Act of 1940 as set forth by the United States Congress of that year." He looked at Miss Schneider. She shrugged.

Three minutes later, I was standing in front of her desk in the outer office while she dug around for the wording of the Oath.

She asked me to raise my right hand. I did so, but then thought that I should take the Oath on a Bible, and I asked for one. For fifteen minutes a guard searched and finally found a Bible across the street in the Hotel Palais Royal.

At twenty minutes past two o'clock, May 25, 1948, I had seceded from the exclusive national state.

My first reaction to this event was that I felt thirsty. Otherwise nothing seemed to have happened. I was merely one passport lighter. I was still wearing the same shoes and socks. My hair was still red and the Macy's label was still snugly sewn in the collar of my shirt. Furthermore, I had not been struck by lightning nor had the ground swallowed me up. Garry Davis, it seemed, hadn't owed his existence to the little green folder issued by the U.S. State Department after all. My humanity required no documentation and it could not evaporate by crossing artificial frontiers. And yet I was still as much affected by world events as the most rabid nationalist. World War Three might yet engulf me as readily as a soldier in uniform or a newborn doe in the forest.

As I walked out of the Embassy into the little court, I sensed a strange freedom. I remember looking back and seeing the two smartly attired Marines guarding the door. They carried side arms and looked as if they belonged in the Middle Ages. I felt a little sorry for them.

Then I looked up at the American flag flying over their heads. "How many men have responded to that banner, sung its glory, marched beneath it, and died for it?" I asked myself. Flying there alone with no standard above it representing Mankind, it signified for me now only division, aggressiveness, fear, and the terrible consequences.

The American flag on the balustrade no longer claimed my allegiance. The flag that did had not yet been unfurled.

One of the chief objects of my gesture of renunciation was to demonstrate that the nation-state need not be overthrown. For, in fact, it does not exist. Men's minds need only be disabused. The nation-state is a whole-cloth myth, perpetuated by the slavery of tradition, unreasonable loyalties and pieces of paper which at best only pretend to recognize rather than bestow existence upon the individual. If I could show that it was possible for me to survive in the world without papers, cross frontiers without a passport and conduct myself as a free human being without benefit of any national credentials, I would be striking a blow at the very heart of nationalism itself.

So, immediately after my renunciation, I went to the office of the Associated Press to tell the world what I had done. I talked to Bob Wilson, the night editor, telling him I wanted to work in Germany, as had Henry Noel, since I had caused destruction there during the war. He took down everything I said and I found myself becoming a bit nervous. This was my first real taste of the workings of the world press. In the States, our family had become accustomed to publicity, since we were all connected in various ways with show business. But this was not acting from script; this was action from principle. At any moment my welfare, indeed my life, might depend upon my wits and what I told reporters.

I left A.P., wanting to go immediately to the French police to see what was to be done. It was not my intention to break

French law, and being without papers was itself a violation of law. But it was so late in the afternoon that I decided to go first thing in the morning. I slept that night quite illegally.

During the night, at my tiny hotel on rue Blanche, I was introduced brusquely to the fact that A.P. had competitors. My room was on the fifth floor and the phone was on the ground floor. First, United Press called. I gave them my story, then returned to bed. Five minutes later Reuters News Service called. Down I came again. By this time, the little old concierge looked at me as though I were a spy or perhaps something even more intriguing. My story to Reuters was brief. I smiled at the concierge, who had been roused each time the phone rang, and wended my way back to fifth heaven. *Brrrrrinnnng!* International News Service! My story this time was a digest. Dissatisfied with what I had told him, the I.N.S. reporter met me the next morning and followed me around Paris all day.

I went first to the local French Commissariat. There the sergeant told me to go to the Préfecture de Police at the Cité. The I.N.S. man offered to drive me, and off we went.

Once there, a guard directed me to the Bureau des Etrangers, Anglais, Américains. I told him there was a mistake as I was neither *"anglais"* nor *"américain"*, but the guard, listening to my "American Express" French accent, assured me this was the right office. I approached a kindly-looking woman seated behind a large desk. She looked at me inquiringly.

"My name is Garry Davis," I began. "I renounced my U.S. nationality at the Embassy. Now I am stateless. I don't want to break French laws. What shall I do?"

As I talked, her eyes grew wider and wider. There was a moment of silence and then suddenly she began to speak rapidly: "Who are you *really*? Why did you give up your papers? How do I know you're Garry Davis? Anyone could walk in here and say that. Where is your paper that proves your identity?"

I managed timidly, "I have no papers. That's just the point. I've renounced my papers. I think being a human being is more important than having papers. And since I'm here in France as a stranger, I'd like to know what I must do according to French law."

"According to French law," she groaned, "you do not exist. You have no passport, you have no *titre d'identité*. You are nothing, nothing, nothing!"

"Yes, ma'am."

She seemed confused. She looked at her desk. There were ten or twelve rubber stamps stationed there, her "troops" all lined up and ready for action, but she could not command a single one of them into battle now. They were obsolete.

This was my introduction to a civilization in which a man does not exist unless he is supplied with numerous papers: from the concierge where he lives, from the local commissariat, from the Préfecture de Police, in the form of an identity card, food coupons, travelling permits, army certificates, vehicle registration, driver's licence, petrol coupons—until finally, instead of a man there is only a papier-mâché human, a *collage* of official forms in various hues and sizes. The human personality is relegated to third, fourth or last place, and a man's simple word becomes about as useful as a diplomat's smile.

Nobody really "is" in this society, or at least it cannot be proven by his life's breath. One cannot approach an official, no matter how minor, and say, "I am so-and-so." One just thrusts a paper under his nose, and if it is properly documented, notarised, authenticated, stamped, approved and sealed, one springs to life. Otherwise one is in limbo.

This incessant papering, called by the French *"la bataille de paperasse"*, and by the Germans something unprintable, gives one a feeling that papers are actually more important than the individual they represent. The man in France, whose wife in Belgium is sick and needs him, must travel down the cavernous, bureaucratic, subhuman passageway of dots and curlicues, lorded over by rubber stamps, before he can give aid and comfort to his ailing spouse. Families are disrupted, individuals jailed, social life hampered, cultural pursuits strangled, and simple human intercourse narrowed to a trickle by this autocratic world of paper.

It was easy to see from the bewildered look on the lady's face that she was not prepared to deal with me directly. True, she could have stamped my forehead, or the back of my hand, or some place where it wouldn't show, but this was unsanitary as well as unofficial, and at the first good scrubbing I would be illegal again.

"Please wait a moment," she said. She telephoned someone and a conversation ensued in rapid French. She put down the phone, somewhat mollified.

"Mr. Davis—that is, if you *are* Mr. Davis—you must go back to the Embassy and get a receipt for your passport. When one gives something in this life, one gets something in return. We must have some evidence that your passport is at the Embassy. This is the only way we can give you permission to stay in France."

I had to laugh. "Very well," I said, "if that's what's required, I'll do my best. Be back tomorrow."

The next morning I returned to the Embassy. It was a little embarrassing when the two Marines popped to attention as I passed by. According to strict interpretation, this *was* U.S. territory, and without a visa, I was trespassing.

Agnes Schneider was surprised to see me. "Change your mind?" she asked dryly.

"Not quite," I replied. "It's just that the French can't believe it and need some written proof that you've really got my passport."

Miss Schneider sighed and obligingly gave me a letter stating that the Embassy did in fact possess my passport. Back I went to the Préfecture. I handed the letter to my rubber-stamp general. She took it gleefully, glanced at the contents perfunctorily, turned it over, and with a flourish stamped it with an imposing seal.

"*Eh bien*, now you exist," she said, smiling.

On the stamped portion, in the spaces, she marked TROIS MOIS. "This is the amount of time on your tourist visa," she confided.

"But I have no tourist visa," I exclaimed. "That's on the renounced passport back at the American Embassy."

"A detail," she replied, putting the inevitable tax stamp below the seal, "not worth troubling about. Now when you return," her tone became conspiratorial, "perhaps your three months can be extended. In any case, don't lose that paper. One hundred francs, please."

I paid, thanked her and left. When I reached the street, I looked at the paper ruefully. What did I have, in fact, but a receipt for my non-existence from one mythical state which had been accepted for three months of existence by another mythical state?

What intrigued me about my new credentials was that I had not sought them so much as that they had been foisted upon me. Both the American and French governments had been so eager to issue me some sort of document that they had twisted and tortured their laws in order to give me papers declaring that I was paperless, or symbols of existence to verify my non-existence. Who, I began to ask myself, was the beneficiary of this transaction? Surely it was not I. My sense of belonging to the human community, my self-awareness and indeed my self-esteem had not been increased. The true beneficiaries of my papers had been the nation-states themselves, I reasoned. It was they who had gained a measure of existence in the world, or come one human-unit further into being, for having issued credentials which I was willing to bear.

My American passport had been such an austere and formidable-looking document that this point had escaped me; whereas the perfect absurdity of the papers I now held enabled me to recognize the sham for what it was. Papers give status, dignity and privilege to the issuing authority rather than to the bearer—although the opposite is generally assumed—and I believe that this is equally true in the case of passports, drivers' licences, honorary degrees, permits to practise law, licences for marriage or, as Jesus put it, legal giving or taking in marriage, or even certificates of good health. In all such cases the individual unwittingly surrenders his right to assume command, status, or direction for himself in human terms by acknowledging and then accepting an outside authority's right to grant these things to him. When an individual accepts a degree from a college or university, he is not, in this sense, gaining an education, but forfeiting one. A man who hangs a degree on the wall of his office is really displaying the fact that he does not know whether he is educated or not. He is saying that he has transferred this power of discernment to an institution which is willing to say that he is educated. Education itself is thus vested in the institution rather than in the individual. The degree is the graduate's receipt for having sold his intelligence, and thus it becomes also a verification of his ignorance. An academic question? Perhaps. But will the day come when men sell their souls to an institution in exchange for a fancy parchment entitled CERTIFICATION OF INNER SPIRITUALITY?

It was this kind of reasoning which prompted me to drop my receipt for a U.S. passport with its smudgy French visa into a convenient ashcan—with the understanding that thereby I was becoming a little more of a person and that "America" and "France" were becoming a little less presumptuous. I was no longer even concerned about breaking the law. For after all, I thought to myself, I may well be breaking the laws of France by existing without papers, but what is more to the point, France breaks the laws of existence by illegalizing me in the absence of papers.

As the days passed, I began to realise that I had to divest myself of still other appurtenances in order to become more fully human. I had been reading a small Bible which my father had given me just before I left the States. It influenced my next decision deeply. For although my religion was no more orthodox than my citizenship, deriving as it had from one Jewish and one Christian parent, although I was never a regular church or synagogue member, nevertheless I have always revered the Bible—as, in fact, all holy books. And I remember finding Jesus' instructions to his disciples in St. Matthew particularly illuminating at this point in my life.

Provide neither gold, nor silver, nor brass in your purses, read the Scripture, *nor scrip for your journey, neither two coats, neither shoes, nor yet staves: for the workman is worthy of his meat.* I was greatly impressed with this passage and perhaps sensed in it a kind of kinship with the sages of India, who for centuries had renounced their worldly possessions in pursuit of wisdom. I felt the need to give up more than mere papers. Consequently, I bundled up my earthly possessions, such as they were, excepting only two shirts, a pair of army pants, a leather jacket, some underwear, and a pair of shoes, and deposited the lot one day at the door of a charitable organization.

I felt a truly amazing inner freedom. People on the street ogled me, for I smiled broadly at the world. I couldn't help singing, and I practically danced down the street. Fear was suddenly reduced to a childhood apparition; I had simply outgrown it. And so, around the middle of July, I found myself standing in my little room on the fifth floor of the Hotel des Ingénieurs in Montmartre—rent: 30 cents a day—with a declaration of principles in my hand, a briefcase and typewriter by my side, my clothes on my back, and ... nothing else. My meals were provided free of charge by a young Polish refugee who ran a restaurant and who had become interested in my cause. I planned to leave Paris and walk over the French countryside, stopping at villages and farmhouses, to talk, to work, perhaps to write, and one day to cross the Franco-German border. But as it turned out, I had a far more important adventure ahead of me. The three months on my discarded visa were running out.

On August 15th, the day of the expiration of my French "visa", I returned to the Préfecture as requested, but practically shirtless and utterly paperless. At the Bureau des Etrangers, I found my sympathetic friend and smiled at her. She returned the expression perfunctorily.

I waited. People came and went—Italians, Swiss, British, Americans, refugees from Poland, Roumania, Albania—all seeking permission to travel. After about an hour's waiting, my functionary friend nodded to me and sighed, "All right." I moved into the chair beside her desk.

"Let me have the paper I gave you three months ago, and we'll see what we can do."

"Well, I'll tell you," I began, not knowing exactly how to break the news.

"Give it to me quickly," she said, holding out her hand.

"I don't have it any more. I got rid of it because it represented something which I didn't need to recognize."

This didn't reach her at all. She just looked at me, her eyes wide. Finally, she spoke. It came slowly and from way inside: "You ... don't ... recognize ... France?"

"France does not recognize me."

"Not ... recognize ... you," she echoed with resignation. Then I noticed something odd about her expression. There was the beginning of amusement fighting to break through. I think possibly she was getting a glimmer of the absurdity. But she killed the slight smile with effort.

"How could you do such a thing? And after all I did for you! Do you think we work here all day just to have our papers torn up? I must turn you over to another office. And there I don't know what will happen to you."

She picked up the telephone and called "Monsieur le Directeur". I would be escorted to his office, she told me; and then, as we were obliged to wait for my guide, she smiled, this time rather timidly I thought. Opening her desk drawer she carefully unloaded a cache of newspaper clippings. The articles were all about my escapades! Ever since I had come to her three months ago, she explained, she had kept track of my activities through the newspapers. Suddenly I was no longer the pitiful, paperless refugee who was going to be kicked out of the country. I was a celebrity, a person whom one asks for an autograph—which she did. Our positions were strangely reversed. I had been "legalized" by the press. Now I was the authority; she, the subject.

A clerk came in and escorted me to the bureau across the court. There another clerk copied down all vital statistics and told me to return in two days to be photographed. I gathered from this treatment that I was going to receive a French identity card. Since I could not protest until actually offered the card, I arrived at the appointed time and was photographed along with many other stateless persons. Then I was taken to another office and told to wait. When my "final paper" arrived, it turned out to be not an identity card at all, but a *refus de séjour* (refusal to stay). It gave me until the 27th of that month to arrange *mes affaires* and leave France. But of course I had no papers which would permit me to enter any other country. This was a serious crisis. Here I called myself a citizen of the world, and yet I was being told either to seek asylum on another planet, die, become a perpetual mariner living in international waters, or go to jail permanently. A fine state of affairs! I wished I could see ahead to the next item my French friend would cut out for her scrapbook.

I went to the police station on August 27, the day I was supposed to leave France. The sub-chief of the bureau, righteously indignant, wanted to know why I was not out of the country.

"You see, there's a world government meeting in Luxembourg on September 6th," I replied, "and to get there I'll need a little more time for arrangements."

He shrugged philosophically and gave me an extension until the 11th.

"What will happen on the 12th, if I do not get to Luxembourg?" I asked him.

"*Eh bien*," he replied, "you will see the inside of a French prison."

Since the doors were closing rapidly in France, I had decided to try Luxembourg. I thought I had a particularly good reason for going there as the World Movement for World Federal Government, a conference of world government organizations which included the United World Federalists, was having its annual convention there. But of course the paper problem was coming up again.

This time I decided to take the bureaucratic bull by the horns. I printed my own papers! It was a simple white card which I called the United World Citizen International Identity Card. After raising a little money for the project, I had 1,000 of them printed, kept one for myself, and sent the remaining 999 to Luxembourg ahead of me should any of the delegates desire to use them.

As soon as possible, I took my U.W.C.I. Card to the police for a rubber-stamp recognition so that I could get a Luxembourg visa. Although the official I met, the same one who handled my *refus de séjour*, exhibited great interest, he said it was not in his province to grant passports and visas.

The next day, I went to the department for *passeports étrangers*. Again there was much interest, but more shrugging. Get a letter from the International Refugee Organization, they said, then we shall see. I didn't exactly class myself as a refugee, but trudged crosstown to I.R.O. headquarters. The office was packed with refugees, all seeking personal attention. I showed my document around, and it caused so much wonder that I was quickly ushered in to see the chief. He was more fascinated with my card than anyone, including the police, since he had to deal with all sorts of strange documents, and a common worldly one seemed to him to slice through miles of red tape with a single, bafflingly miraculous stroke.

The whole staff gathered around to see the strange object, staring at it as if it were the Holy Grail. I told the chief that I needed a letter from him to the French Ministry of Foreign Affairs, stating that I belonged under his jurisdiction. He complied willingly.

By then it was about eleven o'clock on Saturday morning. The Luxembourg convention began on Monday. Therefore I had to get all of my papers in order that morning to be at the convention on time. I needed both a *titre de voyage* from the police and a visa from the Luxembourg Embassy. Both offices closed at noon. But to get the *titre de voyage*, I was told by the I.R.O. chief, I first had to get a letter from the Ministry of Foreign Affairs to the Préfecture de Police after I turned over his letter to the Ministry of Foreign Affairs. I had no objection to amassing "papers" now, because all of the credentials I received were to be based on my own "home-made" United World Citizen International Identity Card rather than on any national passport. The problem I faced was strictly one of time and space.

Scurrying across town, I burst into the Ministry of Foreign Affairs office and asked in breathless pidgin French for a letter to the Préfecture. I think my impatience did the trick for, ten minutes later, I had the letter in hand. It classed me as *Apatride, d'origine américaine*. To my knowledge, this status is unique in France, and this was the first of its kind. It was, anyway, the first official title I had been given in France.

I dashed—it was now 11:30—back to the police, but taking one look at the line at the window where I had to apply, my hopes sank. The office would close long before I reached the *fonctionnaire-en-pouvoir* behind the grillework. I decided to chance the Luxembourg Embassy with just this letter and my "passport".

The consul at the Embassy—whom I caught at the door—told me that if I could get my "passport" stamped by the French, he would visa it. I looked at my watch. Noon! Maybe in an emergency, I thought, the French would stay open long enough for one flick of a rubber stamp. I hurried back. When I arrived, a clerk informed me that it would take three days to get the necessary papers to leave. Trapped in the Bataille de Paperasse! I was still in Paris, exhausted by now, and under orders to leave in eight days but with nowhere to go.

Perhaps I was getting just what I deserved, I thought to myself. Once I succumbed to the world of papers—any papers at all, even papers of my own making—I seemed destined to become inextricably snarled in red tape as had so many thousands of refugees in the postwar years. And yet I thought it right and proper to have created my own papers. The idea of one individual issuing papers to himself had seemed to be logical *reductio ad absurdum*. Nevertheless, this time I was stuck. Maybe my own document just wasn't "official-looking" enough.

I spent the evening with Don Livingstone, a young Scotsman whom I had met several months earlier as a result of his letter expressing interest in my renunciation of citizenship. We had become fast friends at once, and our discussions of brotherhood, world government, socialism, child care, immortality and family life carried far into many nights. His lovely and charming French wife, Denise, gave me needed sustenance and also warm friendship throughout my stay in Paris.

During dinner we discussed my predicament exhaustively without finding a solution. At the last stroke of midnight I was to become illegal, a hunted man with literally no place to live. Sensing for the first time my real problem, Don offered me asylum in his own flat.

"You might be stuck with me the rest of your natural life," I told him jokingly.

We were standing by the window just then, sipping after-dinner coffee, when I happened to glance down at a copy of the morning *Herald Tribune*, Paris edition. On the front page was a photo of Robert Schuman, the French delegate to the United Nations, handing Trygve Lie, the Secretary-General, a golden key symbolizing the ceding of the territory of the Palais de Chaillot to the U.N. for the period of its meeting in Paris. I grabbed the paper. Don began reading over my shoulder. Trygve Lie, the story went on, had declared the territory "international".

We looked at each other, bursting with excitement. I sat down. International territory . . . in Paris? *In* France but not *of* France? It seemed heaven-sent. What better home could there be for a homeless citizen of the world? The more we talked about the idea, the more fascinating it became. Not only did "international territory" provide the perfect asylum for me, but my camping out at the U.N. would dramatize the need for world law. Naturally, I would ask for "international law" to govern me on "international territory", but there would be none.

Perhaps in this way I could focus attention on the inadequacy of the U.N., suggesting that if it could not provide for one lone human being, it would not be able to provide for the whole of mankind. It was a desperate plan to be sure, but a beautiful argument for world government.

We drafted a statement, made copies, and I delivered them by hand to all the major wire services that night. Then I went home, set my alarm for six and fell asleep.

This unique document tacitly sanctions the right of the individual to govern himself. As such, it is as revolutionary in character as the Magna Charta, the U.S. Bill of Rights and the U.N.'s Universal Declaration of Human Rights. (Further evidence of its revolutionary character is the addendum in the lower left-hand corner.)

Activities at the U.N. On September 17th, 1948 (*above*) my tent and I were forcibly ejected from U.N. territory in Paris. On November 19th, (*below*) my attempt to deliver the Oran Declaration from the balcony of the Palais de Chaillot's Great Hall was thwarted, but the entire speech was made in my stead by Robert Sarrazac.

3

The day dawned beautiful and clear. Packing my typewriter, a copy of the Bible, and a few personal items, I set out on the subway to Trocadero, arriving at the Palais de Chaillot at about seven.

There was no one about, and I began to scout the premises for a good campsite. The street was not blocked off, so apparently I would have to consider it still French territory. I could not get into the Palais itself. The only place to go was the restaurant across the street, which also belonged to the U.N.

I moved onto the steps. The doors were already opened, though the building was deserted. Good—there were lavatories. I had been wondering about that problem.

I explored upstairs. Apparently the building was also to be used by the Secretariat. Office equipment was scattered everywhere. It was actually the week before the sessions were to start, and the building was not yet completed, though meals were being served in the restaurant. I sat down in a conspicuous spot to await events.

"*Eh bien*, monsieur, what are you doing here?" My first encounter with a guard.

"I'm waiting for the session to begin."

"But you are a week too soon."

"Yes, I know."

He went away, scratching his head. Two minutes later he was back.

"But see here, you can't wait here. It's against the rules."

I pointed to the streets. "For me, *that* is against the rules." Then I showed him my *refus de séjour*.

"But you can't stay here."

"It's international territory, isn't it?"

"*Mais oui* . . . but. . . ."

"That means it isn't French territory."

"Yes but. . . ."

"I have left France then, *n'est-ce pas?*"

"*Mais non*, you are still in Paris."

"*Mais oui.* This may still be Paris, but for the moment it is international Paris."

"*Paris c'est Paris.* Move along." He tried to push me off the steps.

"Do not force me to break your own law," I said quickly. "You will get into trouble." This stopped him. "Don't you see," I continued, "I had to leave France on the 11th, and here I am on international territory on the 12th. Within regulations...."

"*Mais alors....*"

He went away for instructions. I entered the dining room, my heart pounding from the first round, picked out a table, and started to type. Workmen were arriving. I received many curious glances. This is what I wrote:

9.00 a.m.
PALAIS DE CHAILLOT
SEPTEMBER 12, 1948

I am in the restaurant of the U.N. headquarters. Guards have been passing back and forth giving me covert glances. Two helmeted police are standing about ten feet away, probably debating whether they should ask me for my papers ... I am sure that the uniform and the official looking typewriter have scared them off. . . . Another man is now approaching but he has turned away now as have the two policemen. I seem to want to put off this meeting with the world or rather with this tiny world here until the very last minute. I realise that at ten o'clock there will be photographers and reporters here, but now I feel quite alone. Alone with a great avalanche about to break over my head.... This void I am standing in is quite exciting. I sincerely feel that I can be a force toward achieving some measure of world peace....

Around ten o'clock the first newsmen arrived. Also the photographers.

"What's up, Davis?"

I told them of my encounter with the guard. Most of the newsmen were delighted with this unusual story. Others were cynical and regarded me as a meaningless crank. But they were also cynical about the Cold War and diplomatic gobbledegook.

A few were looking ahead to possible implications of my stand. What effect might it have on the U.N. itself and on general public opinion? One of these was Dave Schoenbrun of CBS, a student of history and current world affairs. We had a lengthy talk on the steps under the warm September sun. I returned to my typewriter.:

I have just been through the mill with the photographers and now they are all taking pictures of my typing here. . . . I am now in a goldfish bowl. Everything I do will be recorded by word and picture. If I thought that the renunciation was an act capable of drawing attention, it was merely a tiny ripple to what I feel will happen now. I must prepare carefully. Much is at stake. Many people are watching. I perhaps symbolize a great ideal to many people without hope. I must not in any way destroy that principle. But on the other hand, I must not assume too much. This is perhaps a greater danger than the other. If I talk myself into the proposition that I am a superman, or another Jesus, I will get delusions of grandeur which will not be consistent with that which I want to effect. . . . The photographers have just left. I am being made more and more aware of the power of the press and the . . . *Life* is now taking pictures. Oh brother, history is being made today. Keep your equilibrium, Garry. Great things can happen today. And tomorrow . . .

A reporter from A.P., Bob Munsel, asked me if I had eaten anything. I told him I hadn't, and he promised to bring me a sandwich for lunch. People had begun to gather by this time, and I explained to one and all why I was there, *refus de séjour* in one hand, the United World Citizen International Identity Card in the other. They would listen, amused for the most part, and hurry away to their work.

The newsmen returned in the afternoon to find out whether U.N. officials had approached me. I told them no. Bob Munsel brought me a ham sandwich and a cup of coffee.

Then one of the newsmen went to interview an official of the Secretariat. He came back to say that the matter had made its way up to one of the two assistant Secretary-Generals, Konstantin E. Zinchenko of the U.S.S.R., the highest official on hand. Zinchenko was quoted as having said, "Davis is a world baby. The U.N. Charter did not foresee being a nursemaid. States may join; diapered citizens, *niet!*"

Around four, someone from the Quakers offered me a sleeping bag, which I accepted gratefully. Food was beginning to come now, much more than I could eat. Little old ladies pressed cheese, bread, and a bottle of red wine in my hands, murmuring "*Que Dieu soit avec vous.*" One elegantly dressed lady, accompanied by a dignified gentleman with a small moustache and cane, perhaps having finished cocktails at one of the cafes on the Trocadero, offered me a tin of *pâté de foie gras* and some English biscuits. I didn't want to risk hurting the feelings of the donors by refusing, yet fruit, bread, wine, cheese, and meat were piling up. I stacked all the provisions on the shelf in the coat room, planning to call a welfare organization to take away the surplus.

By this time, the guard had assumed a benevolent attitude toward me. Knowing his bosses hadn't molested me, he felt he could safely take me under his wing. He kept people out of the restaurant when I was tired, and let those in that I wanted to see. But eventually even my good-intentioned guard became engulfed. Both morning and evening papers had carried the story and all Paris now seemed to be aware of the U.N.'s first "citizen". Every time I sat down, more newsmen and more people streamed up to me. This continued until 11 P.M. Then the guard told me, apologetically, that the doors of the restaurant had to be locked. I said, "All right," and got my sleeping bag from the coat room. I went outside on the little porch and unrolled it. Photographers set the little sign FOR U.N. EMPLOYEES ONLY on the door behind me and flashed this picture around the world. I was dead tired, my feelings numbed and knotted, and glad to get to sleep. After the pictures were taken I was left alone . . . for about ten minutes.

"Are you awake, Davis?"

"No, damn it!"

"Okay, be back tomorrow."

I was awakened at about 6 A.M. by two night firemen. They were standing a few feet from me discussing my situation.

"... *mais non, il n'est pas Américain . . . citoyen du monde . . . c'est curieux . . . tout à fait idiot bien sûr . . . mais alors . . . c'est pas mal comme idée quand même . . .*"

I got up. It was another beautiful day. Across the Seine stood the spectacular Tour Eiffel, above it a clear blue sky, and around me the expansive white marble of the Palais. Workmen began to arrive. Two of them offered me bread and cheese. I asked them what they thought of world citizenship as we munched together. "*Eh bien, ça dépends, tu sais . . .*"

People began to appear at about nine: students, housewives, businessmen on their way to work, a Catholic priest who just stared, a nurse wheeling a baby carriage, two turbanned Sikhs, and a top-hatted, bemonocled Englishman who told me haughtily that "The British Empiah *is* a world government, sir." Then along came Robert Sarrazac, a man who impressed me deeply at this first encounter, and who was later to become one of my chief counsellors. With his eyes deep-sunk and compelling, a V-shaped face gave him somewhat the appearance of a theatrical Mephistopheles.

Sarrazac asked me politely what my plans were.

"I am requesting the delegates, through the Secretary-General, to convene a constitutional convention, under Article 109 of the U.N. Charter, to draft a world constitution."

"I see. Eet weel not work," he said matter-of-factly.

"Why not?"

"Do you not understand? Zee Nations Unis eez nozzing more zan zee old League of Nations weeth a new name. How can nations unite? Eet ees impossible. Zey would be out of beezness."

He suggested I build a tiny white cabin beside the majestic Palais de Chaillot to represent humanity. He and his friends would help me.

"You see, zee man in zee street eez complètement disregarded here. And are you not an '*homme de la rue*'?"

"I guess so," I admitted, "since I'm practically sleeping on the *rue*. But I still think I must go through with my petition. After all, I assume the delegates want peace too. They'll see the wisdom of my petition."

"Ah, Monsieur Davis, you are naïve," he said, "but we weel see what we weel see." Then he left, promising to return later in the week.

I noticed a little fellow outside the glass door of the restaurant jumping up and down trying to get my attention. He was sporting a goatee and seemed to be perpetually smiling. My guard kept shaking his head. I had left instructions not to let anyone in without a U.N. pass unless I okayed it.

"Better let him in," I called to the guard, "before he shakes the building down."

It turned out to be Guy Marchand, who had just returned from a personal world-wide "peace tour", a man looking in his own way for his own answers. He believed he had found one on his doorstep upon his return. He offered me his services in any capacity. It was a unique offer, considering the fact that among other accomplishments Mr. Marchand was the world's champion glider pilot.

At around two in the afternoon, when the crowds had thinned

out for lunch, a tall, lanky, serious-looking American approached me, a small smile playing on his lips.

"Are you Garry Davis?" he asked.

"I think so," I replied.

"I'm Rufus King . . . from Washington."

"How're things at the Pentagon?" I asked warily.

"I wouldn't know, I'm just a lawyer," he replied, smiling.

"Well, glad to know you, Mr. King," I said, holding out my hand. "I could do with some professional help."

He had just returned from Norway, he told me, where, with Fritjof Nansen's son, he had petitioned the Norwegian Government to turn over or cede a dot of land to them, just a longitude and latitude point, after which they would declare their allegiance to this dot symbolizing all the dots throughout the planet—that is, the entire world territory. The Norwegian Government, however, would not even part with a dot. Returning to Paris, Rufus King read in *Le Monde* that I had acquired a whole acre of dots, more or less, along the same general lines.

"I'd like to help you put this over," he told me, "you know, world constitution, bill of rights, pledge of allegiance and so forth." Mr. King in his field was as unique as Guy Marchand and Robert Sarrazac in theirs. He was an expert on "Individual Secession Into The World Community," which he claimed I had performed and now exemplified.

We had no further time to talk as an interruption came in the form of a loud checked coat, a raucous voice, and a crooked smile.

"Great show, great show! Jesus, what a stunt! Got the whole goddam world lookin' atcha. Burn the pants off the Commies. Yer not a Commie, are ya? Knowyer old man. Great guy, but a sonofabitch to work for! Shake, name's Minevitch. Christ, what a stunt!"

He was Borrah Minevitch. I knew from the movies and stage that he had once played the wickedest harmonica a man ever got halfway into his mouth. Now he was a correspondent for *Variety*.

"Whaddya need, kid? You name it, ya got it. Yer all right. Whaddya need?"

"How about mimeographing this letter to Trygve Lie?" I asked.

"Ya got it." He grabbed the letter and rushed off.

All through the day, there were crowds and reporters. Leg men and feature writers from all over the world were congregated in Paris for the coming sessions. Apparently they had been sitting around looking for pre-session copy and soaking up Scotch at Charlie's Bar. I was copy.

Late in the afternoon, a U.N. postal clerk slipped over to me furtively from the main building and deposited a sack of mail at my feet. He scurried back as if I were a "fence" handling stolen "ice". I looked at the mail. It was addressed to *Garry Davis, Steps of the Palais de Chaillot,* or *Garry Davis, U.N. Restaurant,* or just *Garry Davis, World Citizen, Paris.*

It was mostly from France and Germany. I put it in my sack, intending to open it later that night.

Don Livingstone showed up toward evening with fresh fruit, and sandwiches made by his wife. I was due for a newsreel shot the next day.

"Don, how about standing in on a newsreel shot tomorrow as the announcer?" I asked him. "I'm nervous and would feel better if you were throwing me the questions."

"Well, it's not my cup of tea," he said, "but since it's for a good cause, I'll try my best. Now here, eat some fruit."

The police had blocked off the street section between the Palais and the restaurant, thereby making it "international territory" too. *Life* photographers and Fox Movietone News took pictures of me crossing the Place du Trocadero. Now I could collect my own mail. Don came along and we did the newsreel question-and-answer show. When the film played at Radio City Music Hall, my family saw it, and my father wrote, "I didn't understand what you were talking about. Keep your explanations simple. And smile!"

He was right. I was beginning to feel the pressure around me as if I were in a giant goldfish bowl with a hundred searchlights playing on the water. Though I was constantly surrounded, I felt utterly cut off from reality. I was confined to 75 square yards and inside me a great hunger was building to go to a movie, walk in a quiet garden, sit down to an evening meal with friends, or just plain crawl into a hole. Small wonder I was not simple and smiling.

Borrah Minevitch returned on the third day with one thousand mimeographed copies of my letter to Trygve Lie. I held a press conference at four o'clock, an open-air affair, with crowds milling about, dozens of newsmen asking questions, and flash bulbs popping. Copies of the letter were distributed and the newsmen rushed off.

"My God, Borrah, take one across the street to Trygve Lie, quick!" I shouted. "We forgot the Secretary-General—Wait, let me sign it first."

The food kept coming . . . but it was all cold. Finally, a sympathetic restaurateur from the Champs Elysées had an entire meal brought up in a delivery wagon complete with Soupe à l'Oignon, Truite au Beurre, Frogs Legs Provençale, Haricots Verts, Coupe Meringue Glacé, and coffee in a Thermos. It was served by a waitress in a brief dress, really more of a costume which revealed her long legs encased in black mesh hose. Every time she served me, photographers took flash pictures! I noticed she would smile prettily, always managing to stand a little behind me—the old "up-stage" trick—so that her face would not be lost to the camera. As it turned out, she was the gift of a French press agent who was bent on promoting his starlet and had engineered the whole operation, meringue and all.

Every night there were hundreds around me discussing *"cette curiosité"*, or *"le petit homme"*. It became *"comme il faut"* to go up to the Trocadero to ogle at *". . . le premier citoyen du monde, très amusant, n'est-ce pas?"*

Behind the hullabaloo, however, I felt the significance of what was happening. The world was weary of peace talk; it wanted peace. This was most apparent from my mail, now coming in by the sackful from all over Europe.

"You have concretized our hopes for peace."
"Bon courage, continuez."
"We are with you in our little village."
"May I represent you in Germany?"
"Good luck, God bless you."
"We pray for you every night."

On the morning of the sixth day, September 16th, Borrah brought me a tent. I had slept outside that night on a cot donated by some Quaker friends. I told the press boys, who by this time considered the U.N. restaurant steps a regular beat, that at noon I would pitch the tent. This caused considerable excitement and all newsreel companies were alerted.

There was a tiny plot of ground beside the steps which

seemed to be just big enough for the tent. At noon, stakes in hand, I came out of the restaurant, having just spent half an hour in one of the booths in the men's room to get some privacy, and moved on to the new territory. Several thousand people crowded around, stretching throughout the wide plaza. Three newsreel cameras on mobile trucks ground away.

Two Frenchmen helped me. Others held back the crowd, including the policemen on duty who had obligingly blocked the tiny area with wooden horses. After many fumblings, we finally got the tent erected. A great cheer went up. The World Citizen had a proper home!

At one o'clock that afternoon, I was officially recognized by the Secretariat of the United Nations. A Mr. Wood came to see me in the restaurant. He told me the Secretariat had called the French Ministry of the Interior to request for me a *titre d'identité*. The Ministry had obliged.

"But, Mr. Wood, I didn't ask the U.N. to go to all that trouble," I told him.

"It was no trouble, Mr. Davis. Now will you just go along and pick it up?"

"But one moment, Mr. Wood. Is it true that this so-called *titre d'identité* is really a sort of favour to me?"

"Yes, yes. Now if you'll just get your things together—"

"Do you mean to imply," I continued, "that there is no law behind this gracious offer?"

"Well, you see . . . it's sort of a favour to us too."

"But it's not strictly legal, is it?"

"Oh, I wouldn't say that. After all, a government has certain rights."

"That may be, but it so happens that I am not now under the jurisdiction of any government. The U.N., as you perhaps know, is not—"

"Mr. Davis, will you or will you not leave this territory . . . I mean, place?"

"Well, I really don't deserve favours of the French Government especially in view of the fact that it has already legally kicked me out. But more than that, I have too much respect for democratic procedures, for representation by elections, for my individual human rights—I still am a human being, you know —in fact, for the law itself, to consider accepting such a dubious paper."

"Dubious paper!" he exploded. "And what is dubious about a *titre d'identité?*"

"Let's save each other's time, Mr. Wood. The only paper I could possibly accept now would be one granting me legal status as a world citizen. That, I presume, is only in the power of the United Nations General Assembly, and has nothing whatever to do with either the U.N. Secretariat, which has no legislative or juridical function, or the French Ministry of the Interior."

He departed. Borrah was with me at the time. "Christ, ya really told 'im off!" Borrah said. "Where'dja get dem words? You oughta run fer President."

I was emotionally exhausted. I had talked, talked, talked all afternoon with so many people. Faces began to blur. At seven-thirty, my face felt hot and flushed. I could take the words and staring crowds no longer. I crawled into the tent and prepared to bed down for the night. Stripping to my underwear, I got into my sleeping bag and tried to shut my ears to the increasing noise of the crowd outside, calling for me to come out and be viewed.

Suddenly the flap of the tent opened. Mr. Wood again. He seemed impatient and tense.

"Mr. Davis, for the last time, will you accept the paper of the French Ministry or not?"

I clenched my teeth and replied hoarsely, "Mr. Wood, do you think my answer would change from afternoon to night?"

"Very well, Mr. Davis, you must be prepared to accept the consequences."

He threw down the flap. I snuggled back into my sleeping bag. Then someone barked a sharp order outside. Two seconds later, the tent was coming down on my head.

I got out of the sleeping bag quickly and grabbed my pants. As I put them on, the tent was whisked away into a waiting police van. Flashbulbs were popping all around, the crowd were shouting at the policemen, and some young boys were picking up stray pieces of wood. Policemen rapidly loaded my possessions into the van. About fifty officers were spread around the area. Two gendarmes grabbed me under the arms and hustled me into the van. We roared away, sirens screaming.

It was all over too fast for me to become indignant . . . or anything else. And underneath I felt immensely relieved anyway. I needed sleep, my head was throbbing and my chest felt tight.

We drove to the local commissariat, and I was ushered upstairs to the inspector's private office.

"Ah, Mr. Davis, please sit down. You are a very likeable fellow, you know. Sit down, please. Well, the Minister of the Interior has the kindness to give you an extension on your permission to stay. It is nice of him, don't you think?"

"It's unlawful," I replied, gritting my teeth. "The minister already gave me a *refus de séjour* which was quite legal. I left the country as ordered. Then I was abducted by your police and returned against my will. It's you who are breaking the law, not me."

"Personally, Mr. Davis, I understand your position and I am very sympathetic, but I have my orders. And I am obliged to give you this paper."

"I'm afraid I can't agree with you, Inspector."

"What do you mean?"

"Obviously you have another choice."

"And what is that?"

"Refuse to carry out your orders."

He laughed uproariously. "*Eh bien*, and then will you give me a job?"

"Yes," I replied. "You can be my first world policeman."

He sighed. "*Mais oui*, it is not easy. My heart is with you already. My wife's too. We have suffered much in two wars. Anyway, the paper is here whether you want it or not."

I left the commissariat empty-handed and returned to the Trocadero. Policemen were spaced every six yards and wooden barriers had been placed around the entire Palais de Chaillot. I met two newsmen while looking forlornly at my former "home".

"What're you going to do now, Davis?"

"I don't know." I shook my head wearily.

"Why don't you go home and get some rest? You made your point."

"That's right," the other said. "One guy can't do it all."

I trudged back to Don Livingstone's where I was packed off to bed immediately. A doctor arrived and diagnosed my ailment as influenza.

"Where on earth have you been," he asked me, "in this beautiful weather?"

4

Paris was then the unofficial capital of the world. All eyes were upon it. The world's facilities for news distribution were centred in the city. World-renowned journalists, top photographers and newsreel men, syndicated feature writers . . . the hotels were swollen with them.

Naturally, Paris reflected mounting world tension. Berlin was the key issue, and the airlift was in full swing. The debate on atomic control was being bitterly fought by East and West. The merry-go-round spun faster. Debates were hotter, tempers shorter. There was talk of running an armoured train through East Germany, and all U.S. foreign correspondents were issued War Correspondents' cards. Delegates wearied of endless discussions which resolved nothing. The plain people were weary too. One wished desperately for something positive to happen, something bright and fresh, something human, and Paris, it seemed, was the perfect setting.

My mail (which was coming in cargo-style) and my friends and would-be advisers, who flocked to my bedside, were full of suggestions for me. My status in France was still wholly illegal or non-legal, but there seemed to be more pressing problems. What were we going to do to advance the cause of world government?

Rufus King wanted me to organize a world union which we would call United Mankind. Someone else suggested that I picket the U.N. There were requests for me to organize grassroots World Citizens' Clubs, since these groups were now mushrooming in Europe, particularly in Germany, and as far off as Libya. Others wanted me to embark on a lecture tour of the world, defying frontier after frontier. Most of the letters, however, were simple requests for the grace of world citizenship.

The idea of a global registry for all who wanted to declare themselves world citizens seemed a natural corollary to these requests, I thought. Not only would such a world-wide registry serve as an exact indication of the popular numerical support of world citizenship for present leaders, but also it would be a potential electorate for future candidates for world office.

As soon as I was well, I moved into temporary headquarters, an office donated by a Russian immigrant who claimed to be a revolutionary and said that my *"geste"* was *magnifique, dans la grande tradition*. A typical day found Ed Morgan poring over my letters, preparing an article for *Harper's* or *Collier's*; Sally Hammond, a young American war widow and federalist, answering letters from journalists who wanted articles in Germany, Sweden, Denmark, Italy, England, and Switzerland; a Lithuanian refugee girl acting as a volunteer; and a Swedish organizer, Anders Clarin, former president of a world federalist group in Sweden, as a sort of jack-of-all-trades.

But of all those around me I listened most closely to Robert Sarrazac, who had just risked his rather estimable reputation on me with an article in *Combat*, the leading French intellectual newspaper, endorsing my actions. Sarrazac would listen to the schemes offered with impatience and then say, his eyes narrowing: "You are all naïve children. Europe is tired. She does not have your energy, but she is years ahead in political wisdom. She does not want mere political machines and super-states. She wants peace and bread and good conversation with friends. She wants neither America's capitalistic imperialism, nor Russia's Communistic imperialism. But also, she does not want her longing for peace to be exploited by fools, no matter how sincere." His deep-set eyes burned brightly.

Sarrazac was particularly contemptuous of any proposal for a popular organization. He had been the leader of a radical group called "Le Front Humain" (The Human Front) which had built to a membership of 18,000, at which point Sarrazac cut it down to sixteen in disgust. He was preoccupied with the idea that the mechanical aspects of an organization inevitably would overtake and befoul its spiritual basis. "Do not worry," he would say gravely, "a popular organization will come soon enough . . . too soon, in fact." He believed that I needed instead a *"Conseil d'Avis"*, a kind of council of solidarity composed of leading French intellectuals.

"But I don't know any leading French intellectuals," I told him.

"Leave everything to me," he replied.

Sarrazac was independent of all political parties and highly respected throughout Paris for his absolute neutrality. This allowed him to approach anyone, and I was bowled over at the celebrities he managed to produce the afternoon we had our first meeting at the Cité Club. The group included Albert Camus, the novelist; André Breton, the poet; Claude Bourdet, editor of *Combat;* George Altman, editor of *Franc-Tireur*; Professor Pierre Giraud, president of the Institut de Biologie; l'Abbé Pierre, Catholic Deputy and a renowned missionary priest; Jean Hélion, the painter; Magdelaine Paz, a director of Radiodiffusion Française; Madame Louise Guieyesse, leader of Friends of Gandhi; Emmanuel Mounier, editor of *Esprit*; Henri Roser, Protestant minister and French secretary for the World Fellowship of Reconciliation; Louis Rosen, well-known financier; Kobloth-Décroix, labour leader; Louis Martin-Chauffier, editor of *Libération*; and at least a dozen others whom I could not recognize.

Jean Hélion, the painter, was to be my translator. Newsmen representing the world press were also present. Sarrazac had forgotten nothing.

When we were all assembled, my supporters sitting in a semi-circle facing the reporters, Jean Hélion rapped for order. He introduced me, and I read a prepared statement in which I declared that I was not a pacifist and would be the first to enlist in a world police force to enforce world law.

Jean translated my remarks into French. When he finished, I asked for questions. Up popped a small journalist with thick glasses and asked me what I would do if Hitler were on the march now. Before I could reply, Sarrazac jumped up and introduced l'Abbé Pierre. After this outstanding humanitarian declared his support for *"le geste de Gaaree Daavees"*, and sat down, up came the bespectacled journalist again. But Sarrazac beat him to it once more by introducing André Breton, then Claude Bourdet, Magdelaine Paz, Professor Giraud, and finally Albert Camus, who had been sitting almost unnoticed at my right. Camus spoke briefly but incisively and seemed to clear the air. And perhaps he saved the day, for there were fierce animosities among those present. Socialists were sitting with radicals, Communists with conservatives, Christians with atheists, Catholic priests with Protestant ministers, deputies with anarchists, and labour representatives with financiers. Unity-in-diversity was the main attraction and a source of awe to many of the journalists.

After the speeches, my persistent interrogator was on his feet, but Sarrazac was already reading a short statement of principles asking the men and women in the semi-circle whether or not they would constitute themselves as a "Conseil de Solidarité" to support my actions in the future. Anxious and hostile glances were exchanged. But Sarrazac was an able strategist. He called upon Albert Camus first. Camus had as much horror of committees and councils as anyone, and this was well known. He was also lavishly admired for his independence of thought and uncompromising integrity to his own principles. He hesitated for the briefest moment. The room was utterly still, the hundred or more journalists sensing the drama of the situation. Not even my bespectacled friend dared break in. Slowly, Camus turned toward me, his eyes direct and quiet. I smiled instinctively, perhaps a little timidly, for while I have never been awed by distinguished actors, scientists or politicians, a great writer has always inspired my complete humility. Suddenly Camus was smiling back at me. He turned to Sarrazac and nodded. There was a burst of applause from the audience. The "Conseil de Solidarité" was born.

I leaned over to Jean Hélion just as things were breaking up and said I would like to make a final statement. I didn't know what it was going to be, but I felt the meeting needed some sort of conclusion. Jean got up, pounded the gavel, and announced, "In conclusion, the first world citizen has something to say." I rose hesitantly.

"Allow me to say a final word," I began and stopped. Everyone waited, coats in hand, scarves half on, impatient.

"World citizenship is like a baby today," I continued. "It is innocent and pure, awkward and helpless. These men and women whom you have just heard sense that innocence and helplessness. Such understanding rises above sectarian interests. Such helplessness is our greatest strength. I admit my helplessness and confess my innocence before you. Yet many men and women of different opinions have risen here to support one man, so that one man now rises, and, speaking for himself only as one human person, declares his support of all humanity as represented by these good men and women of the newly formed 'Conseil de Solidarité'. Such is the key formula of world citizenship. Such is the measure of brotherhood. Thank you all for being here."

After all had filed out, Hélion, Sarrazac, Russell Benedict, who was my American "press attaché", and I made our way to Jean's little Renault. Up stepped the journalist whose question had so persistently been brushed aside.

"Mr. Davis," he began, but Sarrazac had me by the arm and was whisking me into the car.

"Why can't I answer the poor fellow's question?" I protested.

"It is the trickiest question of all," Sarrazac replied, "because he brings up a situation in the past, and expects you to tell how you would act in the present. No matter what you answer, it is a trap. The man is well trained. I know him. He is from Tass."

I did not expect at this time, nor have I ever imagined, that I could "save" the world. At best, I might influence its behaviour slightly. My actions were largely gestures, both dramatic and symbolic. But basically, I guess, I wanted the world to understand the moral nature of what I was attempting. This was the *raison d'être* behind the press conference which Robert Sarrazac had so expertly engineered. The newspaper clippings that I collected as a result of this conference were eloquent proof of the fact that I was finally communicating accurately, really getting through with my message. There now seemed to be a much more clear understanding of why I had renounced my citizenship, why I refused to accept papers and why I had "camped out" on the steps of the United Nations.

At first I had been repelled by Sarrazac's idea of a *conseil* because it seemed as though I would be hiding under the aprons of celebrities. Gradually, however, it dawned on me that I was after all a manipulator of symbols, a press agent for humanity if you will, on a world stage, and, if I were able to employ such status symbols as the French intelligentsia represented to help drive home my points, then I would be justified in using them. I felt that this was especially true when many editorialists, especially those in America, who had been conscientiously ignoring the significance of my actions while idiotically dubbing me "Global Goon", or "Whirled Citizen", began to take my efforts more seriously on learning that I had the support of such eminent persons as Albert Camus and later François Mauriac, Albert Einstein and Albert Schweitzer. Had these same scoffing editorialists troubled to read my statements before the press con-

The World Citizen Identity Card.

Petitioning the Queen in front of Buckingham Palace, May, 1953.

ference, perhaps Sarrazac's recruiting of celebrities would have been unnecessary. But I suppose it is the way of the world that one lone man is seldom listened to, and even then only rarely heard.

At any rate, comment in the world press was enormously exciting to read after the conference. *The New Yorker* acknowledged: "Mr. Davis, whether he acted wisely or foolishly, is in step with the universe. The rest of us march to a broken drum." *Life* noted that I had "aroused a deep longing for peace". Even the sedate *Manchester Guardian* observed that I was "a man to be reckoned with". *Time* no longer saw me as an "eccentric freak" but described me, more than charitably, as someone with "a clear, canny mind which constantly surprises his French intellectual colleagues". Typical of those newspapers which dramatically shifted their opinion of me after the press conference was the Montreal *Gazette* which admitted editorially: "Garry Davis is making rather more of an impact on the world than was generally anticipated."

But it was *Harper's* that actually admitted how impressive was the company I now kept, as if wholly irrespective of what I had been saying all along. "Six months ago," the editorial stated, "young Davis was a pathetic and somewhat absurd figure, staging a one-man sit-down strike on the doorstep of the U.N. Assembly. Now ... he is supported by a group of intellectuals which astonishingly includes Albert Einstein, the novelist Richard Wright, British food expert Sir John Boyd Orr, and a number of prominent French literary figures such as Albert Camus, Jean-Paul Sartre, and André Gide."

Of course I was pleased that I was being taken seriously now, but I was also somewhat disappointed in the journalists who had not been able to understand me until I became fortified with an inescapably imposing list of patrons and sponsors.

The Moscow press was not inattentive either. *Pravda* described me as "a maniac exporting world government from America along with powdered eggs and detective stories". The Communist press called me a "cosmopolitan" and therefore "an agent of imperialist reaction". My aim, Moscow asserted, was "to soften Europe for American colonization, to eradicate from the people's consciousness the desire for national independence and sovereignty, to deafen the feelings of national dignity and pride, to dilute national culture, and to crush under its heel national traditions." How this "line" jibed with the "withering away of the state" was never made apparent.

It was interesting to note that a number of American newspapers regarded me with exactly the same contempt as did the Soviet press. The New York *Daily Mirror*, for example, bellowed, "Why don't global guys, like that world citizen Garry Davis, go to Russia to preach the counsel of perfection." The Birmingham (Alabama) *Age Herald* said I represented "confused and frustrated idealism". And there were others in America claiming that I was obviously a "very clever" Moscow agent just as the Soviet conservatives saw me as "capitalistic propaganda". But this represented, I am afraid, lunatic fringe comment and those same editorial pages have scored every one-worlder from Wendell Willkie to Albert Einstein. I discounted them as such and took courage from the fact that responsible organs of public opinion were now beginning to understand my message and take it seriously.

Thus, with what Madison Avenue might call my "corporate image" restored, I was ready to take on a new project. Edgar Ansel Mowrer, an American columnist who was covering the U.N. in Paris, had given me the tip.

"Trygve Lie has been talking about a world security force," he ventured one day after lunch. "Why don't you offer yourself as its first member?"

I jumped at the suggestion and immediately called Sarrazac at his office. We met the next day, and I outlined the tentative plan.

"Can you help me?" I asked.

He looked at me, eyes deep and profound, yet as usual with latent fire. He seemed amused. "Ah, I see ze pilot eez about to drop heez bombs again."

I smiled. "Something like that."

"*Eh bien, d'accord.*"

We shook hands.

I had been reading Albert Camus' novel *The Plague*, and the name "Oran" was fresh in my mind. Hence this became the code name for the new operation.

Basically the plan was for certain members of the Conseil de Solidarité and myself, along with a team of "operational personnel", to be among the balcony audience of a plenary session of the General Assembly of the United Nations, unnoticed if possible. At some propitious moment, I would get to my feet, pretend to start out accompanied by two "bodyguards", but instead jump the balcony railing, skirt out along the narrow causeway used for lights and, in full view of the delegates, the public and, we hoped, the TV cameras, address the world on the general subject of world government and offer myself as the first world policeman. Other council members would then translate my statement into French, Russian, Spanish and Chinese. Needless to say, the whole operation would have to be planned and executed with great secrecy. If the U.N. security police caught on, we would all be whisked out of the Palais de Chaillot without ever having been heard.

Other members of the Conseil were to be stationed across the street in a café, to hold an immediate press conference to explain the significance of the event and then give it their support. Albert Camus volunteered for this assignment.

We now became engrossed with clandestine meetings, smoke-filled-room planning, and the endlessly intricate preparations necessary to co-ordinate such an operation. Sarrazac, of course, was the chief strategist. Since it was rumoured that the U.N. might recess for the Christmas holiday on December 10th, we decided that Oran should take place between November 10th and 20th, in order to allow time for follow-up action while the U.N. was still in Paris.

Ten days after the press conference, the Conseil de Solidarité met with me at Hélion's to discuss Oran. I read a draft declaration. Camus and Breton said it was too long and not sharp enough. They wanted no frills. Just plain talking, and as little of that as possible.

"Eet must bite," Camus told me.

Some others, however, especially the women, thought the declaration already too severe. But all agreed that it was excessively long. So the police force was cut in the interest of brevity. "We weel *be* the world police force, anyway," said Sarrazac, "beginning November 19th, so why talk of eet?"

He then took the floor and explained the plan of Oran as far as it had been determined. There was general agreement, so all that was left for me to do was to reword the declaration.

Suddenly it was Friday, November 19. O-day! At 12 noon we had our last organizational meeting. Twenty-five Frenchmen, Russell Benedict, Meyer Levin, the novelist, with whom I had become friendly during the past month, and I met at Mme Kellerson's elegant house on Avenue President Wilson, just below the Trocadero.

Sarrazac had mapped out the plan on a great white sheet of paper which he tacked to the wall. It looked like the Grand Strategy for the War Between the Worlds. As he explained its execution in crisp, short sentences, I thought of our pilot briefings at the 92nd Bomb Group in England before our raids over Germany. Positions were assigned. Meyer Levin said someone would have to move the balcony lights so that the TV cameras would not be over-exposed. Sarrazac refused to let any of his men take care of this detail, so Levin volunteered.

Benedict observed that a man had to be at the upstairs stage door opening on to the small balcony where I was to speak in order to head off any U.N. security agents coming up the back stairs. Sarrazac pondered a moment, said *"D'accord"*, turned to d'Herbemont, his assistant, and said, "Well, you are the pigeon." D'Herbemont nodded gleefully.

Then Roche and Rimajou, who had started World Citizen clubs in the Paris suburbs, begged for assignments. Roche offered himself as my personal bodyguard because, as he said, he was an expert in ju-jitsu, and Rimajou was appointed in charge of the group of youngsters distributing the mimeographed text of the declaration to the newsroom.

The usual French confusion continued all through this as an undercurrent. *"Mais alors..."* *"Moi? Je suis absolument d'accord, mais quand même..."* *"Bouge pas, c'est réglé..."* Tickets were finally distributed and the first *de facto* world police force straggled out in merry disorder to "police" the United Nations!

I was worried about the text, which had just been completed that morning, and was struggling to memorize it. It had been cut from four minutes to forty-five seconds. Robert, Jeanne Allymand-Martin, Father Monteclard, Romain-Laiter and I were left in the big room.

"Eh bien, mon général," Sarrazac said to me, his smile conspiratorial, "you are back in ze war. How does eet feel?"

"Not so hot," I replied. "In the last one, I was only a second lieutenant."

Finally, it was 2:30: time to advance.

We arrived at our seats in the balcony without incident. At 3, the session had not yet started. Without looking around, I knew there were at least fifty of our people scattered throughout the audience. How many more were in on the plot, I didn't know. I saw Meyer Levin in the box with the Paramount Newsreel men.

I could feel eyes on me from everywhere. I knew the U.N. security guards were alerted. As I had handed in my ticket, one of them had hurried away to the guard section, but I took courage in the fact that our plan included surprise and a tactical feint.

Jeanne was on my left, Romain-Laiter on my right and Roche behind me. I looked directly forward. Suddenly, my attention was caught by a sound man methodically unrolling a huge wheel of wire along the balcony aisle, and on to the tiny side balcony where the great lights were mounted. He bent down and attached something, came back smiling and climbed over the velvet-lined boxes like a kid in a playground. The balcony railing was wired for sound!

After the sound man had successfully and to my horror alerted everyone, the cameraman began to focus on the spot where I was supposed to speak! I sank lower in my seat. Benedict, also in the box, looked excited. Levin was his usual indifferent yet efficient self. Then I noticed the cameraman lean over to Levin and point to the large standing lamps on the balcony. Levin nodded his head, and up came the sound man again with two fellow workers. They climbed over the railing once more, grabbed the first two lights from the left balcony, and, in full view of the whole wide world, moved them to the right balcony! I broke out in a cold sweat. Did they want me to be surrounded with security guards before we began? Yet there it was, a neat little space, all microphoned, lighted, and trained upon by camera. It was no tip-off; it was a proclamation!

Someone came in and sat down in front of me. Clothed in a huge, conspicuous overcoat, this individual was trying to look nonchalant and crossed his legs casually. What a sorry security guard this is, I thought; a disgrace to the profession. Then slowly the figure turned around and winked broadly! It was Camus. It was his way of saying, *"Bon courage."* He got up and left quickly.

Two newsmen approached me. "Hey, Davis, what's going on?" I secretly marvelled at their professional instinct.

"Search me."

"Going to make a speech?"
"A speech? Why that's against the rules, isn't it, boys?"
"Yeah, like camping across the street."

Just before the session started, Pierre Pichou, assistant head security chief, and his two assistants, came in the side door and walked down the aisle a little way. Spying me, they smiled sheepishly and waved an embarrassed greeting. When Benedict spotted them, it threw him into a fit. He jumped out of the box and engaged them in animated conversation. Finally he coaxed them into his box and held them there with his brisk if vacuous monologue.

All at once, Dr. Herbert Evatt, President of the U.N. Assembly and Trygve Lie, the Secretary-General, filed in with the delegates behind them. Evatt opened the session. The atmosphere was electric. The question for debate was atomic control. First, the Polish delegate was scheduled to speak, then the Yugoslav delegate. Everyone knew what they were going to say. I looked around. Sarrazac was neatly cached away in a box, and Crepey, son of an African chief, drafted to deliver the declaration in his native Togoland dialect, was discreetly ensconced in another section, looking dignified and calm. Directly above him was the ascetic Father Monteclard, priest by day and world citizen by night. I wondered what his parishioners would think of him now. Then, on the other side, were the Maquis musclemen, Sarrazac's "police" force, who were to block off the U.N. security guards. I had insisted on blocking tactics only . . . no violence.

The Yugoslav was thirty minutes into his speech and sounded as if he would be good for thirty more, accusing the West of warmongering. But suddenly he was leaving the podium. I glanced at my watch: 4:45. This is it, I decided. We're past our deadline. Now or never.

I stood up. Jeanne and Romain-Laiter rose with me. I started down the aisle toward the left exit. Then I heard Father Monteclard's booming voice: "And now, the people have the floor!"

Quickly I jumped the railing, ran to the middle of the balcony and ripped off my coat. Dr. Evatt was just looking up, wondering what wild man had dared to interrupt. The crowd in the balcony started to applaud. The cameras began to grind. The "World Police" Maquis had silently moved into place, but somehow the security guards were slipping through.

"Mr. Chairman and delegates. I interrupt in the name of the people of the world not represented here . . ." The delegates were spread out in front of me in long rows. They were taking off their headsets, shaking them, not quite sure where the voice was coming from. Then their gaze followed the President's and they too looked up, attentive.

Dr. Evatt saw me and made a motion with his hand for me to continue.

I looked at him in amazement. A hush fell over the crowd. I actually *had* the floor! But in an instant the flying squad of police were upon me. I was so startled, or perhaps so unnerved at being manhandled, that I departed from my speech and shouted desperately such slogans as "Pass the word to the people!" "One government for one world!" and "I speak for the people!" as I was hustled out.

Then the "second act" began. Sarrazac jumped the other railing and made the entire speech with every proper oratorical flourish in front of the cameras. Next, Crepey stood up and delivered a rousing declaration on the rights of man. The show went on for a half hour.

Back in security headquarters, I was handled with kid gloves. "Why do you make so much trouble for us?" Pierre Pichou asked. "We are your friends. Why do you embarrass us like this? Try to be sensible."

"Nothing personal, Pierre," I told him. "You have your duties; we have ours. *C'est la vie.*"

After several hours of confinement and after everyone had gone home from the U.N., I was released. Significantly, no charge was made against me. A French regular policeman accompanied me to the street. He seemed nervous, as if he had something pressing on his mind. I turned to go.

"Ah, Monsieur Davis," he said hesitantly.

"Yes?"

"May I ask you a personal question?"

"Certainly."

"How much does a world policeman earn?"

5

If one judged by the headlines the next day, Operation Oran was a spanking success. *Franc-Tireur* and *Combat* gave banner headlines to it, though this was to be expected since both editors were members of the Conseil. Even the conservative *Le Monde*, however, gave the event front-page coverage.

The newsreels played all over town and even on my own long-lost Broadway too. My father sent me a photo of the Trans-Lux theatre at 45th Street with a special sign in front: GARRY HECKLES U.N!

Albert Camus played a major part in the bistro across from the U.N. during the subsequent press conference. *Franc-Tireur* screamed his quote in giant inch-high type: WE ARE WITH HIM! Camus told the newsmen to take our action seriously or he personally would belay any snide or ridiculing commentator with his own pen. His prestige among working journalists in Paris was of sufficient stature to guarantee serious treatment, since he had given our movement his unqualified support.

Sarrazac and I sat down the following day to discuss the next "battle" in the "campaign".

"How about another council meeting?" I suggested, now more reconciled to collective support. "Maybe they've got some ideas."

"*Eh bien, d'accord*," said Sarrazac and five days later the "World Citizens' General Assembly" was called to order once more in Hélions' studio, surrounded by his semi-abstract nudes on rue Michelet in the Latin Quarter.

"Now we must get the people of Paris to endorse our declaration," said Sarrazac to the group.

"We should introduce the Conseil de Solidarité to the public too," added Father Monteclard.

We discussed this suggestion and decided that a big meeting was in order. The Salle Pleyel, the Carnegie Hall of Paris, was chosen as the locale. But the time was desperately short. Spectacular advertising methods were necessary.

"Why not distribute handbills from the streets ourselves?" said André Breton. The idea was novel and intriguing. I began to admire the daring of these public figures. I wondered how well-placed men in New York or London would have reacted to such a suggestion, for I had heard even less unorthodox ideas called "undignified" by self-styled one worlders in the States.

All agreed. The handbills were printed and, at noon three days later, I emerged from the Métro at Blvd. des Italiens and Blvd. Haussman to see André Breton, Paul Monteclard, Sarrazac, Romain-Laiter, Kobloth-Décroix, the labour union representative, and many others ready to "hard sell" the Salle Pleyel meeting through hand-to-hand distribution. It was then that I learned how really daring this action was.

"Give me some tracts," I said to Sarrazac.

"*Mais non*, do you want to get arrested?"

"Arrested?"

"*Bien sûr*, it is against the law," he said, and gaily threw a handful in the air.

We arrived at Place de l'Opéra, which at 12 noon is like Piccadilly at the dinner hour, or Broadway just after the theatre break. People were streaming in and out of the Métro, the Café de la Paix was filled to overflowing with American tourists, and pedestrian traffic was heavy.

A crowd had gathered around Breton, Sarrazac and myself. Sarrazac kept nudging me to do something. But with no handbills, I had nothing to do except an old tap routine from *Let's Face It!* He, Breton and Monteclard were madly throwing handful after handful of leaflets over the heads of the crowd. The people standing around would brush them tolerantly from their heads as they came floating down, grinning at us as some truck-mounted newsreel cameras recorded the scene.

Finally, when the ground was solidly covered with paper, we retraced our steps. The newsreel trucks followed us religiously until we disappeared into the Métro. I think Breton was sorry that the gendarmes, eyeing us apprehensively at Place de l'Opéra, did not arrest anyone because of the publicity it might have given us.

In the meantime, the world government movement was spreading to other parts of the world. On November 29th, a large meeting was held in Central Hall, Westminster, London, initiated by the "Crusade for World Government". More than

2,000 people attended, an extraordinary number for Britain, to endorse the "Oran Declaration". A resolution was drawn up and adopted, to be presented to Dr. Evatt along with the French resolution which was to come from the Salle Pleyel meeting. The British proposal was signed by 45 members of Parliament plus other leading British personalities.

From the United States came a telegram of endorsement from Dr. Albert Einstein, whom we had chosen to preside symbolically at our meeting.

"Union Fédérale" of Belgium, leading world government organization in that country, was represented by Maurice Cosyn, its executive secretary, who came down personally to attend the Paris meeting.

"Garry, there is a new group forming in Brussels," he told me. "It is called 'Les Amis de Garry Davis'. So far there are 12,000 members."

In Germany, over 500 World Citizen clubs had sprung up. A vast network was building to incorporate all the world citizenship activity there. No one knew its numerical strength; no one had time to count. Stefan Zickler, one of my "representatives" in Germany, estimated that the German unit had several hundred thousand members. "You must come here," he wrote. "The movement is growing too fast not to have a leader."

There were letters from Switzerland, Finland, Iceland, Poland, and Capetown; Japan, Iran, Ireland, and Indochina. They came from all corners and from every walk of life. Many people wanted me to bestow world citizenship on them; others wanted merely to be registered as world citizens; still others wanted to work actively for the full realization of the goal. One day I was visited by fifteen Libyans all wanting to become world citizens.

Amid this hurly-burly, the business of preparing my speech for the Salle Pleyel meeting was a trial. I asked Jean Hélion to help me, and one afternoon two days before the meeting we sat in his studio, he at his battered typewriter, while I paced the floor, trying to put the speech in order.

"Just explain, very simply, your story," Jean said.

"Yes, fine," I answered. "But my story is about as simple as *The Ice Man Cometh*."

Word by word, sentence by tortured sentence, we toiled our way through.

"Have you thanked the people who brought you food at the United Nations?" he asked.

"Well, I suppose I thanked them as they handed it to me," I replied.

"Thank them again publicly."

Just before the meeting, Professor Giraud tutored me on the French tongue-twisters of the speech.

On the day of the meeting, December 3rd, I drove from Neuilly, where Sarrazac lived, with the professor and Hélion in Sarrazac's Renault. It was raining and yet there was a great line of people waiting in front of the Salle Pleyel to get in. Hawkers of all sorts of peace bulletins were going up and down the line shouting their wares.

In the "green room", the Conseil de Solidarité was gathered and in great confusion. Carlo Levi had come in from Italy, and Patrick Armstrong, Henry Osborne's executive secretary for the Crusade for World Government, from England. We greeted one another in a profusion of grasping hands. Sarrazac began to explain the resolution in which were three questions to pose to the U.N. The meeting was to endorse this resolution and then forward it to the U.N. Assembly. Meanwhile, I received a note from Radiodiffusion Française that a "hot" mike was waiting outside and would I say a few words? I went out and, in my state of tension, muttered something into the microphone.

Finally, the signal came for "curtain". The Conseil got up and filed on-stage to the strains of Beethoven's Fifth. When they filed in, the audience began to applaud. As more and more illustrious personages were recognized, the applause built into an ovation. The hall was jammed, and there were three thousand more waiting outside to get in. I was left alone in the darkened wings, leather jacket on, speech in pocket, heart in mouth.

In the middle of the stage was a vacant chair, left for Einstein, our symbolic chairman. There was no flag, no banner; neither would have been appropriate. The Conseil finally was seated. The applause died down. An air of expectancy filled the theatre.

The lights dimmed, went out. The music came up. Suddenly a screen, lowered in the blackout, came alive. The Paramount Newsreel film showed the U.N. guards converging on me on the tiny balcony overlooking the U.N. delegates, then Sarrazac finishing the speech. There was a brief shot of Molotov fumbling with his headset. All through the film, the music built to a crescendo.

Then the screen went blank. The music stopped. The hall was utterly silent. My heart was pounding loud in my ears. The electrician on the backstage board light looked down at me from his precarious balcony and winked. Then a tiny light signal flashed above the stage right door.

I stepped through, a small spotlight picking me up. The build-up had been dramatic and the timing exact. The effect on the audience was electrifying. A clap of thunder burst from them, and built into a sustained roar. It hit me like a wave and I almost retreated in fright back through my little door.

I moved across the centre stage and sat down in a vacant chair. Flashbulbs were popping all around and brilliant arc lights for the TV cameras were blinding my eyes so that I could see no audience at all. My smile was broad, however. The applause built into a frenzy. Then the arc lights turned off, the applause died away, and Jean-Jacques Agapit opened the proceedings.

Camus' speech coming after five or six others, all interpreting "*le geste de Gaaree Daavees*," ripped to shreds those pessimists who declared that we were simply Utopians and not practical men. In short, crisp sentences, often humorous, Camus exposed the duplicity of the diplomatic world. His delivery was professional, his pauses effective. He received an ovation when he sat down.

Then it was my turn. I rose shakily but determined at least to be understood. My speech was simple and direct with little rhetoric. Also, it was short. As I talked slowly, feeling the words roll off my tongue easily, I felt better. Toward the end of it, I stated that I didn't intend to wait until it was too late to do anything about world peace . . . that I was acting now. My conclusion seemed to unleash anew the pent-up feelings of the audience. When I finished with "*Peuple de Paris, la parole est à vous !*" they took their cue and demonstrated for about ten minutes.

After Sarrazac's speech the electrician, with typical Gallic independence, took things in his own hands. The Métro closed at 1:30 and it was then 1:15. So he turned out the lights! There we were, on stage, the audience still in the house and in semi-darkness, the only light coming from the lobby through the open doors. Slowly we began to file out, audience and speakers alike, like tired revellers in the early morning when the masks are off and the ball is over.

It was still raining slightly when we got to the street. I said good night to Sarrazac and the others and started walking to the Métro. A beggar was huddled on the steps as I hurried down, his thin hand outstretched. I reached into my pocket and found it empty. I stopped. The train was coming into the station. I watched it load and pull out. Then the attendant came from his cage and moved toward us on the demi-dark steps.

"Well, that's it," he called to us. "That was the last train. Move along now."

We climbed the stairs slowly together and when we reached the top, the beggar hobbled along in his direction, I in mine.

Next morning, there remained the question of how the Salle Pleyel resolutions were to be brought to the attention of the U.N. The press had carried the full story of the meeting. Still, the actual documents had to be delivered.

I had written Dr. Evatt explaining the reasons for the November 19th balcony interruption and had received from him a gracious reply in which he stated that he would be happy to circulate among the delegates whatever petitions or documents I had. I wanted to meet and discuss the whole situation with him as soon as possible.

But this plan met with strong objections from my French supporters, particularly Breton, Camus, and Sarrazac. "Speak with the enemy! Sit down at the same table with diplomats as if you were friends! What are you thinking of, Garry? Do you want to betray the people?"

That morning, Dr. Evatt's secretary called to arrange an appointment for me. Russell Benedict set the date for the following Monday. We had not yet spoken to Sarrazac about delivering the petitions and the resolutions from Salle Pleyel but began nevertheless to gather together such items as we thought pertinent. There was the "Oran Declaration," the "Salle Pleyel Declaration", the British petition, a letter from Professor Giraud and Sarrazac acting for the Conseil de Solidarité, and a covering letter from me as chief messenger boy.

Then came a telephone call from Sarrazac.

"How about the petitions?" I asked him. "They've got to be delivered, you know."

"*Mais bien sûr.*"

"Why don't we just walk up there and deliver them?"

"*Pourquoi pas?*"

"Okay. Cosyn is still here... and Pat Armstrong to represent Great Britain..."

"And the Empiah," added Benedict.

"We'll all go up together, right?"

"*Tout à fait d'accord.*"

"We'll let you know when we've got all the stuff together."

"*Entendu.*" We hung up.

Russell got Dr. Evatt's secretary on the phone to inform him we would be up there directly.

"But I don't understand, Mr. Benedict," he said with a thick Australian accent, "I just spoke with someone from your office and informed him that an interview today is quite impossible."

"You didn't inform anyone in our office," said Russell.

"Isn't this the world citizen group?" he asked.

"It is," replied Russell.

"And isn't there a Mr. Sazzarac there?"

"Uh-uh. Yes, that is, it's Sarrazac. Well you see, that's the secretariat office and this is the office of the president," said Russell quickly.

"What's up?" I asked. He put his hand over the mouthpiece. "Sarrazac got to him first. Says he told him 'no dice'."

"Tell him we'll be up anyway. Say the people can't wait."

"Sir, would you be good enough to inform Dr. Evatt," Russell said into the telephone, "that our mandate is from the people and it is our duty to deliver our documents today whether we have a formal appointment or not."

I felt annoyed at Sarrazac. Why hadn't he told me what the secretary had said? Was he planning something behind my back? Or perhaps he hadn't understood the thick Australian accent. I would ask him about it that evening. But somehow, as in many other minor points of dissension, I never did. The public pressure on us both, like soldiers in battle facing the common enemy, made us overlook personal differences. Worlds apart in background, temperament and education, the miracle was not that we had misunderstandings but that we were able to work together at all.

It wasn't until seven o'clock that evening that everything and everybody was ready. Then off we went, the five of us driving to Palais de Chaillot.

At the wooden barriers surrounding the Palais, I asked for the security chief. When the chief, my old friend Pierre Pichou, arrived, I told him of our mission and asked whether Dr. Evatt was still there. He told us both Dr. Evatt and Trygve Lie had planned to go grouse hunting that weekend but had stayed in town expressly to receive our documents.

"They waited for you until five o'clock," he continued. "Then they left instructions with me that when you arrive, I am to bring your material to them immediately where they are dining."

"You see"—Sarrazac turned to me with an attempt at camaraderie—"you are more important zan zee birds."

"And you too, my friend," I said soberly, thinking that at least we had saved the lives of some grouse as I handed the chief our documents. "Take good care of them," I added. "They represent the conscience of humanity."

That Sunday evening, Hélion, Romain-Laiter, Robert Robin, another labour representative to the Conseil, Benedict, Sarrazac and I met at Louis Rosen's office at rue Marboeuf. Mr. Rosen was our financier member of the Conseil. It had been announced in the late Saturday papers that the U.N. would leave Paris on Saturday next, December 11th, for Christmas. Obviously we would have to let the public know the answers to the Salle Pleyel questions before then. It gave us one short week.

"But where? At the Salle Pleyel again?" asked Hélion.

"No, it proved too small the first time," I replied.

"What about that big stadium, the Velodrome d'Hiver?" suggested Benedict timidly. It was the Madison Square Garden of Paris. Besides the six-day bicycle race, only two figures in France could fill it: Thorez and de Gaulle.

"Are you crazy?" exclaimed Sarrazac in astonishment.

"Well, why not?" Mr. Rosen wanted to know.

"Too beeg," replied Sarrazac. "It seats over twenty thousand and takes months to organize a meeting for it. We 'ave only four days at the most. What if we 'ave a failure? And it cannot help but be a failure."

"Not if twenty thousand people show up," I ventured.

"I'm for it," Robin said. "The iron is hot. Let us not be afraid to strike."

"But it costs almost one million francs to rent," Sarrazac

returned weakly. He knew the organizational details would be in his lap.

We all looked at Mr. Rosen, who alone could raise such a figure. He wiped his brow.

"But may be it is not free on Thursday night," he said hopefully.

Benedict called the management. It was free. The air in the room was tense. We now had the chance—if we dared to take it—to demonstrate the tremendous pulling power of world citizenship. Or to fall flat on our faces! We had only four days to organize. I was thinking also of my own predicament. To address three thousand Frenchmen in their own language was bad enough; to address twenty thousand people in a cavernous arena could well be a catastrophe. But I had long since given up the illusion that my fate was in my own hands. I think all of us felt more or less the same way. Finally Mr. Rosen shrugged.

"Well, why not? Life is short."

"Bravo!" said Robin and we all trooped out for a *vin blanc* to celebrate the big decision.

On Monday, I arrived at the Palais for my interview with Dr. Evatt. My French advisers had pumped me full of advice on what to say and what not to say. There seemed to be a sharp difference as to when I was speaking for myself or speaking "officially", that is, as the "First World Citizen". To my claim that they were one and the same, there were sharp protests.

The guards were waiting to receive me, and I was immediately ushered into Dr. Evatt's office. After cordial greetings, I asked him if we could have answers to our questions by Wednesday of that week, apologizing for the shortness of time, as we wanted to announce the replies at the Velodrome d'Hiver.

"The Vel d'Hiv, eh?" he mused, a twinkle in his eye. "You people trying to compete with us?"

"No sir," I replied stiffly, "we're just concerned with peace for all of us . . . U.N. delegates included of course."

"Of course. Well, I shall see that the delegates receive your questions," he said in his thick Australian accent, "but I doubt seriously whether you shall have replies by Wednesday. After all, you raise some rather large questions, you know."

"You mean like world peace?" I asked. "Perhaps that is a naïve question, but who is to answer it if not the United Nations?

Isn't that what it's for? And if not, isn't it better to admit it now rather than wait for another war, with the U.N. as a sort of smokescreen? I'm not speaking only for myself, Dr. Evatt, but for all the people of Paris as well as for many throughout the world who have already supported us, including many from your homeland, Australia."

"Well, I guess I'll have to get a letter off to you myself, not as the President of the General Assembly, you understand, but as a private individual. Will that do, do you think?"

I thought it would do fine. To the public, Dr. Evatt was Dr. Evatt; the public does not appreciate the diplomatic hair-splitting of a man saying one thing officially and another—usually the opposite—unofficially, when both statements are meant for public consumption.

We parted cordially. The wind bit through my leather jacket as I crossed to the restaurant steps on which I had lived for six memorable days, three months before. I went into the restaurant and ordered a coffee. Though I was by no stretch of the imagination a U.N. employee, the manager and waitresses knew me well.

An elderly waitress with tired eyes but a proud chin approached me as I sipped, and waited timidly. I smiled and she came closer.

"Mr. Davis, my husband is a Roumanian refugee . . . he has no papers . . . the police will not give him permission to work. I could only get work here with the U.N. while it is in Paris. But next week? . . . I thought perhaps . . . that you . . ." she faltered.

"I wish I could do something," I told her, not quite able to meet her eyes, "but I myself have no papers . . . and no money. I'm just as illegal as your husband."

She walked away slowly, the U.N. waitress's uniform looking crisp and clean, but her shoes old and worn.

My coffee was cold. I got up and left. Her husband was not legal; I was not legal. How long will it be, I wondered as I hurried into the Métro, before humankind itself becomes legal.

6

After my meeting with Dr. Evatt, there began a rash of activity which made the preparations for the Salle Pleyel rally look like the announcement of a checkers match between two inmates of the Old Folks Home in Dry Gulch, Montana. A million leaflets were printed and distributed throughout Paris by youthful world citizen groups—on the *grands boulevards*, in the Métro, in the side streets, in restaurant lavabos, on theatre seats, inside napkins—everywhere. Someone procured a plane, and the pilot, a friend of Sarrazac, Inc., dropped thousands of leaflets illegally, risking arrest. Sarrazac had daily, almost hourly, meetings with his staff. He was like a man possessed. The French in general have a peculiar talent of organising in an aura of seeming chaos. Robert Sarrazac had raised this talent to the level of a science.

To add to the excitement, we decided to hold a press conference to publicize the meeting further and to call for funds. Debts were mounting along with the tension.

I had numerous interviews and on Thursday itself, the day of the rally, two photographers from *Noir et Blanc*, a popular weekly, pursued me all day long. The dailies, *Franc-Tireur* and *Combat*, gave front-page coverage all week to our activities.

Dr. Evatt's reply was duly received, not on Wednesday as expected, but at one o'clock Thursday afternoon—a catastrophe for me! I had just seven hours in which to write, translate and rehearse a speech in French to be given in a mammoth auditorium before, we hoped, close to 20,000 people. Speaking in the Vel d'Hiv was difficult under the best of circumstances.

Again I was closeted with Jean Hélion and once more we tortured our way through my script. By six-thirty, my voice was hoarse from rehearsal. Pegeen Hélion, Jean's wife, popped in every twenty minutes with a glass of pineapple juice to mollify my tired vocal chords. But what could I drink to improve my accent? I asked her.

I arrived at the huge stadium with Jeanne Allymand-Martin at about eight-thirty. As we passed the front entrance, I saw people by the hundreds streaming in, the hawkers outside selling French fries and hot chestnuts along with peace pamphlets. We waited in the room where the wrestlers, hockey skaters, six-day bicyclists, boxers, basketball players and other entertainers rested before their entrances. We were gathered in a tense, uncertain group. I was carefully anaesthetizing myself for the occasion. There was a conference. The aftermath of the meeting was in question. The whole Conseil was not present, for many members thought the venture ill-advised, hasty, and did not feel justified in lending their active support to it.

L'Abbé Pierre was present with a tape recorder and had me tape my speech while in the green room. At about nine, my guides and I traversed the cold, dank corridors underneath the main area. The others had gone on ahead. The rumble of the crowd in the huge arena came through to us. Stepping out behind the podium through a short corridor into the vast auditorium, I was struck by the immensity of the audience. Every seat, except for the topmost tier, was filled.

All the other speakers were already on the platform. I mounted the steps quickly. In my leather jacket I was easily recognizable. My presence on the stand seemed to be a signal for the crowd. The first bursts of scattered applause gradually melted into a massive rumble, which in turn gave way to a roaring chant: "GAAARRR-RRREEEE DAAAAA-VEEEESSS . . . GAAA-RRRR-RRREEEE DAAAAA-VEEEESS."

Broadway had accustomed me to the stage and audience applause, but this was a shock wave of sound. My eyes became wide and dilated; my hands rose automatically in the air, fists clenched. Flashbulbs were popping; huge arc lights were beating at us. People moved up and down the aisles, many praying on their knees. Then the chant slowly lost its power. The emotion began to ebb, releasing us from its tyrannical grip. The sound receded into a restless whisper throughout the hall. On the platform, we were still in a state of stupefaction, and it was with effort that I pulled my thoughts into focus. I had tasted a powerful drug, perhaps the most powerful of all, and, for a brief moment, I had succumbed to it. I could not look at the audience for a while.

Jean-Jacques Agapit again presided over the meeting. There was a vast undercurrent of impatience, of waiting, of hoping to hear or witness something more than words. This unnerved

Jean-Jacques. He announced the orators one by one. Then he sat down, relieved that his chore was done. Sarrazac leaned over to him in a frenzy.

"Announce that Garry is to speak!"

After all the preparation, the publicity, the tremendous ovation, he had forgotten to mention my name! But now it was too late. He couldn't mention it as an afterthought. Besides, the first speaker was mounting the rostrum.

The highlight of the evening was to be Dr. Evatt's answer to our declaration in his "personal" letter to me. Kobloth-Décroix was to read it, and I was to comment on it. But for some reason, he was first on the speakers' list and I was last. Obviously no one in between could make any mention of it out of respect to me. This left an unmerciful gap to be filled with sheer rhetoric.

The audience, having heard most of this before, grew increasingly restive. They wanted a crusade and were getting a tea party. They were already convinced about what the speakers were trying to convince them of. Peace was being talked about once more instead of being acted upon.

Halfway through the evening, a young man jumped to the speaker's podium, his eyes wild, his hair streaming. He began appealing to me directly, while "official" hands sought to pull him down. He persisted and won the sympathy of the audience. This was action—unorthodox, spontaneous and unrehearsed, like the chant. In horror, I saw my own interruption at the U.N. mirrored in this young rebel.

He screamed: "All right, we want peace! Now what? What shall we do? Shall we refuse to bear arms? Shall we refuse to be conscripted? We are tired of mere words. You . . . you yourself are a man of action. Lead us! We will follow you. For God's sake, there's a war approaching. Tell us what to do!"

He was finally pulled down, the "rebellion" squelched, our own "security guards" doing their ironic duty well. Orthodoxy moves fast, I thought. The audience applauded him for a solid minute.

At last it was my turn to speak. I rose grimly, shaken by the young man's fervent interruption. I knew beforehand that my written words were inadequate to the occasion. And my command of French was not sufficient for extemporaneous speaking. Behind me I could hear all sorts of whispered conversations, with Sarrazac scurrying to and fro, talking to various members of the council. The young rebel had stolen the night. The high point of the evening seemed to be past.

As the microphone picked up my words and hurled them forward, full-blown from ten enormous speakers, I realized that we were doing the very thing that I had argued against. We wrote world constitutions, declarations of rights; we passed bills and laws that spoke of freedom and equality, and even happiness—and what did they mean? If not followed by deeds, they were sterile, empty, flat marks on paper with no genuine relationship to life. The only deeds that night had come from the audience, the people: first, the vocal support at the outset, and then the "rebel" who begged for dynamic leadership and got pulled down and thrust aside like an unwanted delinquent.

My speech finished, suddenly the meeting was over. As the mammoth crowd left the Vel d'Hiv, I felt utterly drained and as loose-jointed as a rag doll. The atmosphere in the hall seemed to be a massive "So what?"

I returned, despondent, to my tiny room over the kitchen of the Hôtel des Etats-Unis. I looked at the bare walls, the solitary bed. In my pocket was an advertisement of the meeting. Slowly, almost shamefully, I tore it to pieces and crawled into bed. But as I fell asleep to the strains of the sad, tinkling piano from the restaurant below, the news channels of the world were swelling with the word of a breath-taking success.

I had been dead wrong. The meeting itself was the deed. It joined with the Salle Pleyel meeting in becoming a historic landmark in the evolution of world citizenship. While in my opinion, and perhaps in those of a few others who attended, the meeting was a failure because we seemed unable to give the audience anything tangible to take home, it was regarded as a tremendous feat by millions throughout the world. The farther away from Paris, the greater attention it received. *Life*, for instance, gave it a four-page spread. People saw only headlines screaming GARRY DAVIS SPEAKS BEFORE 20,000 AT VEL D'HIV; or, CROWDS CHANT WORLD CITIZEN'S NAME; or, 20,000 PARISIANS IN ACCORD WITH DAVIS.

No, it was only my pride which made me feel I had to "give" something to the fellow citizens attending. Who was I to be able to give something? I later wondered. Yes, the drug had been powerful.

Indeed, if world citizens were born at the Salle Pleyel meeting, that night at the Vel d'Hiv they had begun marching.

The General Assembly of the United Nations left town as scheduled on December 11th. The Palais de Chaillot became "French" territory once again. The world continued as before. It was as if ghosts had peopled the halls for the past three months. Armaments piled up faster than ever; Korea was reaching the boiling point, concentration of troops being suspected in both North and South; Trieste was still demanded by both Italy and Yugoslavia; the Indo-China war, the fighting in Malaya, were in full, bloody swing; Berlin still endured the airlift; the United States was still building air bases, and the Soviet Union was still engaged in its insidious encroachment policy, capitalizing on human misery wherever it existed. Malan still practised restrictive segregation in South Africa, denying human rights to those humans born with brown pigment in their skin; German and Japanese rearmament was openly espoused and about to become a reality; the refugee problem was daily growing worse, with ten million in Germany alone; crime, political corruption, juvenile delinquency, divorce rates, all were on the rise. Four-fifths of the human race were still ill-fed, ill-clothed, and ill-housed. Nationalism was in full, deadly flower, spreading its poison everywhere, and the United Nations had gone home for the holidays.

One bright spot appeared on the horizon just before its departure, however. On December 1st, the Draft Declaration of a Universal Bill of Human Rights was proclaimed to the world. It was approved on December 7th and adopted on December 10th by the General Assembly. Forty-eight countries were in favour, including the United States, Great Britain, France, and India; none were against, and eight abstained: namely, the Communist bloc.

The Declaration contended in its first article that all men are born free and equal in dignity and rights; that they are endowed with reason and conscience and should act toward one another in a spirit of brotherhood.

The General Assembly stated that all people should seek to put into practice such sentiments not only as a duty but as a human right. Then the diplomats went home to get further instructions from their separatist monolithic sovereign-states.

Le Monde asked me for an article of comment on the U.N. deliberations. I obliged and summed it up simply: 10,000,000 words versus 0 deeds.

The U.N. was gone, but we were still there. My new deadline was coming up again. On December 23rd I was to be expelled once more from France. No one knew what would happen —least of all the French Government. There were government communiqués to the press, counter-communiqués by us to the press, comments and counter-comments by the Paris dailies, conjecture by weekly news magazines, personal contacts in governmental circles from the Minister of the Interior to the President's advisers, articles by Conseil members, articles by opponents, assurances that the Préfecture de Police was "against me officially" but "for me personally", and all in all, taken for what it was, an incredible expenditure of energy, time and intelligence over nothing.

On the 17th of December, the police called me down to the station. I went alone and quietly, feeling the whole business a side issue with little or no bearing on major problems. Unfortunately I could not have appreciated at the time the incessant frustration which plagued the average man in postwar Europe over the business of papers. I couldn't realise, not having been subjected daily to that degrading experience in the United States, what a phenomenal status I enjoyed as a paperless person. I was literally the symbol of frontierlessness and one recognized by a so-called sovereign government, able to move about, free to speak, hold meetings, and write and publish. I was a symbol of a brave new world-to-come wherein all would enjoy such freedom. It was enough for the present that one man had managed to achieve such a status. He must be protected and preserved at all costs. He was *le porte-parole*.

"*Eh bien*, Monsieur Davis, *citoyen du monde*, what are we going to do with you?" asked the sub-chief when I was seated.

"Why do anything with me?" I returned.

He leaned back in his chair. "I have heard that you are difficult to get along with."

I said nothing.

After a moment's silence, he leaned forward and asked intensely, "Why do you make so much trouble for us? Why don't you go back to America and talk to them of peace? Or why don't you go to Russia? They could use your world citizenship there. *Mais en* France . . . what have we to do with peace ?"

"Plenty," I said. "And the minute you think you don't, you're licked."

He reached into a drawer. Out came a *carte de séjour*. "Now, Mr. Davis . . ." He looked at me pleadingly.

I shook my head.

"Three months," he said hopefully.

"Make it thirty years," I said.

He withdrew it quickly. "Humph. I am just following my orders, Mr. Davis. It is here in case you change your mind."

Later in the week, le Préfet de Police himself, M. Leonard, sent a communiqué to the three governmental newspapers stating that he would personally receive me on the 21st to hand me my *permis de séjour*, but only after I had asked for it.

This veiled threat threw our camp into a fit of indignation. "*Quelle audace!*" exclaimed Sarrazac. "Nothing less than an audience with the Président de la République can wipe out such an insult, an insult not only to you personally, but to the entire Conseil and the people of Paris who support you. Besides, an audience with M. Auriol will give proper '*hauteur*,'" he continued, "raising you from a hapless, stateless person, '*d'origine américaine*' caught in police regulations, to the level of a proper sovereign."

I had been sleeping at a friend's house for the past two days rather than at the hotel, for Sarrazac, who had a spy complex hung over from the war, believed that there was danger of my being kidnapped, though who would want me he declined to say.

The dailies carried the story on the 23rd that I had requested an audience with M. Auriol, President of the Republic of France. My council assured me it would be at least ten days before an interview would be granted, if at all. The main thing for the moment, they told me, was that the police now had been stalled.

The next morning at 7:30, therefore, I was prepared to leave for the countryside for a needed rest at Don Livingstone's farm, 130 kilometres from Paris. As I was going out the front door my concierge came rushing in with the early morning edition of *Combat* in her hand. "*Félicitations*, Monsieur Davis!" she exclaimed breathlessly. "*Regardez.*" There on the front page in a little box was the news that the President would see me at five o'clock that afternoon!

№ 000001

IMPORTANT

This passport, properly issued, is valid for travel in all countries unless otherwise restricted.
It is not transferable. It is for use solely by the person to whom issued and is valid for five years.
The person to whom it is issued must sign his name on page 3 immediately on its receipt. This passport is NOT VALID unless it is signed.

GRAVA

Ĉi tiu pasporto, kun oficialaj vizoj, validas por vojaĝo en ĉiuj landoj.
Ĝi ne estas transdonebla. Ĝi estas nur uzebla de tiu persono al kiu ĝi estas oficiale donita kaj estas valida por kvin jaroj.
La persono al kiu ĝi estas oficiale donita devas subskribi sian nomon sur paĝo tri tuj je ricevo. Ĉi tiu pasporto estas VALIDA NUR se ĝi estas subskribita.

Page 1

I, the undersigned, hereby request all whom it may concern to permit freely and safely to pass, and in case of need to give all fair and lawful aid and protection to

Mi, la subskribinto, per ĉi tio, petas al ĉiuj koncernaj personoj sekure kaj libere pasi, kaj en okazo de bezono doni justan kaj leĝan helpon kaj protekton al

HEAD OF GOVERNMENT

GARRY DAVIS

de facto citizen of the world
efektiva civitano de la mondo

The bearer is accompanied by his
Kun la posedanto estas

Wife (Edzino) _____
Minor Children
(Neplenaĝaj Gefiloj) _____

Given under my hand and seal _____ in the name of the Absolute
Donita kun mia subskribo kaj sigelo

at (ĉe) NEW YORK, N.Y.   Garry Nakarajan
JAN. 1,
19 56.

Page 2

DESCRIPTION OF BEARER
ASPEKTO DE POSEDANTO

Height (Alteco) 5 feet (futoj) 11 inches (coloj)
Hair (Haroj) Red Eyes (Okuloj) Blue
Complexion (Vizaĝkoloro) Fair
Distinguishing marks (Markoj) None
Place of birth (Naskiĝloko) Bar Harbor ME USA
Date of birth (Dato de Naskiĝo) July 27, 1921
Occupation (Profesio) Writer
Home address (Hejma adreso) _____
_____ Street (Strato)
New York N.Y. USA
City (Urbo) State (ŝtato) Country (Lando)

Garry Davis
Signature of bearer
Subskribo de posedanto

The undersigned certifies that the above signature and the photograph on Page 4 are those of the bearer of this passport.

La subskribinto certigas ke la subskribo supre, kaj la fotografo sur paĝo kvar estas tiuj de la posedanto de ĉi tiu pasporto.

Alexander [signature]
Signature

Place of issue
Loko de donita NEW YORK, NY
Date of issue
Dato kiam donita 1. 9. 1956

Page 3

Samples from the
World Passport.

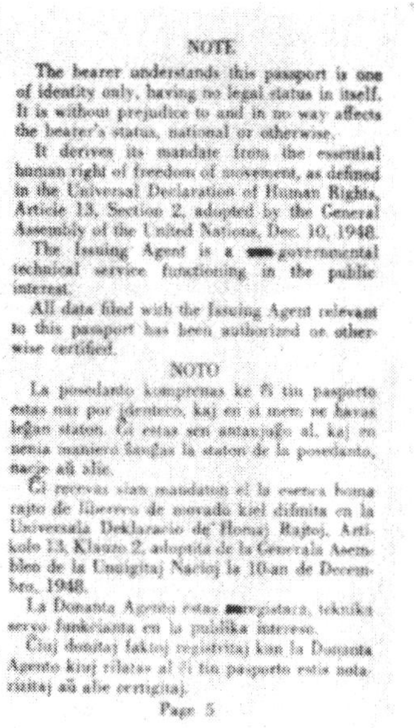

Photograph of bearer
Fotografo de posedanto

Page 4

NOTE

The bearer understands this passport is one of identity only, having no legal status in itself. It is without prejudice to and in no way affects the bearer's status, national or otherwise.

It derives its mandate from the essential human right of freedom of movement, as defined in the Universal Declaration of Human Rights, Article 13, Section 2, adopted by the General Assembly of the United Nations, Dec. 10, 1948.

The Issuing Agent is a non-governmental technical service functioning in the public interest.

All data filed with the Issuing Agent relevant to this passport has been authorized or otherwise certified.

NOTO

La posedanto komprenas ke ĉi tiu pasporto estas nur por identeco, kaj en si mem ne havas leĝan staton. Ĝi estas sen antaŭjuĝo al, kaj en nenia maniero ŝanĝas la staton de la posedanto, nacie aŭ alie.

Ĝi ricevas sian mandaton el la esenca homa rajto de libereco de movado kiel difinita en la Universala Deklaracio de' Homaj Rajtoj, Artikolo 13, Klaŭzo 2, adoptita de la Generala Asembleo de la Unuiĝintaj Nacioj la 10-an de Decembro, 1948.

La Donanta Agento estas neregistara, teknika servo funkcianta en la publika intereso.

Ĉiuj donitaj faktoj registritaj kun la Donanta Agento kiuj rilatas al ĉi tiu pasporto estas notariitaj aŭ alie certigitaj.

Page 5

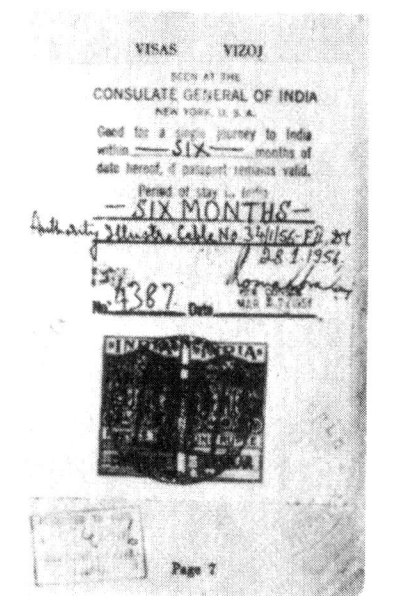

VISAS   VIZOJ

SEEN AT THE
CONSULATE GENERAL OF INDIA
NEW YORK, U. S. A.

Good for a single journey to India within ——SIX—— months of date hereof, if passport remains valid.

Period of stay in India
——SIX MONTHS——

No. 4387

Page 7

Samples from the World Passport.

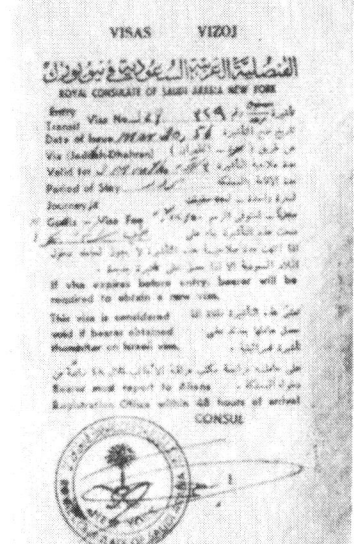

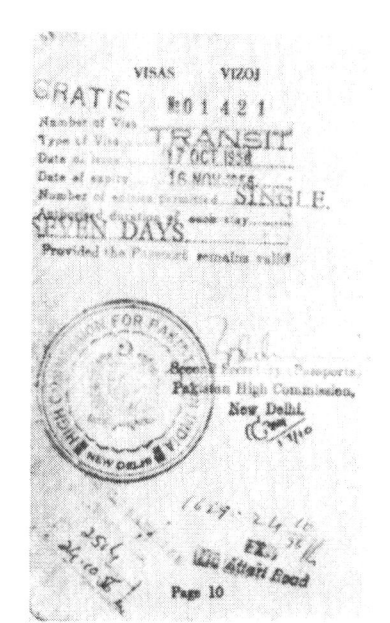

Samples from the World Passport.

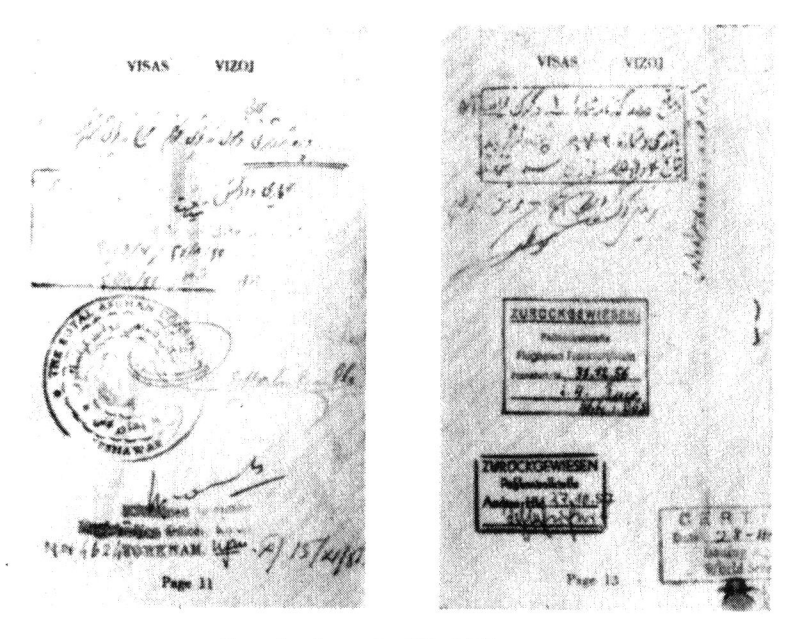

Samples from the World Passport.

I hurried back to my typewriter and prepared a short statement of my position, and, with Sarrazac, Professor Giraud, and Hélion, who kept mumbling that nothing less than such an emergency could have gotten him, a philosophical anarchist, to enter the Palais de l'Elysée, we taxied to M. Auriol's state home. A welcoming committee of photographers and newsreel men was waiting for us on the steps.

The President's secretary turned out to be an old school chum of Sarrazac's and a Socialist to boot, so he was quite interested in the whole affair. After a half-hour talk with him, we went in to see Monsieur le Président. Professor Giraud presented me, and I read my hurried declaration, which explained my reasons for refusing the still illegal extension.

"I am prepared to obey all French laws," I said, and I then asked for the President's *"bienveillance"* which, in translation, means something like "good fellowship" or "benediction". Then the professor and Sarrazac asked for a special letter giving me permission to travel freely throughout the French Empire.

M. Auriol explained that as the titular head of the French Republic he had no power to grant such permission even if he wanted to. Besides, he was symbolically appointed to protect the Constitution, he said, not to grant extrajuridical status. Sarrazac delicately pointed out that I had been "brought back" into France by the French police at the behest of the Minister of the Interior and thus the Government was in fact responsible for me. He added that this action by the Government gave me a unique symbolic status unlike his own and that such a gesture from the head of a great state might create a precedent which would be a giant step toward world unity. Professor Giraud then reminded the President that the French Constitution provided for an extension of sovereignty to a world government, provided reciprocity was guaranteed.

M. Auriol listened patiently, finally expressed his *"bienveillance"*, but reminded us that from a practical standpoint he could not really help.

We thanked him for the audience, wished each other a Merry Christmas, shook hands and departed.

On Christmas morning, after putting through a transatlantic telephone call to my family, I left for the Livingstone farm for a week. I had prepared myself for a short period of meditation to calm my jagged nerves, but at that moment this so-called farm had no plumbing, no electricity, no heat, no fuel, no food, and little of anything else. Keeping warm in the draughty living room in itself was a production. I bought wood in huge chunks from a local wood chopper, sawed it into handy lengths with an eight-inch hand saw which wiggled and waggled in the cuts, then kindled a fire in the fireplace with chips and brush, carefully feeding the bigger pieces as the fire blossomed, and settled down to enjoy the process of thawing out. Meditation came second to keeping warm.

At night, I put the iron bed outside and curled up in my sleeping-bag with just enough vision to see the magnificent starry sky above. The myriad, distant twinkling diamond points were immensely calming.

Sometimes, when the wind howled and the rain drove down, I would walk long miles along the deserted country roads. During these walks, such was my relief that I would fall to my knees and great sobs would pour forth. All the tension and suppressed emotion of the past months would come boiling to the surface, and I would rent the empty countryside with the anguish of one humble cell of humanity groping its way toward freedom and dignity.

7

Sarrazac drove out from Paris on January 3, 1949, to retrieve me. He looked haggard. I discovered why when I arrived at my hotel on Blvd. Montparnasse. As I walked into the dingy lobby, there on the wall was a large sign: GARRY DAVIS ET SES AMIS—PREMIER ETAGE: RECEPTION; 2EME ETAGE: ENREGISTREMENT; 3EME ETAGE: PEUPLE DU MONDE ET CORRESPONDANCE; 4EME ETAGE: PRESSE; 5EME ETAGE: GARRY DAVIS.

When I left the hotel, we had had one room above the front office and one room above the kitchen. Now I was a blooming corporation!

At our first staff meeting the next day, Philip Robichon, who handled the incoming mail, gave the first report: "*Eh bien,* so far 56,493 letters . . . 40 per cent from intellectuals, students, professionals, writers; 30 per cent from middle-class workers, in factories, stores, small shops; and about 10 per cent from workers in the lower class, farmers, miners, et cetera. 24,000 from France, 17,000 from Germany, 4,000 from Belgium, 2,500 from Italy, 1,700 from Scandinavia, 900 from England, 675 from the United States, 450 from Communist countries, and the rest from Latin America, Canada, Australia, Africa, the Middle East and Far East. Classifications are: requests for registration as world citizens; offers of aid; peace plans; *Peuple du Monde* [our newspaper] subscriptions; goodwill; organizations; and world citizen groups. But I need a larger space for filing, and the turnover in volunteers is too rapid and they are not checked thoroughly enough beforehand."

Robichon also observed that to answer 56,493 letters would cost $1,692.69, just for the stamps.

Jean-Jacques Agapit, our treasurer, reported gloomily that we were deeply in debt and that contributions were not sufficient to cover the mailing or even the telephone bill. As it turned out, however, we were soon to receive a loan of one thousand pounds from the British Crusade for World Government which relieved Agapit's consternation, at least for the moment.

Then we heard from Russell Benedict about the press.

"Well, so far we've got only 1,873 articles on file, but that's because we haven't got the dough to check clear 'round. Most of the stuff is from France and Germany. Let's see"—he checked figures—"1,924 individual articles on Garry in France since September 1948, and 472 from Germany, though we know for a fact there's a great deal more in the German press right now. Lots of Stateside coverage, but we haven't got figures on that."

I was dumbfounded by the reports. During the past few months I had been so preoccupied with the task of speaking out that I had lost touch with the reaction. Now I had to catch up. During the next few months, therefore, I kept as regular and as busy a schedule as any railroad president. I was in the office at eight every morning when the mail arrived. Charlie Eichler, my young German personal secretary, would join me in sorting the mail as we discussed the day's docket of appointments, broadcasts, personal appearances, and messages to meetings in various parts of the world.

At 9:30, my private secretary, Ruth Allanbrook, came in to take dictation. Ruth was a young American girl from Boston who had worked for the United Nations as a secretary. We would spend the morning together with correspondence. Early afternoon was devoted to interviews. Russell Benedict, as my press attaché, had a peculiar job. Gradually, rather than arranging interviews, his main task came to be postponing them. A typical afternoon might find me closeted with a French political writer discussing disarmament, when Benedict would poke his head in the door.

"Want to talk to a couple of journalists from Egypt?"

"No, Russ, your Egyptian's better than mine."

"Came 2,000 miles to see you. Got a string of papers. Might be good."

"You brief them. I'll pop out and say hello."

"Okay." And his head would disappear.

Other visitors included a Swiss journalist who wanted to "organize all Switzerland"; a Miss Horst, who had renounced her Dutch nationality "to work for children"; a British girl, who considered me—somewhat hysterically—the saviour of world peace; American students on the G.I. Bill of Rights pitching in to help now and then; movie directors wanting to know whether I would film *The Life of World Citizen No. 1*; and an occasional American journalist such as Billy Rose, who was then covering the world for his syndicated column.

The remainder of my afternoons and evenings during these months was consumed by special projects. These included issuing some 650,000 identification cards from our "International Registry"; a protest to the Atlantic Pact (because of its supranational militaristic partitioning); the drawing up and publicizing of our Pact of World Citizens; and, most interesting of all, my first attempt to reach the millions of people behind the Iron Curtain.

Having been denied permission to address a huge Communist rally in Paris that April, I decided to address a meeting a week later organized by the anti-Communists. Since the meetings came so close together, I knew that many Communists would attend both—and this would provide my first chance to slip my message through the Iron Curtain. As it turned out, however, I was the one who learned a lesson, not the Communists.

Sure enough, the night of the meeting the Vélodrome d'Hiver was packed and I was told that there was a large block of Communists and anarchists present—traditional enemies of each other in France but jointly enemies of all "bourgeois" meetings. Among the speakers to precede me was Dr. Carl Compton, the American atomic scientist, who proposed to defend not only the bombings of Nagasaki and Hiroshima but also the present stockpiling of atomic weapons. Needless to say, he had chosen the wrong time and the wrong place to make such a speech. Just to make matters worse, Dr. Compton's French was even more ghastly than mine, and after his efforts to make himself understood failed, his speech was handed over to the chairman, George Altman, editor of *Franc-Tireur* and member of my Conseil de Solidarité, who read it aloud, scowling occasionally over his shoulder at having been made to read such an unpopular statement. Once Dr. Compton's speech was comprehensible, there were boos, catcalls, whistles and hisses from the audience.

Noise begets noise in a meeting. Directly in front of the podium, the Communists struck up the "Internationale"; the anarchists, oddly enough, the "Marseillaise". The crowd edged toward the platform. Hands grabbed the giant arc lights focused upon it. The standards began to sway dangerously. Cameramen were snatching up their apparatus and running for safety. And as they are apt to do whenever their citizens signify the desire for a rumpus, the good French policemen disappeared.

George Altman tried to placate the crowd through the microphone, but merely added to the uproar. A full-scale riot was suddenly under way.

Obviously the Communists and anarchists were out to break up the meeting—the Communists as a matter of policy and the anarchists as a matter of principle. That meant diverting the crowd, breaking it into segments, making members of the audience want to leave, and creating so much confusion that orderly processes could not continue. Yet many could be hurt if the crowd stampeded to the exits, and the arc lights could easily have started a terrible fire.

Friends began urging me to leave, but something stayed me. Suddenly I was on my feet and, moving to the front of the platform beside George Altman, I shouted for the microphone. He looked up at me, saw something in my face, and gave it to me. I stood on an empty chair next to his, putting one foot on the velvet cloth covering the speaker's table. Then, raising my arms high above my head, palms out, I remained motionless.

As the highest figure on the platform, I stood out. My leather jacket and grey army pants were a familiar sight to most Parisians. While I remained motionless, some of my friends down below swung several of the giant spotlights around to illuminate me. The riotous crowd-noise was gradually replaced by a familiar chant: "Gaaareee Daaaaveeeees, Gaaareee Daaaa-veeees." As the chant rose in volume, both the Communist and anarchist groups were revealed to be only vociferous minorities.

I took out the speech I had in my pocket and, asking for quiet, with a mike in one hand, read it from my perch on the speaker's table.

As soon as I had finished, I stepped down. George Altman took the mike and the meeting continued. Leaving the hall immediately, I went home shaking. This was the first time I had ever seen organized Communists in action and it was one of the first times I realized the depth of the spiritual power I represented.

Office work had never been my cup of tea. As a result, Sarrazac and I planned a lecture tour of the provinces and ultimately Belgium and Switzerland—all to be accomplished in my naked illegality, for I was still under the spectre of an official French *refus de séjour*.

Undaunted, Sarrazac and I turned our Paris offices over to our fellow workers, leaving Jean-Jacques Agapit in charge, and departed Paris in May. One of our first significant stops was a town named Trouilla, in the south of France. I addressed a group of labourers, among whom was the town's mayor, while they were at work building a house. Then most of the workers gathered around while the mayor and I discussed world citizenship for thirty minutes. A month later, I read in *Time* that Trouilla had declared itself a "World Town", since a majority of the people had declared themselves world citizens. The town council also adopted a statute declaring that anyone caught making atomic bombs in this town of 300 would be prosecuted severely!

We also spoke at Carcassonne, Perpignan, Nimes; Montpellier, the university town; Toulouse, where we competed with a model airplane show and came out second best; Nantes, on the west coast; St. Nazaire, Besançon, and Montbeliard, on the east frontier. In Lausanne, Switzerland, I spoke at a large meeting of Swiss co-operatives. I entered Switzerland without papers, in the car of the president of the co-operative. When the Swiss guard questioned my right to enter, he was told, "But this is the World Citizen; you know, he travels everywhere without papers!" The guard was not confused enough to forget to charge me five francs for an entrance fee. I also entered Belgium—to speak at Nivelles—by Piper Cub and then returned to France the same way, all without mishap and without so much as a postage stamp of national identification.

Finally, on the 10th of July, we reached Cahors. The Cahors meeting was especially significant because Cahors was the first town to write us that it wished to take part in our movement as a town. With its population of 15,000, Cahors was chosen to become the first town to be *"mondialised"*.

For Cahors, *mondialisation* meant no visible break with the French Government. No world citizen renounced his French citizenship; young men were still conscripted for the national army; and everyone still paid taxes for armaments . . . officially, that is. But a majority of the population registered themselves as world citizens and pledged their vote to a People's World Assembly. They asked citizens of other towns of comparable size to join them. During the next few months, *mondialisation* spread to many such French towns. Soon I was hearing reports of *mondialisation* in Germany.

Germany had been beckoning to me ever since the day I renounced my citizenship. When I first spoke to Bob Wilson of the Associated Press that fateful day in May, I told him that I wanted to work with Henry Noel in Kassel, Germany. Now, almost eighteen months later, I felt the moment for my visit to Germany was drawing near.

On November 25th, I learned that in March 1950 the East German government planned to push through a law for two years' compulsory military service for all men of military age. No doubt the American authorities in West Germany would follow suit. Thus German youths were to be conscripted to march in battalions against each other. The U.S.A. and the Soviet Union were about to arm the very people against whom they had both fought, and arm them in supposed defence against their fellow countrymen!

Here was a great opportunity, I felt, to give the world an example of the power of unity. Germany could only be united through recognition of the larger whole of the world community itself. Villages, towns and small cities had now declared themselves *"mondialised"*. Why not a country? I would go to Germany to see about getting it *mondialised*. An encouraging fact was that while there were only 50,000 World Citizens in France, Germany had 125,000.

A year earlier, I would have left Paris unknown. This time however, as I thumbed a ride outside Paris on the road to Strasbourg on the morning of December 17th, two newsreel trucks followed me and four journalists were busy asking questions. The night before, I had released a statement saying that, since the occupying authorities in Germany had refused me entry permission, and since I felt it my duty to go to Germany anyway in response to the many invitations I had received to speak, I would simply go to the west bank of the Rhine and take my chances there.

I arrived at Strasbourg late in the evening of December 19th. Earlier that day I had made a side trip to Gunsbach to the home of Dr. Albert Schweitzer, who I thought was still in Europe, and to whom I had written while in Paris. Learning from his housekeeper that he had left a week before for Lambaréné, I hitchhiked to Strasbourg, arriving tired and hungry. I happened upon a cafeteria-style restaurant, filled with literally hundreds of young people. As I passed my tray along the slideway, a young man behind the counter looked at me curiously, then asked, "Aren't you Garry Davis?" I told him I was, whereupon he let out a whoop that was heard throughout the dining hall: "Garry Davis *est ici!*"

It was the University of Strasbourg dining hall.

As I ate, the crowd around me grew. I was asked whether they could have a meeting that evening with me. "Why not?" I replied. Tables were immediately pushed to one side, chairs lined up, and in fifteen minutes the hall was transformed into a makeshift auditorium. Apparently the news had gotten around the campus, as students were streaming into the hall by the dozens.

I stood on a table, surrounded by hundreds of expectant young faces. Questions came to me from all sides about my world citizenship activities. After making a short statement about human rights, and the freedom to travel, I told them I would be going to the Kehl bridge the next morning in order to cross the Rhine into Germany.

"May we come with you?" called out a dozen young voices.

"Well, I might not get that far," I told them, "as actually I have no papers to enter Germany and, as a matter of fact, no permit to return to France once I leave."

That was all they needed. They would champion me. We would meet at ten o'clock at the Kehl bridge, five miles from Strasbourg, and march triumphantly across into Germany.

There was only one hitch; the small town of Kehl, on the other side of the Rhine, was still under French jurisdiction. The real Franco-German frontier was beyond the town's limits. In fact, all persons were permitted to cross the Rhine into Kehl, there being no sentry posted on the west side of the river.

That evening, as I learned later, the students, enjoying that spontaneous immodesty in action known only to university students, surged out on to the streets of Strasbourg, overturning empty streetcars, marking up store fronts, and shouting imprudently, "Garry Davis to power!"

As I got off the trolley at Kehl bridge the next morning, I was met by what looked like 5,000 sudents, some of whom were carrying sticks apparently for the coming "battle" with the police. Alarmed by this display of weapons, I looked toward the bridge and there saw, stretched across the near side, a cordon of policemen, their bicycles forming a roadblock before which stood several French officers in uniform and a small waspish man in a brown derby.

"Listen, please," I called to the students in French. "I thank you most heartily for being here. This is full evidence of your support for my principles. These principles, however, will not be served by violence in any form. If they are right, they will prevail of and by themselves. I ask you all to support me in this. If one finger is raised against the authorities, all our moral power will vanish. Your self-control in this respect will be the only witness to your understanding of what I am saying. I have full confidence in you. Now, let's go."

I marched up to the waiting officials, the students massed behind me. As usual, the press photographers were on hand. The waspish man stopped me three paces from the bicycle barricade, and asked me in French if I had papers to leave France. I replied in the affirmative, taking out my recently acquired *titre d'identité et de voyage*, on which was stamped a permission to leave France. He examined it carefully, handed it back and said, "*Eh bien*, you may leave France."

I took one step . . . eastward.

One of the uniformed officers stepped in my way, demanding to know whether I had permission to enter Germany.

"No, I have no permission to enter Germany," I told him.

"*Alors*, you may go no farther," he said imperiously.

"Is this then the frontier?" I asked him.

"Yes."

At this, the students let out a yell, knowing full well the actual frontier was beyond the town of Kehl.

"But I have no permission to re-enter France, and I have just left," I told him. "I must then be standing on the line between France and Germany."

The waspish man stepped forward. "Line? Line? But there is no line between France and Germany, that is, no actual *line* . . . I mean . . ."

"No line?" I asked. "But if there is no line, how can there be two countries? You have just given me permission to leave France, which I did. I have witnesses. And as you know, I have no permission to re-enter France once out. Now I learn I cannot enter Germany. Obviously I'm stuck on the line between the two countries."

The students were laughing uproariously at this piece of logic, and even the policemen were trying hard not to smile.

"*Mais non*," the Interior Ministry man coaxed, "you may come back to Strasbourg, now, if you wish."

"Oh? Then will you give me a visa to re-enter France?"

"Visa? But there is no question of a visa. You are still in France."

"Ah, then please tell me where the frontier is because this gentleman here"—I indicated the French occupation officer—"informs me that Germany is just on the other side of him."

The Interior man looked uneasily at his French compatriot. From the crowd were coming cries of "He's right!" "There must be a line!" and "Bravo, Garry, continue!"

Seeing their hesitation, I said, "Well, until I have permission to enter Germany, or a visa to re-enter France, I shall be obliged to remain here ... on the line between two countries," whereupon I moved to the side of the road, parked my backpack against the small guardhouse on the sidewalk, sat down, took out my typewriter, and began typing the above conversation.

The reporters were questioning the Interior man and the French officer, both of whom remained non-committal as to what action, if any, would be taken in my regard. Finally they went off to file their stories, after the photographers had taken pictures of my latest vigil. The students crowded around asking questions, slapping me on the back, and generally being friendly.

"But what will you do this evening, Mr. Davis?" asked a young moustached Frenchman. "It will be very cold."

"I don't know," I told him, "except that I will be here."

"I shall see about getting you a tent," he said. "I have a small sports shop in Strasbourg."

That would be a great help, I told him, thanking him for his thoughtfulness. A special guard was posted at my end of the bridge to make sure I didn't cross, the ludicrousness of the situation being revealed fully in that everyone else—men, women, and children, dogs, cats, horses, cars, trucks, baby carriages—could cross Kehl bridge into Kehl without surveillance.

The day passed eventfully enough, with a constant stream of visitors, some stopping only to say hello, others getting into serious conversations, such as one André Fuchs, a free-lance journalist from Strasbourg who wrote an article for the *Nouvel Alsacien* in highly sympathetic terms. Some students from the University returned around six with a large pot containing enough hot soup to last me a week. A volunteer food brigade had been arranged, they told me, which would supply me with the necessities as long as I remained at the bridge. A little later, the sports shop man returned with a small pup tent. One of the girl students, sitting by while I ate the thick soup, asked me if I had a sleeping bag. When I informed her that I hadn't, she said she would borrow her brother's and bring it to me later that evening.

"You do not know me," she said in good English, "but my mother was your governess in Philadelphia when you were a child." Her name was Esther Peter. I was delighted to make that personal contact in such trying and unusual circumstances. The Peter family proved wonderful and helpful friends in the following days, Mrs. Peter, little Esther, and Raoul, who generously lent me his sleeping bag for my "Watch on the Rhine".

Sighting a line from the bridge to a small field directly to the side, I pitched the tent that evening on the stateless "line," digging a small trench around it as best I could with a toy spade donated by a neighbourhood child. The wind from the Rhine was damp and chill, necessitating a fire for warmth. After scouring around a bit in the open area, I came across what proved to be tar-soaked logs which crackled and burned brightly, giving off vast rolls of smoke into the ashen sky.

Each evening the students appeared with the soup kettle and several *petits pains*, Esther usually being among them. I had advised friends to write me to: "No Man's Land, Pont Kehl, Between Strasbourg and Kehl, France-Germany." Sure enough, mail began trickling in, delivered by a talkative, highly amused French postman who informed me there had been quite a debate at the post office as to whether that address would be recognized.

On Christmas Eve, students brought out two small Christmas trees which I placed on either side of the tent. As the field on which my tent was pitched was a favourite natural playground for the kids of the neighbourhood, I had made many friends among them, taking part in their after-school games and trying desperately to translate Grimm's Fairy Tales into an understandable French as we gathered around the fire in front of the tent. To my great surprise and delight, when they saw the two trees they went rushing off, returning shortly with decorations from their own trees.

It was a merry if somewhat soggy Christmas for me that year.

In the mail were invitations to speak at the universities of Cologne, Heidelberg, and Baden-Baden. Twenty thousand world citizens at Stuttgart had signed a petition inviting me to visit their town. When Dr. Adenauer was approached by a world citizen delegation to find out his disposition of my case, he gave them his personal approval of my entry, saying that all men advocating peace should be welcomed into Germany. The special guard, however, was still posted on Kehl bridge.

As it began raining at around eight o'clock on December 26th, I retired into my tent early, somewhat tired and discouraged, my body reacting sluggishly because of the continued exposure. No matter how large the fire, I couldn't seem to shake off the chill that day.

"Oh, Mr. Davis, are you there?" a voice drifted in to me above the patter of the rain shortly after I had fallen into a fitful sleep.

"Who is it?"

"We're from the Council of Europe, British delegation. May we have a word with you?"

"I'm sorry. I've had a trying day and I just can't make it out again," I told them.

I heard nothing more. Later I learned that Dr. Hugh Dalton had expressed a desire to see me, hence their trip to "No Man's Land".

On the evening of December 27th, Esther noticed my pallid look and rasping voice. She entreated me to see a doctor, and when I refused, brought one out to see me. He advised immediate hospitalization. I wouldn't hear of it because it meant giving up the "line", though I realized I was in poor shape physically. Esther, mistaking my hesitation, assured me that the hospital expense would be taken care of by a leading merchant in Strasbourg whom she had already approached.

"No, it's not that," I told her, touched by her thoughtfulness. "You see, once I relinquish the position I've already established here, I couldn't regain it without sacrificing the logic of it."

At that moment, up walked a tall young man with glasses who announced himself as a world citizen from Basle, Switzerland. Without preliminaries, Esther asked him, "If you are a world citizen, will you take Garry Davis's place in his tent while he goes to the hospital?"

"But of course, with pleasure," he replied.

Esther looked at me. I looked from her to him.

"Shake," I said. "You have just enlisted for the 'Rhine Campaign'."

Esther jumped up, ran to him and gave him a little hug.

"I am so happy. Now come, Garry, we must go quickly. There is a police car outside. Maybe they will take us."

Such were the incongruities of the situation that the very police assigned to check up on me were drafted into driving me to the Strasbourg Hospital, while the Swiss World Citizen waved adieu from the "Line"!

During my three days there and one night in Strasbourg at the Peters', not only the Swiss, but an Egyptian, a Frenchman, and an American took nightly turns under the tent at Pont de Kehl in order that the "line" be always occupied. So much curiosity had been aroused among the Strasbourgeois that a meeting was arranged for the day that I came out of the hospital.

The hall was full that evening and a long table on the stage at which I was seated was surrounded by members of the local world citizen committee plus leading Strasbourg pacifists. When I arose to speak extemporaneously, by chance my eye fell upon a lovely red rose in a graceful vase somehow placed in the middle of the long table. Carrying it to the front of the stage, I christened it a "world rose", as its beauty and fragrance could be appreciated by one and all alike. The idea of one humanity naturally flowed from this simple illustration.

I finished by saying that I would return to Pont de Kehl the next morning to continue my vigil, but that in order not to run the risk of further physical disability, I would attempt to construct a small cabin in place of the tent so as to be protected from the weather. Any and all who wished to aid me in this task, I said, would be welcome.

The next morning when I arrived at ten o'clock at the bridge, a crowd of several hundred had already gathered, a covey of policemen eyeing the group from afar. Many carpenters were on hand with tools; two young architects had shown up; and an old lady carried curtains for the as-yet-unbuilt windows. There were also stacks of lumber, a roll of roofing paper, a small keg of nails and a potbellied stove complete with chimney. Dozens of young boys were ready to be conscripted.

That day's work at Pont de Kehl remains in my memory as a monument to Gallic efficiency above and beyond the call of duty—national duty, that is. Oblivious to the strict building code which prohibited the erection of any house, including a doghouse, without a licence, and under the combined direction of the serious-looking architects, who conferred on a drawing made on the back of a world citizen registration blank I gave them, we laid a foundation and floor, erected four walls with cross-bracings, and by afternoon began nailing down long planks wedged together to form a roof. At dusk a neat little one-room bungalow marked the razor-edged new line between France and Germany.

During the next few days, the neighbourhood children proved a great source of comfort to me. Directly after school they would make a bee-line for the cabin. To them it was a large-sized doll's house which they could take over in playful abandon. One Sunday afternoon, I was discussing with a group of learned visitors possible names for the cabin. "World Wigwam," "Humanity's Hovel," "People's Perch" were suggested, when a little seven-year-old girl with a dirty face, large dark brown eyes and red cheeks, standing almost in front of me, raised her small hand as if in class. Kneeling down, I asked her if she had a name for the cabin.

" *Oui*," she said in a barely intelligible whisper. "*La Cabane du Bonheur*."

From then on my address was "The Cabin of Happiness," Pont de Kehl, Franco-Germany.

One of the letters I happened to receive at this address was from Albert Schweitzer, in response to my request for philosophical guidance. The sage of Lambaréné wrote that perhaps now was the time for me to step out of my life of action and deeds and embark on a contemplative excursion. He said he believed that I probably needed a period of meditation which would not be possible as a leader of the world government Movement. "Seek to have a clear judgment of things," Schweitzer wrote, adding, "You wanted to act by exterior means instead of acting by spirit. You must abandon this way."

Schweitzer's words preyed on my mind during my days at the Cabin of Happiness. In one way, spiritually I suppose, I was anything but happy. Meditation here was impossible; there were too many visitors. And I knew Schweitzer was right. I hungered for the privacy and calm to explore the deeper meaning of my life and of world citizenship itself during the past two years in France.

I think there is a point one reaches, a point of sheer and utter surfeit with involvement in action, at which more involvement becomes meaningless. If one allows this process to go too far—and I imagine this is the lesson of Oedipus and Macbeth—one develops a kind of callousness and insensitivity to all deeds, events, peoples and relationships and then pursues the life of involvement with desperation and ultimately tragic and spiritless abandon. I felt all of this about myself as a continuous undercurrent at the Cabin of Happiness—as though I were crossing such a threshold—and it was there that I decided that sooner or later, and the sooner the better, I would return to America to collect myself.

Meanwhile, of course, I was still a pilgrim to Germany and an unlikely one at that. But fate was soon to take a hand in the matter. I was eating dinner in a little restaurant near the bridge one evening when someone burst in shouting, "The cabin is burning!"

I hurried out, and there, about 200 yards off, the tiny cabin was blazing away. I had left the children playing inside! Breaking into a cold sweat, I covered the ground in seconds. The cabin was covered with tar paper to keep out the cold and it made a brilliant blaze. Half the walls were afire. I ripped open the door. Empty! Thank God! Then, oblivious to the heat, I thought of my meagre possessions. But what could I save now? I rushed in, reached up on the shelf and grabbed my briefcase, then dashed out into safety. By then a crowd had gathered. Someone had called the fire department. Seconds later, the walls collapsed, the flames now a cluster of licking tongues.

As we watched helplessly, a wave of sadness swept over me. This foolish little cabin had been a symbol. I had even pictured a little community of cabins around it, all built in the same spirit, a microcosmic world community. Now all seemed gone. I could imagine how the accident had happened. The children must have loaded the stove to the brim, against my implicit orders not to touch it, and then, when it grew late, the policeman on guard had chased them home. The wind had blown into the chimney, thrown a hot coal on to the wood floor, and the blaze started.

The Cabin of Happiness lay at my feet in ashes. And so indeed lay my hopes and ambition. I wanted now only peace—the peace in which to prepare.

And so I returned to Paris to confer with Sarrazac and told him of the letter I had received from Albert Schweitzer. "Seek to 'ave a clear judgment of things," he mused. "Yes, Garry," he said after a pause, "the moment of action for you is past."

Sarrazac accompanied me back to the site of the cabin a few days later. Word of my return had preceded me and a crowd had assembled at the bridge. Police were there too, and once again they had placed their bicycles as a barrier to close the bridge.

I walked up to the site where the cabin had stood. The floor was still there. I stepped upon it, turned around and faced the crowd. I told them that I had wanted to enter Germany to help rebuild that country, since I had helped destroy it as an American bomber pilot. I then recalled the events of the past two months —how I had been granted permission to leave France but refused permission to enter Germany, how the citizens of Strasbourg had built my cabin and how together we had held the line for two months.

I did not mention the letter from Schweitzer nor my own inner craving for peace and meditation to renew the life of the spirit. Instead I said that I was only one among over 600,000 who had expressed a desire to become world citizens seeking to create, among other things, a world without frontiers. "The world is in your hands as well as mine," I said, "and I have decided to return to my homeland." My remarks wound up with my calling upon "the community of those who carry the card of world citizenship" to help "create a world with no frontiers."

There was little comment and no applause from the assembled people. The policemen with their bicycle frontier seemed equally disappointed. With some embarrassment they disengaged the barricade and rode off authoritatively, leaving only a skeleton force to take care of emergencies.

A great weight had rolled from my mind. I felt really free for the first time since camping on the U.N. steps. It was a supreme luxury. Esther, sensing my need for rest, had arranged with a Strasbourg merchant for a month loan of his skiing lodge in the Vosges. There I caught up on my correspondence, brought my diary up-to-date, read, took long walks and had many stimulating conversations with this delightfully bright and alive young girl who had generously agreed to keep house and do the cooking. In March I returned to Paris immediately to apply for entry to the United States. Walking into the Embassy, I nodded to the pair of Marines whom I had not seen since the day of my renunciation of American citizenship. Mrs. Agnes Schneider was there too. She looked up and smiled blandly. Everyone was exceptionally courteous. Without delay I was classified as a "French non-quota immigrant" who was to become a "resident alien" in the United States.

Three days later I was aboard the S.S. *America* waving to a crowd of friends and well-wishers. The waving continued as the *America* cruised out into the bay, and then suddenly, some of the crowd who had moved to the outermost promontory of land unfurled a huge banner which read, GOOD-BYE GARRY MERCI.

8

From Marco Polo to Rudyard Kipling, men from the materialistic West have travelled to the contemplative East to study philosophy and to acquaint themselves with the deepest meaning of life. Since my main purpose in leaving Europe was not only to explore the philosophical premises of world citizenship, but also to unravel the dispirited and restive enigma that was Garry Davis, I had begun at least vaguely to think about a trip to India even before embarking for the United States.

Strangely enough, aboard the S.S. *America* was a south Indian philosopher by the name of Dr. P. Natarajan, the founder-head of the "Gurukula Movement" which was dedicated to the teaching of "spiritual understanding". We met on our second day at sea in the third-class lounge.

"I tried to see you in Paris," this roly-poly, brown-skinned man told me, "but you were too surrounded with people. I decided to let Tao arrange a meeting. And here we are, together on the neutral sea." The notion of world citizenship, he said, was grounded in an ancient, unitive science-philosophy known in India as Advaita Vedanta in which he was a specialist or "guru".

"Citizens come before governments," he added, "but men come before citizens. Until men are educated to have a global or universal attitude toward all life, there will be no true world citizens."

At first I was sceptical of this strangely garbed, self-styled guru, who seemed to promise absolute truth in ten easy lessons. On the other hand, his manner of speaking impressed me deeply. He used ordinary words and yet somehow they became extraordinary and "new", almost as if they had acquired another dimension of meaning merely by a subtle rearrangement. I could not help being reminded as he spoke of St. John's comment that Christ spoke with gentleness yet with authority.

I was later to learn that Dr. Natarajan was the disciple of the great teacher Shri Narayana Guru, of Travancore, South India, who, when he died in 1928, was mourned by millions of followers throughout India and the Far East, and who was accorded recognition as a *jagat guru* or universal sage from Romain Rolland, the brilliant French writer. The Doctor also carried after his name various professional degrees including a Ph.D. from the Sorbonne.

"Come to India with me," the Doctor suggested. In the back of my mind I decided I might indeed visit him in India if only to challenge his bold assertion, but as it turned out it took me years to travel the 12,000 miles between his home and mine.

Dr. Natarajan's nearest disciple, Harry S. Jakobsen, the Norwegian philosopher-machinist on Schooley's Mountain, New Jersey, confirmed the guru's message and invited me to stay with him and work in his small shop while we discussed Indian philosophy. Coming after an unsatisfying return to the theatre, during which I appeared in *Stalag* 17, it was a welcome offer.

In August 1952, therefore, I left the cast of *Stalag* 17 on its road tour to move in with Harry Jakobsen in his rural West Jersey "Gurukula" (home of a guru). While grinding steel shanks for cutting tools for the Jet Age, I listened to, disputed and absorbed the major premises of the venerable wisdom-science of Advaita Vedanta with this blond, rough-hewn Viking. My brain was thoroughly shaken in the process. Both fascinated and repelled, I wanted to flee this dread inquisition into my innermost soul, yet I was equally desirous of achieving the sureness and serenity which marked both Dr. Natarajan and Harry Jakobsen. Jakobsen's practical wife, Mary, complained that we talked more than we worked, and she was right. But that kind of talk was the hardest work I had done in my life till then.

In January 1953, after studying and working with Harry Jakobsen for four months, I decided to go to India, now hungry for more philosophy. Though Jakobsen had proved a titan in his grasp of fundamental principles, he continually reminded me that he was only a novice compared to his teacher. "I have only roughed you out," he told me in his machinist vernacular. "Dr. Natarajan will polish you up, but good!"

For travel papers I acquired an affidavit in lieu of a passport, a six-month Indian visa with a three-day British transit visa stamped on the back. The day before I was scheduled to sail, I met a fellow actor in New York who informed me that *Stalag* 17 was about to be produced in London and that the management was desperately looking for an actor to play "Harry Shapiro". Five hundred members of British Equity had been read for the part, he said, and not one displayed an authentic Brooklyn accent!

Playing in London's West End in a Broadway hit during Coronation Year was a jolly good idea, I thought. My finances were desperately low, and, though I would be Dr. Natarajan's guest, still I thought it wise to arrive in India with some funds at least. I could sign up for six months, earn some needed pounds, attend the Coronation and then continue my way eastward. I cabled Sam Bird, the American producer, that I was available and en route via the *Queen Mary*. On the third day at sea, I received a cable: YOU'RE HIRED DISCUSS TERMS HERE LABOR PERMIT NO. 576807 LACHIEM BIRD.

Sam was upset to learn at Southampton that I had entered England on my transit visa rather than on the labour permit number he had cabled. "We'll have to hop down to the Home Office tomorrow," he told me, "and get you changed from a transit into a working visitor."

London had changed since I knew it during the war. I remembered it pock-marked, grim, blacked-out and peopled by resolute if frightened citizens. Now London was gay, decking itself with Coronation colour and pageantry. "Coney Island with a monocle," said Sam. I was delighted to be there.

The Home Office, in view of the forthcoming job, obligingly changed my status from that of a three-day transit to a three-month visitor. "What happens after three months?" I asked the clerk. "Why by that time, sir," he replied smiling, "I suspect you'll be such a toast of the town, the Home Secretary himself will stamp the paper." It was a prophecy of a sort.

The show opened at the end of February in Edinburgh, to good notices. From there, we played Blackpool, Hull, and Brighton for a week each. Three days before we were scheduled to open in London, however, tragedy struck the House of Windsor. Queen Mary died. London went into mourning, the black wreaths and drapes sharing public space with the Coronation decorations. The management decided to postpone our opening for a week.

At last, with high hopes for a long and lucrative run, we opened at the Princes Theatre on April 5th to a full house. The laughs were long and loud; the applause at the final curtain solid and reassuring; the notices next day short and sweet.

We closed Saturday night. Our kind of hilarity, it seemed, just did not mix with London's sense of bereavement.

The actors imported from the States had been guaranteed passage home according to Actors' Equity rules. But I had been "in transit" when I arrived and it was therefore my responsibility to "transit out". However, the closing notice found me embarrassingly impoverished, without a job, and with but three weeks remaining on my combined labour and resident permit.

As I contemplated this sorry turn of affairs in my dressing room after the last show, there came a knock on the door. It was a Mr. Boulting, an independent producer for Metro-Goldwyn-Mayer in England. He praised my performance and proceeded to offer me a role in the forthcoming Gene Kelly film *Crest of the Wave*, to be filmed in Scotland. Delighted, I accepted and was told to report to the M-G-M offices on Monday to discuss salary and to pick up my script.

As I left the M-G-M offices on the Monday, shooting script under my arm, everything settled except the actual signing of the contract, Mr. Boulting said casually, "Oh, by the way, Mr. Davis, we're awaiting final approval on you from our executive offices in Hollywood. Just a formality, you know. Automatic, rather. They approve anyone we okay here. We'll be signing the contract directly we get official word. In the meantime, just consider yourself signed."

Two weeks and five days later, the next day being my legal last in Great Britain, there was still no word from the studio. I called Mr. Boulting and explained the situation. "We're frightfully embarrassed, Mr. Davis," he told me. "There seems to be some difficulty from the Hollywood end. Can't get approval somehow. But we want you and are fighting for you. Just consider yourself signed."

"But Mr. Boulting," I replied, "I may consider myself signed and you may consider me signed, but your Home Secretary won't consider me signed unless I *am* signed."

"Yes, well, why don't you pop over to Paris for a few days? We'll surely get approval by then. We can sign you there, and you can pop back here with a new permit?"

"That would be okay except that the French won't let me pop in unless I can guarantee a return to England."

Deciding pressure was needed from my end, I took my remaining precious pounds and placed a transatlantic call to my father, who was at the moment on the seventeenth tee of the Greenbriar Hotel golf course in White Sulphur Springs. He promised to call friends in Hollywood immediately. At four P.M. I returned to the Home Office to request an extension on my labour-residence permit.

"We are not permitted to extend a labour-residence permit," the clerk informed me, "unless the alien has a position already."

"But tonight my permit runs out," I wailed. "And tomorrow, without a permit, I can't get a position."

"Tomorrow," he returned ominously, "you must be out of England!"

"What?"

"You must leave England tonight . . . by midnight."

"Leave England? But I have no money."

"Well, Mr. Davis, that is not the problem of the Home Office, is it now?"

Here was my first experience with the theoretical right to work and its actual practice as regards a so-called alien. I couldn't work if I didn't have a labour permit, yet if I didn't have a job, I couldn't get a permit. Furthermore, not being legally able to work, I had to leave the country. It was a closed circle. And at midnight, April 28, 1953, I would be outside the circle.

I pulled out a crumpled copy of the *Universal Declaration of Human Rights* which I kept in my pocket and turned to Article 23. *Everyone has the right to work,* I read, *to free choice of employment, to just and favourable conditions of work, and to protection against unemployment.*

"I should like to speak with someone of higher authority," I told the clerk.

"I have instructions not to refer you to anyone else," he replied.

"I see. Well, in that case, I shall make my protest to you. In the name of human rights—"

"Please, Mr. Davis, we are very busy," he interrupted with a cold smile. "You will no doubt be given three or four days' grace before being apprehended by the Alien Police. Good day, sir."

Later that evening, wandering about London and wondering what to do, I arrived at Marble Arch where the penny-whistle orators peddled their much-abused panaceas. I stopped to listen. There were Biblists and anti-Biblists, Communists and anti-

Communists, anarchists and constitutionalists, agnostics and deists, racists black, white and mixed, and a young man with long hair, a red beard, and a flowing white shirt ranting incongruously against modern art. But one fellow's words attracted me. In high humour, he destroyed the basic premises of the other speakers one by one. Then he launched into a dissertation on the importance of nothing, or nothingness.

"And do you know what nothin' is?" he asked his audience indignantly and then receiving no answer went on: "It's what's behind all the somethin's, that's what! And do you know where you'd all be if it weren't fer nothin'? Why you'd all be squashed t'gether like jelly in a puddin', that's where you'd be. Why it's nothin' which makes the 'ole bloomin' world go 'round, that's what!" Intrigued, I invited him to tea and over the hot brew found myself explaining my predicament.

"Cor! That's one for the books, that is," he said and added as an afterthought, "or for the Queen."

My ears pricked up. "What do you mean, 'for the Queen'?"

"Well, she's the Queen, ain't she?" he replied. "I mean, the 'ole bloomin' government 'as turned you down, 'asn't it? Seems to me as if you 'as to ask 'er Majesty fer 'elp. What's she up there for anyway?"

"But she's just a symbol," I replied. "She has no power . . . no authority."

"Well then," he returned laughing, "you're both in the same bloomin' boat!" He paused. "Ere, wait a minute! I think I read somewhere where the Magna Charta says if you've got the coppers after you and you can touch the throne and claim sanctuary, you know, like the 'unchback did at Notre Dame, the Crown 'as got to protect you."

Nat Schaffer, Hyde Park seer, earthy voice of The People, and dabbler in Magna Charta law, had, I thought, a point. A man's fundamental right to work was being denied by Her Majesty's government practically within stone's throw of Buckingham Palace. Obviously Her Majesty, busy with Coronation details, knew nothing about it. Not to inform, nay, petition the Sovereign for a redress of grievances in so basic a matter would be a serious breach of duty not only to oneself but to the Crown *itself*.

I returned to my "digs" in West Kensington to compose my petition to Her Majesty. After asking her to intervene in my behalf, in that I found myself "deprived by Your Majesty's servants of the fundamental human rights to exist by earning a livelihood, and to freedom of movement . . ." I outlined the facts of my plight starting with my departure from the United States on January 23rd and ending up with that afternoon's chat with the Home Office clerk. "Thus, as of April 28th," the paragraph concluded, "I find myself in direct violation of British law, being in fact, yet by necessity, still a resident of England. As such, I face either jail or deportation."

Then came the direct appeal: "Therefore . . . I hereby petition Your Majesty most humbly and sincerely for Her Royal Intervention on my behalf."

I concluded by saying my petition was "not only in the name of a single individual, a world commoner, without power and means . . . but also in the name of an awakening world civilization."

The letter was dated May 1, 1953, and it was mailed to Queen Elizabeth on that date by registered post. From the post office I went directly to the pawnshop, where my camera and watch already resided, to pawn my remaining suit for the room rent while I awaited a reply.

But I received no royal word.

Since my rent was due on May 7th, I packed my remaining clothes in a backpack, took an underground to Victoria Station, then walked the remaining distance to Buckingham Palace to await some response personally. Nat Schaffer had come along joyfully, now boned up on sixteenth, seventeenth, eighteenth, and nineteenth century cases in which individuals had sought asylum from persecution in the throne's shadow. That some had been beheaded deterred him not a whit. "It's the bloomin' principle—what's right," he affirmed, and urged me to see it through "to the bloody end" if need be!

We arrived at the Palace about eleven. The sky was blue, the tourists and Coldstream Guards in full regalia. I parked myself on the narrow concrete shelfing forming the base of the high enclosure surrounding the outer court and opened my typewriter.

"You can't type 'ere," Nat exclaimed. "What will people think?"

Nat was magnificent. Petitioning the Queen from in front of Buckingham Palace was perfectly proper, but carrying on business as usual at the same time was socially reprehensible.

"We must let the Queen know I'm here," I argued, inserting a piece of paper, "otherwise she wouldn't know where to send the reply."

"You're dead right!" he said. "And I'll take it in meself."

"Thanks for the free delivery," I told him, "but it's better you don't get personally involved. We'll mail it special delivery."

While Nat was off mailing the short note, he dropped word of my stand in front of Buckingham Palace to the press. Fifteen minutes later, I was surrounded by buzzing reporters. Photographers took pictures. When they left, policemen eyed me suspiciously, tourists with curious or amused glances, and the Palace Guards—*klomp-klomp*—not at all. I glanced at the outer court longingly. Maybe I could get there at least. On the street, I was definitely illegal. But once inside the Palace enclosure . . .

"Come along now. Out of here. This is the Palace Court, you. Move along now." He looked six-foot-six bearing down on me as I gently laid my pack against the concrete shelfing inside the court.

"You don't understand," I said hurriedly. "You see, I'm a petitioner to the Queen and waiting for a reply."

"And I'm the Prince of Wales. Now get along before I have you arrested."

"Oh, you can't do that," I returned, "because I'm already outside the law. Look here." I showed him the back of my travel affidavit with the expired visa. "The Queen knows all about it, and so does the Home Office," I continued. "If you put me out on the street, I'll be breaking a British law and you'll be an accomplice!"

He stopped and scratched his head. "You wait right here. We know where to send you." He hurried away.

A voice called out, "Hey, Davis, what's up?" I turned and saw a reporter, pad and pencil in hand. I started to go to him when a burly figure with sergeant stripes emerged from the guardhouse. He strode rapidly to me, grabbed my hand, and before I could protest had it around my back in a ju-jitsu grip and was hustling me off toward the police lodge. The reporter, from one of the major wire services, filed a story that I had tried to break into Buckingham Palace with a petition in my hand shouting, "I want to see the Queen!" Friends around the world berated me years later for my "publicity-seeking stunt" so lacking in judgement and decorum. Only once again did I neglect to issue a statement to the press *before* involving myself in public action and that time too I suffered misinterpretation and condemnation; but that chapter came years later in my story.

Inside the little police lodge, an inspector with a grand moustache approached me while I was seated on the wooden bench typing. He stood in front of me, legs spread, arms behind him at "Parade Rest," looked down and said, "Have you ever been in a hospital, Mr. Davis?"

I stood up hesitantly. "I beg your pardon?"

His steel-grey eyes bored into mine. "Have you ever been in a hospital?"

"Why do you ask?" I returned.

He blinked his eyes and his moustache twitched. "Do you refuse to answer the question?"

"No sir, I don't refuse to answer. I just wondered what your reason is for asking it, that's all. I suppose there is a reason for asking it, isn't there?"

He hesitated an instant, then turned on his heel with a mighty "Humph!" his moustache dancing, and strode back into his office, the sound of Khyber bugles echoing in the distance.

Moments later another officer appeared, this one with silver insignia on his shoulders. He was kindly-looking; elderly, with a shock of white hair. He approached me with a smile and sat down on the bench beside me.

"Now, lad, we understand we're in a bit of trouble, eh?"

"Yes sir, we are."

"Well now"—he edged closer—"let me ask you a wee question, lad: have you ever been in a hospital?"

"Sir," I replied, "I was just asked this very same question by another officer. I inquired why he had asked, and he didn't even give me the courtesy of a reply. Now, in all frankness, I am beginning to suspect the motive behind the question. What in the world has a hospital to do with my petitioning the Queen for the right to work?"

He looked thoughtful, was about to say something, stroked his chin and retired to his office.

After a bit, the sergeant told me I was to be examined for "mental unbalance". I asked him why.

"'Cause you might be balmy for all we know," he replied.

"Well, tell me," I asked, "what evidence do you have that calls for this accusation, and who gives the evidence?"

"I give the evidence, that's who," replied the man at the desk making out the order.

"How can you give the evidence," I asked him, "when I haven't spoken to you before?"

Apparently not appreciating this line of questioning from someone he had been ordered to send away for a mental check-up, he barked, "Look here, Davis, shut up and sit down!"

I sat down, then in a quiet voice asked him why he wouldn't tell me what evidence there was that I was mentally unbalanced.

"It's your attitude," he replied angrily. "You're nothing but a troublemaker. I can spot 'em a mile off."

"Well, I really can't see much to commend your attitude now," I told him. "I merely asked for information, and not only are you refusing it, but you're also shouting and being extremely rude. I ask you to treat me with the respect due a fellow human being." I was standing again by this time.

The sergeant advanced toward me threateningly. "You sit down, Davis, before I push you down!"

I sat down.

Taking me to a mental hospital, I thought, was mighty close to arbitrary detention without due process. The more I thought about it, the worse it sounded. After a half hour, the second inspector passed by, all officiousness. I called to him. "I beg your pardon, sir, but I am obliged to ask for the right of due process rather than this arbitrary detention which could land me in an asylum without a trial."

"This decision is final, lad," he replied coldly. "There is no appeal."

My worst fears were confirmed. I could be committed to an insane asylum and the key thrown away!

When the sergeant came to fetch me, I told him that in protest to this unreasonable and illegal detention, I would remain utterly inert. If he wished to move me from the station to a hospital, he would have to do it without my aid.

He called four policeman to lift me. "You will not be able to lift me," I told them. Not really wanting to, they couldn't.

The sergeant, disgusted, turned to an orderly. "Get the chair." A moment later, a camp chair was produced and I was half dragged, half lifted into it, whereupon the four policemen easily lifted the unquestioning chair and transported it on to the back of a waiting police van.

My room at the hospital was private and quite pleasant. An orderly had popped in to inform me that "You're going up before 'is nibs tomorrow morning. 'E's clever, 'e is. Takes down every word ya say. Do try to act normal, won't ya?" I assured him I would do my best.
Nat had arrived bearing the evening papers and was looking around fearfully. "What are they doing to you?"
"They want to find out whether I'm crackers or not."
"Naw, it's them what's crackers. They just don't know what to do with you. You've caused a proper stir, you 'ave. 'Ere, 'ave a look." Sure enough there were pictures and stories in the papers.
Nat saw things as they were. He was not concerned with dogmas or platforms. He had nothing to sell. Nat's philosophy was *no* philosophy, just being Nat. And in being Nat, he wasn't fooled into becoming anything else. Self-sufficient, a keen if rough intelligence, a light heart, and a good soul—that was Nat Schaffer.
The next morning at eight, I was ushered into a small office to see "'is nibs." He was young, about my age I thought, and sported a jaunty goatee. My strategy was to feign a manic-depressive condition, then suddenly switch to a schizophrenic, then explain what I had done to illustrate that I was sane, or at least that I knew the difference between the classic symptoms of psychic disorder and rational conduct. His goatee, however, waggled so ludicrously when he spoke that I lost my composure. When in desperation I confessed to him that I was petitioning the Queen in order to make some money, he called me a "scoundrel... as sane as the rest of us" and ordered my release for the next morning, adding that the police had asked him to hold me for at least three days.
My next visitor, as I was dressing the next morning, was elderly and had a kind face.
"Is it not true, Mr. Davis, that you were found inside the forecourt of Buckingham Palace?" he began.
"That is true, sir."
"Do you consider such conduct quite er—proper, sir?"
"Quite, sir, under the circumstances."

"And what were the circumstances, sir?"

"I was destitute and faced official persecution, sir."

"Ah, I see." He paused. "Do you know, Mr. Davis," he continued with a twinkle, "there is an old statute, more of a common law, I should say ... sixteenth century ... which says that a man who is destitute may repair to public property, and if, by the rise of the sun, he has managed to construct a domicile of sod with smoke coming from the chimney, well sir, the property is his! Good day, Mr. Davis, Godspeed." I watched him depart, open-mouthed.

Nat was waiting for me after I was released that afternoon.

"What you goin' to do now, Garry?" he asked.

"Well, I am still in merrie olde England, still without the right to work, and still broke. Add that I've now got a clean bill of mental health, and just been released from the police without papers. Looks like the Queen is still the only one to solve this one."

"What, go back to the Palace?"

"What would you suggest?" I asked.

"But they'll pick you up again."

"I'm illegal anyway, so what difference will it make where I wait, in jail or in front of the Palace?"

By this time, I had many well-wishers and even some volunteers to help with my paper work. When I showed my petition to Peter Ustinov, who was then playing in *The Love of Four Colonels*, he thought it grand and wanted to know when I was going to "make the movie". Marie Bryant, the singer-dancer, appearing in a new revue and an old friend from show business days, offered me hospitality at her house at Baron's Court. A young volunteer named Muriel Tredwell became my Girl Friday, proving invaluable in typing letters, memoranda, and communiqués. Then, of course, there was ever-faithful Nat.

The weather was brisk in front of Buckingham Palace now. Along about 10 P.M., the last news reporters left and I was alone. Across the street was a small park, the green grass beckoning and almost daring me to construct a "domicile of sod". All along the Mall, Coronation stands were under construction and there were huge sheets of plywood and stacks of lumber scattered about in great disarray. My vigil seemed rather ridiculous now with the wind whipping through my thin coat, particularly in view of the fact that Queen Elizabeth was not at Buckingham Palace at all.

This sorry fact was brought home to me when Nat showed me a "News of the World" picture of me typing in front of the Palace. The caption read, WHY DOESN'T SOMEONE TELL GARRY SHE'S AT BALMORAL?

It would be a simple matter, I thought, to build a small lean-to out of the scattered lumber and it would keep the wind out during the night. Suiting action to the thought, I crossed the deserted street, fashioned a lean-to and crawled in. It was snug and warm.

I must have dozed off, for a light in my eyes woke me up. "All right, come out with your 'ands up, and no funny business," a voice commanded. I crawled out blinking to encounter an armed night watchman.

"Blimey, an American!" he said seeing my A-2 jacket. "You can't stay 'ere, young fellow. What's the idea?"

"I have to stay here. You see, I'm petitioning the—"

"I'll get the bobbies after you, that's wot I'll do."

"Go ahead," I said. "They won't do anything. As a matter of fact, I left them this afternoon. They know I'm here."

It was the usual overnight cell all police stations have for night pickups. I was booked for vagrancy in spite of a protest that I was not a person before the law. The night sergeant was not concerned with subtleties. I refused to go to a welfare home; I was penniless; *ipso facto*, I was a vagrant. Whatever else I was he did not care.

My trial was brief and unfortunately the matter of the right to work never came up. I was convicted of vagrancy, sentenced to seven days in Brixton Prison, and Sir David Maxwell Fyfe, the Home Secretary, signed a deportation order in my behalf, deeming such action as "conducive to the public good". I was told that I would be deported to the United States, and this was reaffirmed despite the fact that I immediately renounced by mail my United States resident alien status, thus severing all legal connections with America. The British Government simply did not know what to do with me. I was soon to find out just how desperate it was.

Eight weeks later, with the works of Shakespeare, Schopenhauer and Lin Yutang fresh in my mind—for these had been my companions in prison—I found myself being escorted by two detectives aboard the *Queen Mary*, bound for New York. The boat sailed at 9:30 A.M., made a stop at Cherbourg to pick up passengers from Europe, and then steamed out to open sea. At this point my cabin was unlocked and I was given the freedom of the ship—until we arrived at New York on July 27th. Then, accompanied by the ship's sergeant-at-arms, I was brought before a U.S. Immigration official.

"Welcome home, Garry," he said cheerfully.

"Welcome home is it!" I spluttered, trying to hold back my anger. "What law is there that allows you to welcome me home against my will?"

"Aw come on, Garry, don't be like that. We're trying to play ball with you. Play ball with us."

"I don't like to have to remind you of your own duty, Officer, but I must insist on knowing the legal basis of the entry."

"Well, you see, Garry, there's really no law to handle you. You're a unique case. We're just going along with the British."

"No law!" I exclaimed. "Then it's collusion."

"Yeah, something like that," he admitted blandly.

I was so overwhelmed by this blatant admission from an officer of the United States Immigration Service, I was speechless for a minute. Finally I said, "Well, if you respect your uniform so little as to admit to collusion, I assure you I will be no party to it."

"Mr. Davis, what do you want me to do? Look, I got a wife and two kids. Give me a break, will ya?"

"I'm sorry, Officer, I refuse to enter the United States as a deportee. That's final."

"Oh, we don't have you down as a deportee," he said. "You're down as a traveller as far as we're concerned."

"Down? Down where?" I asked. "Where does it say I'm just a traveller?"

He looked at me sheepishly. "Well, there is a kind of paper . . ." He reached into a folder. "Yeah, here it is. See?"

Lo and behold, he handed me a British paper entitled "Document of Identity Issued to an Applicant Who Cannot Obtain a National Passport." I stared at it in amazement. There was my picture and physical description. There was the legend which read:

> Mr. S. Gareth Davis, holding Identity Book No. —, who resides at London and is registered as of Stateless (formerly American) nationality, desires to travel to America. This document must, when necessary, be visé for the journey to the country above men-

tioned by the appropriate authorities in the United Kingdom. It is valid only for a single journey.

Below was the seal of Her Majesty's Chief Inspector, Immigration Branch, dated 20 July, 1953, and signed by one W. Seggie for *H.M. Chief Inspector.*

The document also carried my signature!

A signature cut out from a letter I had written from Brixton —the prison stationery was obvious—was *pasted* under my photograph! I was amazed.

"I do not accept this paper," I said.

"Well, whether you take it or not," he said, turning it over and stamping it with his seal of admittance to the United States, "this is your entry paper. Now if you will kindly disembark, Mr. Davis."

"I categorically refuse to leave the ship under these conditions."

"Then we'll see to it that the ship leaves you," he said, and turned to an assistant who hurried off.

Ten minutes later, the sergeant-at-arms turned me over to two burly New York City policemen who gently but firmly "imported" me on to the New York City pier.

9

I was boiling mad. Mad, both because I had been handled like a sack of meal, and because I had no means of rectifying the injustice. When one is victimized by a government, I thought to myself, there is nowhere in this world of international anarchy to turn. Nowhere except to another government. *Another government!*

Now, if ever, I thought, is the time to proclaim *world* government. I needed representation. For the past five years, I recalled, I had simply assumed world government by virtue of having declared myself a world citizen. Yet all the time, I had been a citizen without the advantages of government simply because it had been assumed rather than proclaimed. Now, after having spent nine weeks in prison for absolutely no legitimate reason, shanghaied by one nation in collusion with another, and then dumped ashore like contraband, I saw more clearly than ever what must be done.

I regarded the proclamation of a government as consistent with the general principles of political philosophy as I understood them.

In order to be sure of my legal underpinnings, however, I went to see Arthur Garfield Hayes, the eminent civil rights lawyer. When I told him what I proposed to do, Mr. Hayes pressed his intercom button, barked "Staff meeting!" into the speaker, and admitted seven top-flight civil rights lawyers into his office that busy weekday afternoon to listen to my story.

The group questioned me sharply on all aspects, particularly on my most recent entry into the United States and my voluntary renunciation of resident alien status at Brixton Prison.

After a short pause, one of them ventured, "Seems to me you're something of a legal enigma."

"More of a *non*legal enigma," a colleague said.

"Yes, but he isn't *il*legal," said another, "since he's actually been recognized and admitted by the Government."

"Recognized yes, but under what statute?" asked the first.

"That's just the interesting point," Mr. Hayes broke in, using his pipe for emphasis. "The United States Government, or at least the State Department as well as the Immigration Department, it seems to me, has recognized this young fellow as a sort of legal entity in himself; that is, he incorporates the elements of sovereignty as do governments. He may be in the United States *de facto*, but I fail to see how he is here *de juris*. Hasn't happened since the end of the Revolutionary War when the U.S. made a treaty with the Delaware Nation of American Indians."

"If you're a government, Mr. Davis," one serious-looking young man suggested, "you could sue Great Britain and the United States in the International Court at The Hague."

"Or better yet, declare war on them," another chimed in. "In that way, when you're conquered they must support you." Everyone laughed.

"One moment, gentlemen," I interrupted. "Doesn't a government have to be declared publicly first? And then doesn't it have to have territory and popular support?"

"A government must indeed be declared," said Mr. Hayes, "to warrant recognition from other governments and to obtain citizen support. Also, it must fill a public need. The need in this case, as I see it, is to provide you with some law. As to territory, a newly declared government need not *have* territory though usually it *claims* territory. What you could claim for yourself, I have no idea."

"Why not the entire planet?" I asked.

"Yes, of course," he laughed. "Why not? What can you lose?"

"Then you can issue your own world passport," someone suggested.

"And print your own money," another added.

"But first you must define the principles of the government and state publicly why you are declaring it," Mr. Hayes advised. "From there on, may I say, play it by ear. Great Britain doesn't yet have a constitution or a bill of rights, and many governments never do get around to popular elections. Laws usually are made by decrees at the beginning. I happen to be a democrat, however." He reached behind him and pulled a thick book from a small bookshelf.

"Here, glance through this," he said, handing it to me. It was *Democracy Works*, by Arthur Garfield Hayes.

With these ideas boiling away in my mind, I retired during August for a short rest to my parents' home in Sorrento, Maine. Then I decided to give a "lecture" on September 4, 1953, and chose the city hall of Ellsworth, Maine, fifteen miles away. My "lecture" was entitled, "I Am a Government." Don Stewart, publisher and editor of the *Ellsworth American*, gave frontpage space to the announcement of the meeting. An old sea captain's chart of the locale pin-pointed the precise spot where I would stand as 68° 25' 30" longitude, 44° 32' 30" latitude. I would claim that crosspoint as legal world territory.

When I brought the posters advertising the event out to my family's house on Sorrento Point, my father and mother just stared.

"*You* are a government?" my mother asked bewildered.

"That's right," I replied. "Have been since July 27th, 11:25 A.M." Then I told them of my conversation with Mr. Hayes and his staff.

My father thought the whole idea outlandish. "People don't go around declaring governments," he said, "much less declaring themselves governments. Craziest nonsense I ever heard of. And in Maine, too! Why, they'll laugh you off the platform—that is, if anyone shows up."

"But this isn't only for local consumption," I argued. "In fact when I stand on that platform, it won't be Maine any longer; it'll be just plain Mother Earth!"

"Garry dear, why don't you write to Margaret Chase Smith and ask her advice?" my mother suggested.

I placed posters in stores throughout the surrounding countryside and of course throughout Ellsworth. Most of the "summer folk" would be gone, or going that weekend. They would undoubtedly be more concerned with closing the house, packing the car, making sure the telephone, gas, electricity and water were turned off than listening to a modern Don Quixote tell why he was a government.

I had a flag made: a green map of the world and the figure of a world citizen inside on a yellow background. It was decidedly makeshift, but serviceable for the occasion. I attached it to a wooden stand.

The hall cost $25 to rent and seated 1,000. Forty showed up. Tom, the local Ellsworth policeman, stood at the back. My speech ran for two hours, being 22 single-spaced typewritten pages. At the proper point I unfurled the flag, and there was a monumental silence from the exhausted forty—world veterans by this time. What they had expected to hear, I don't know. Some were friends of the family; others, local townspeople who had no doubt wandered in for lack of anything better to do; others were probably curious about the title; and still others, that blessed rare few, were genuinely interested in the subject matter.

After filling in the details of the previous five years, I declared: "Here in this Town Hall, in Ellsworth, Maine, in the sovereign United States of America, I, a world citizen, exist in a world anarchy. I am no longer able to tolerate such a condition. By the authority vested in me as a world sovereign, it is my duty and responsibility to myself and to my humanity to hereby proclaim for myself a world government with full legal powers and prerogatives based on the three prime laws of one God, one world, and one mankind. This government for the moment exists only in my person, but since all men are world citizens with full world sovereignty based on the recognition of the three prime laws, if they but affirm them, the proclamation of world government is every man's right, privilege, and responsibility. . . ."

Remembering Arthur Garfield Hayes's words regarding the claim of territory, I boldly claimed "in humanity's name . . . the territory of the entire earth as the proper home and rightful possession of all mankind." Then as a symbol of ownership, and recalling Rufus King's unique strategy, I went on to claim "here in the soil of my birth, the dot of land on which I now stand, as World Territory. . . . Let it be henceforth known as 'World Citizens' Point.' "

"Ya mean yer goin' to live in the city hall, Garry?" one of the townsfolk asked.

"Well, I guess I'll have to," I replied laughing, "unless Tom back there arrests me. The spot I'm standing on no longer belongs to the United States of America."

Tom uttered an embarrassed "Heck!" and fidgeted with his badge self-consciously.

When I finished and sat down, exhausted, someone shouted

"Amen!" the others applauded, and Tom, Ellsworth's symbol of law and order, stepped out quietly for a short beer.

"Every man . . . possess[es] the right of self-government . . ." wrote Thomas Jefferson in 1790. ". . . Individuals exercise it by their single will . . ." I felt I had affirmed this inalienable right in the truest sense and in an area vital to the security and well-being of all men. The task before me from this moment forward then was to test this "right" and thus make it available to all those who might wish to invoke it.

Accordingly, I returned to New York, and after recouping my finances a bit through a machine shop job in Bloomfield, New Jersey—procured through the good offices of Harry Jakobsen—in January I set up a world government executive agency, the United World Service Authority. Through this agency I organized a world citizens' political party, continued to register world citizens and began co-ordinating the various one-world activities begun in 1948 from Paris. The most important project of the agency, however, was the issuance of a World Passport. This document was a green-covered information and identification booklet with space provided for visas, not unlike the U.S. passport. The text was in English and Esperanto. Thanks to a loan from my father, I had one thousand printed on May 10, 1954, and I immediately filed one copy with the Security Division of the United Nations and one with the U.S. Department of Justice. Sample passports were also mailed to the Washington ambassadors, consul-generals or plenipotentiaries of the 79 extant national governments of the world as well as to leading travel agency federations.

To cap the mailing, I sent other samples to the High Comissioner for Refugees, Dr. G. J. van Heuven Goedhart, in Geneva; to President Eisenhower, and to Mrs. Eleanor Roosevelt.

By August 25th, seventeen national governments had either acknowledged receipt of the samples or had sent them on to their foreign ministries. Three governments, Ecuador, Laos and Yemen, wrote that they would recognize the passport on a *de facto* basis. Dr. José R. Chiriboga, Ambassador of Ecuador, wrote on August 5th: "My Government believes your idea is interesting and, providing all requirements are complied with and security maintained, Ecuador would accept such documents for purposes of being used instead of a passport."

Mr. Ourot R. Souvannavong, Ministre Plénipotentiaire and Envoyé Extraordinaire of Laos, wrote on August 19th: "The world of centralization . . . undertaken by U.W.S.A. is not only of the highest moral importance but also an effective instrument coming to the aid of the efforts of governments in their legislative work concerning this field of action." He added that "the Government of Laos welcomes favourably the initiative and is ready to give all desirable attention to it when the necessity presents itself."

By late July, I had received acknowledgments from twenty-eight governments. Not one government had rejected the World Passport. Even Mrs. Roosevelt accepted hers with "many thanks".

All that remained now was for me to test the passport. I was still anxious to go to India to study with Dr. Natarajan and this project seemed ideal for testing the efficacy of my new document.

My first attempt was abortive. I wrote to President Eisenhower asking for his signature on my own World Passport No. 000001. When I received no answer, I decided to try somewhat the same strategy with the U.S. Government that it, in collusion with Great Britain, had foisted on me. I rubber-stamped a facsimile of President Eisenhower's signature on my passport after advising the President of my action, then boarded the S.S. *United States* bound for Southampton, from which port I hoped to continue to India. British Immigration, however, took a dim view of both passport and signature and I was sent back home on the *United States*' return trip. When I arrived at New York, U.S. Immigration ignored the passport, claimed I had never left the United States, and I was politely but firmly escorted off the boat.

My second attempt to get to India was equally unsuccessful. Unable to get a renewal of my visa from the Indian consulate in New York, I stowed away aboard the S.S. *Liberté* bound for Le Havre. After five days of tea, sandwiches and sleeping in deck chairs, I was apprehended in the French port, returned once more to the U.S.A. and put on trial as a stowaway. Upon hearing my "defence", which was that I did not come under his jurisdiction, the judge smiled in a fatherly way, sentenced me to a week in jail, suspended the sentence and released me in my own custody. This same day I learned from India House that my visa had been authorized by cable from New Delhi the very day that, in exasperation, I had stowed away on the French flagship. I practically ran over to India House to pick it up. This time I was determined not to fail.

"There's just one small matter that must be taken care of before I can issue you your visa," Mr. Abrams, the consular officer, began. He looked at me with embarrassment. "We must have a letter from you stating that you intend to leave India after six months."

I groaned. "You know that I don't have a re-entry permit for the States?"

"Yes."

"And no papers for any other country?"

"Yes."

"And still the Indian Government insists on limiting my stay?"

"Those are my instructions."

"Am I to believe then that the Indian Government wants me to perjure myself for the sake of a visa, or does it impose such a condition deliberately in order to keep me out?"

"Please do not think either, Mr. Davis," he said. "It's just that you present such an unusual problem . . . the Government doesn't know quite how to handle it."

"I'm a problem simply because I'm only human," I thundered, feeling the bitter frustration of the past months welling up in me.

He became all Consul. "Well, Mr. Davis, if you are not prepared to give us such a letter. . . ."

I thought a moment. "I will agree to such conditions if you agree to a condition of mine," I told him.

"Oh, and what is that?" he asked with interest.

"For me to have the possibility of leaving after six months, I will have to have your visa affixed on my World Passport," I said.

The light left his eyes. "But I have no authority to do such a thing."

Disgusted, I wound up by writing and signing the letter stating that I would leave India in six months. When I was given the Indian visa, however, I had it photostated and simply pasted the photostat in the passport myself. If the Indian Government would not visa the passport, I would save it the trouble, I thought. The document had to be tested. Since, in terms of human rights, a visa itself is a fraud, as indeed is a passport, I felt I was committing no crime by using both to *remove* the restrictions to my free travel. In establishing precedents for world law, there were bound to be conflicts with existing and arbitrary rules supposedly governing the area between nations. Having suffered from them, I had no compunction about establishing my own rules with the qualitative difference that they were grounded firmly in universal principles.

In view of the British refusal of President Eisenhower's facsimile signature, I next made a rubber stamp of U.N. Secretary-General Dag Hammarskjöld's signature, stamped my World Passport with it, and then advised Mr. H. of my action. A reply from Mr. Leo Malania, an executive assistant to Mr. Hammarskjöld, thanked me for my recent letter to the Secretary-General, but said that it was "not advisable" for me to affix his signature to my World Passport. The S.G.'s position did not allow for such use, he added. I went the next day to the U.N. to see Mr. Hammarskjöld personally as this was, I thought, not a matter which could be handled by an assistant. But Mr. Hammarskjöld was not available, so I was packed along.

On April 1st, T.W.A. informed me I must have a transit visa for Dahran, Saudi Arabia. Armed with their letter stating that I was on Flight 422 the next day, plus the World Passport No. 000001 with Dag Hammarskjöld's facsimile signature, I went to the Saudi Arabian consulate on Madison Avenue and applied for a transit visa. The secretary took the passport and the letter with the application forms, went into an inner office, and closed the door. Ten minutes later he returned, handed me back my passport and the T.W.A. letter, turned and went back to his desk and a pile of papers.

I put the passport and letter in my pocket without a glance, gave the secretary a perfunctory "Thank you," as if world passports were handed in every day of the week in every consular office throughout the world, and sauntered out, closing the door behind me. Walking down the long hall, scarcely daring to breathe, I rang for the elevator. The door opened and I slipped inside. I dug into my pocket, pulled out the document, opened it hurriedly, and turned to the second visa page.

My heart took a leap. Sure enough, there was a Saudi Arabian transit visa for three days! Historic day! Here was the first official recognition of the World Passport and from a nation whose jealousy over its frontiers was almost a matter of fanaticism. The T.W.A. girl who gave me the letter had informed me sweetly that Saudi Arabia "never gives visas to stateless people".

Arriving at the airport dressed in my world citizen uniform, patterned after a U.S. pilot officer's battle jacket and trousers, but with the world citizen patch sewn on the left sleeve, I checked in at the T.W.A. desk. It was Easter Sunday. Everyone seemed in a particularly buoyant mood. I turned in my passport at the counter. The young man took a long look at it with its pasted Indian visa, its Saudi Arabian visa, its Hammarskjöld signature and my passport picture with the Notary Public seal.

He looked up. "You're a U.S. citizen, of course, aren't you?"

"Now that's a strange question. Why do you ask?" I replied guardedly.

"Because of your transit stops," he said, writing in my ticket. "Your passport doesn't actually say whether you're a U.S. citizen or not, so I thought I'd ask."

"Well, funnily enough, I'm not!"

"You're not?"

"Oh, now really, what's the matter?" I asked.

"Well, if you're really not"—he looked at me intently as if he hoped to see U.S. citizenship somewhere on my face—"then we'll have to see about transit visas for Canada, France, and Switzerland."

I moaned.

"Don't worry, Mr. Davis, there won't be any trouble," he assured me. "We'll just have our representative in New York contact the three embassies . . . uh-uh, it's Sunday."

"It's also ten minutes before flight time," I reminded him.

"Just a moment, please." He hurried off. The T.W.A. press agent moved in. "Would you care to give us a statement, Mr. Davis? There's a press room here at the airport and I can get it to the wire services."

"I don't even know that I'm leaving," I told him. "There's some question of transit visas."

"Yeah, I guess you're always running into stuff like that, huh?"

"Sure am."

"Well, let me know if you want to make a statement, Mr. Davis."

"Sure will, thanks." He moved off.

The young T.W.A. desk sergeant called to me from an office. "Our rep in town can't rouse anyone at any of the embassies. Do you want to talk with him?"

"Yes," I said, grabbing the phone. "Garry Davis here. Now I really don't understand all this need for transit visas when we only touch down at these places for half an hour at the most. I've already been to France and Switzerland without papers, and as for Canada, who would want to jump ship at Newfoundland at this time of the year?"

"I agree, Mr. Davis, but we've just got to get okays from them first."

"Why wasn't I told this when I bought my ticket?" I asked, visualizing all my plans going awry again over those damnable visas. "I could have gotten those visas myself."

"Yes, we should have let you know," he agreed. "We'll have to put you up until the next flight goes out on Tuesday. In the meantime, I'll personally clear with the embassies first thing in the morning as well as with Washington."

"Washington!" I yelled into the phone. "What the devil has Washington to do with this?"

"Well, we just don't want there to be any more slip-ups, do we?" he chatted.

"But listen," I urged desperately, anticipating more delay, and possible cancellation, "the reason you're going to call the other embassies is because I'm *not* a U.S. citizen; then, what is the point of disturbing Washington over something that is none of Washington's business?"

"Now, don't you worry, Mr. Davis," he purred, "we'll get you off on that Tuesday flight. You just leave everything to me." He hung up.

"Can we take off, fer Chris' sake?" someone shouted into the office. The young sergeant looked at me. "Can we take off, Mr. Davis?" It was twenty minutes past flight time. I nodded dumbly. He turned. "Take it away, Charlie. He's not on this one."

I left the office and took a cab to New York after getting a T.W.A. overnight hotel chit. Monday, April 2nd, I spent at the T.W.A. office listening to an executive call various embassies in Washington about "a rather unusual situation that has come up, and we need your help".

115

Around 4:00 P.M. I was informed that Canada, France, and Switzerland had waived their visa requirements in my case on the condition that I confine myself to the transit lounge of the airport in each of their countries.

"Fine," I said. "What about Washington?"

"All clear," he replied. "I called the Justice Department." He paused. "They rather gave me the impression you can go to the moon for all they care."

"I'll bet, and go native," I said getting up. "Well, it looks like I might get off tomorrow after all."

"You're as good as in Bombay right now."

The new flight was scheduled for 6:00 P.M. the next day, so someone at T.W.A. had told me. I decided in the morning to go around to the Swiss Consulate on Madison Avenue and try to coax a visa out of them for the World Passport. I arrived at noon wondering whether a letter from T.W.A. like the one for the Saudi Arabian consulate might not do the trick. I dialled the T.W.A. number, asking for the young lady to whom I had spoken previously.

"Where are you talking from?" she asked me when I had told her my request.

"The Swiss Consulate," I replied.

"But aren't you on Flight 600?"

I began to sweat.

"Yes, why?"

"Your plane leaves in twenty minutes!"

"What!" I shouted. "Let me speak to the Tower Control Chief."

"Right."

A moment later, "Tower Control Chief here."

"This is Garry Davis. I'm scheduled for Flight 600 from Idlewild and I've been held up in town till now on some business that cropped up at the last minute. Can you hold that flight for me?"

"Just a moment, Mr. Davis, I'll get the tower on another phone and see." I waited nervously. Someone *had* said 6:00 P.M.

"Okay, Mr. Davis, they'll hold twenty minutes."

"Right." I slammed the receiver down and became a blur from then on till I got to Idlewild 35 minutes later. A whole squadron of T.W.A. officials was lined up at the kerb waiting for me.

I was rushed through checking-in, and clutching my portable typewriter and briefcase, raced through the gate and out on the asphalt where a huge DC-6 impatiently waited.

As I settled into my seat, the giant engines started and I automatically reached for my seat belt. Was it possible? Was I about to take off for India? I wondered incredulously. We taxied on to the ramp and moved into the warm-up position beside the take-off runway. My heart was pounding, my throat dry. I looked at the busy airport scene, the blue sky . . . a plane was on its final approach. When would I see it all again, if ever? Then I felt ashamed of my sentimentality. There's no road back, I thought to myself, only the road ahead—an ancient road trod by kings, conquerors and vagabonds alike, each seeking enlightenment. The giant engines were going through their magneto and run-up checks, drowning out all passenger conversation.

We taxied on to the take-off strip, a green light flashed from the tower and the idling engines sprang into a full-throated roar, sucking in huge gulps of air hungrily as the big machine moved forward, ponderously at first, then faster and faster as the props raced in their endless circles. I looked down at the speeding runway and for some reason felt my eyes moisten as we gained airspeed and our spinning wheels left the ground.

A long-held dream was about to be fulfilled. I was travelling halfway around the world on a World Passport to study with a wisdom guru.

10

Flying above the clouds at 15,000 feet, one is always impressed by the brilliance of the sun. We passengers had to adjust ourselves to it. Our eyes squinted. We all reacted in the same way—we Germans, Japanese, Chinese, Russians, Americans and Indians. "*Jus soli*," I said to myself, "by right of the sun"; that is the manner in which we humans endure. The sun seemed to make a mockery of our vaunted national frontiers, illuminating whole hemispheres of the earth in a sweep; it tanned our skins to an approximately uniform pigmentation; it could feed us or it could blind us all in the same way. . . .

At 15,000 feet these were natural thoughts, at least for a world citizen. Back on the crust of the earth, however, one was faced with the bureaucrat, the rubber stamp, and policemen with professionally suspicious eyes. Flight 600 stopped briefly at Shannon, Paris, Geneva, Rome, Athens and Cairo, and at each stop-over I trooped down the ramp with my fellow passengers to turn in my passport. Just before boarding, an official would return the passports and mine was usually returned with a smile or a scowl—the scowls diminishing and the smiles broadening, it seemed, as we approached Bombay.

Soon we were circling the airport at Bombay. When we landed I was on India but not yet *in* India, for the airport itself was "international". If the Bombay authorities did not wish to admit me on my World Passport, T.W.A. would be obliged to ship me back to New York. I knew the rule book would have to be disregarded in my case. There was nothing in it yet about world citizens nor about world passports.

I was third in line to hand in my passport to a brisk young officer with jet black hair, black eyes and beautiful tan skin. In front of him were several rubber stamps. My mouth was dry. Such a tiny piece of energy was needed to pick up a stamp, ink it in the pad and print an impression on a piece of paper. Hardly any effort at all was required. It certainly was not heavy labour, nor did it require any creative ability. Even a monkey could be trained to do it. Yet, that casual gesture, that flick of the wrist, might start a chain of circumstances which would lead to changes in jurisprudence throughout the world. Much of Western law originated with just such casual precedents.

When my turn came, I presented the World Passport. The young official took it from its vinyl plastic case slowly, staring at its green cover. My stomach was fluttering. He opened the passport slowly, reading the notice on the first page very carefully. I was insufferably hot and longed to take off my jacket. Then he turned the page and looked at the Notary Public's rubber stamp and seal. The passengers behind me were becoming impatient, but the young official seemed determined to take his time. He came finally to the photostated Indian visa on page seven. Just then, a head popped in the doorway and said, "Mr. Davis, I wonder if you would care to say a few words to the *Times of India*?"

"I'd be glad to," I said, "just as soon as I am cleared here."

"Thank you," he said and popped out.

The young officer glanced at me for the first time. I smiled at him. He smiled back automatically, whereupon he then took a rubber stamp marked PERMITTED TO LAND, rapped it on his ink pad authoritatively, and pressed it to the bottom of page seven directly under the photostated Indian visa!

I was in sovereign India and still a world citizen. The World Passport worked!

Representatives from the *Times of India*, the *Indian Express*, and the Press Trust of India, the national wire service, were on hand to greet me in the next room.

They wanted to know my mission in India. I told them I was there to study Vedanta with Dr. Natarajan and, if possible, to translate the results of that study into hard-core political realism on the global level. There was no problem, I added, made by man which could not be solved by man, and war was definitely a man-made phenomenon.

"But who is this Dr. Nat'rajan?" asked the *Times* man. "We have never heard of him."

I laughed. "So it takes a poor Westerner to point out your wise men to you. Have you not heard of the warrior *rishi* Narayana Guru?"

"Of South India?" the P.T.I. man asked.

"Yes, Travancore," I replied. "Well, Dr. Natarajan is his *parampara* disciple."

Eyebrows raised. To these busy journalists working in the bustling cities with their teletypes, presses, wireless, etc., in touch with the political, social and industrial life of the planet, such things as *guru parampara* and *vedanta*, especially being spoken so casually from a Westerner's lips, were mightily embarrassing.

I was then met by a former student of Dr. Natarajan, Arjuna, who put me up for the night at his home in Bombay. The next morning I boarded a train for Bangalore and proceeded from there by bus up the Nilgiri Hills to Ootacamund, the Newport of India, above which, at the tiny hill village of Fernhill, the Guru Natarajan had his spiritual retreat or "Gurukula."

"How shall I greet him?" I wondered excitedly as the bus chugged up into the mountains. Finally, I arrived at Ooty and there hired an ancient taxicab for the ride to the Gurukula. As the taxi crawled along the narrow dirt road leading to the spiritual retreat, suddenly I could make out the familiar, portly figure of Guru Natarajan standing in front of a large main building waiting to receive me. I recalled Harry Jakobsen's words, "He will polish you up, but good!" and my apprehension increased. But when the taxi stopped I leaped out and embraced the Guru.

Dr. Natarajan's immediate concern was for my complete rest and recuperation, not only from the trip to India, but from "sensational situations" in which I had recently been engaged.

"Here you need only live with nature in freedom and sunlight," he told me. "Cultivate a negative or neutral attitude within you in which you empty yourself of all ideas of action. I would say a minimum of two months would be necessary for this. Feel completely at home in the Gurukula. Calm your nerves by gardening and pastoral activities. Spend lots of time alone, eat alone, walk alone, and shed all the debris of wrong conditioning in the West and of repressions due to artificial conditions of life there. Find the capability here of disaffiliating yourself from the crowd mentally. Prove you can do this to yourself over and over. In brief, cultivate the joy of contemplative self-sufficiency."

Twice daily at 9:00 A.M., after all the Gurukula inmates had their early morning tea and bath, and again at 7:00 P.M. just before the evening meal, we gathered in the main auditorium for what might be called a prayer meeting. In reality, it was more of a classroom, the subject being wisdom and the textbook, the Bhagavad-Gita. We sat on either side of the Guru, while he squatted on the traditional leopard skin with his ochre shawl over his head. Either a fruit or flower offering was the usual centrepiece brought in by a villager or guest. Individually dipping our hands into the scented Siva ashes, we smeared them with two fingers on our forehead.

"This is not to be regarded in the sense of ritual," the Guru told me at my first session, "but simply as a reminder of the perennial nature of wisdom and the contemplative way of life. Also, such harmless gestures tend to soothe the feelings and remind them of a traditional pattern of things as distinct from the relative world of necessity and daily events."

Swami Mangalananda, one of the Guru's closest disciples, would begin these services with an almost sung rendition of a Gita chapter. Then, after a short prayer by Narayana Guru which would be repeated by everyone, we were free to speak when so moved, very much in the manner of a Quaker meeting.

Between these two services I bided my time, walking, talking, thinking and writing. On one of the walks I took with the Guru, he began by singing: "If I Knew You Were Coming, I'd 'a' Baked a Cake" which, he said, he had learned from the teenagers in Bloomfield, New Jersey. Then we came to a small pond which was matted with lotus blossoms. The Guru stopped and contemplated the sight for a moment.

"Do you know why the Indians consider the lotus a holy flower?" he asked me finally.

"No," I replied.

"Pick one up and look at the underside, the part that's been resting on the water."

Reaching down, I picked up the nearest flower and turned it over. I saw nothing unusual.

"Well?" the teacher asked.

"But I don't see . . ."

"Place it back on the water and pick it up again, and remain alert," he advised me.

I did so. Then it dawned on me as I looked at the underside that it was as dry as toast. I dunked it again, and still it remained dry.

"Yes, it rests on the water but does not get wet," said the Guru. "Thus it is like wisdom, or what is referred to in India as the Absolute, which permeates the entire universe yet which is not touched by it. Contemplate this."

We walked along in silence.

During the two months I remained at the Fernhill Gurukula, I learned for perhaps the first time in my life the art of relaxation: how to do absolutely nothing without feeling idle. The pressure of useless activity rolled from me like layers of dirt. Gradually, I became able to "exercise" by mere contemplation—a paradox to the Western mind—and to conceive conclusions and truths far in advance of being able to demonstrate them. From the "negative" or "neutral" attitude I cultivated under the Guru's gentle guidance, I seemed to perceive things directly relating cause to effect, obtaining a strange, wonderful sense of the whole of things. This growing capacity must have changed me a good deal because one day, quite unexpectedly, the Guru approached me. Evidently thinking I had shed the remnants of "sensational situations," the sage offered some positive advice.

"Go see Prime Minister Pandit Nehru," he said.

I wrote to Nehru for an appointment and within a few days received a letter from his private secretary stating that the Prime Minister would receive me on June 7th.

"Ask him for his blessing," said the Guru as I left for New Delhi.

"His blessing! But he calls himself an agnostic."

"Any man has the right to bless another man's work when it is for the general good," the Guru said. "Nehru is no exception. What greater respect can one man pay to another than to ask for his blessing? He will understand this. Furthermore, I think he will give it. Remember, you are the disciple of a guru."

Four days and 1,000 miles later, I arrived at the imposing Foreign Ministry building with a briefcase in one hand, and a small wicker basket with fruit and nuts in the other. The day was excessively warm, well over 100 degrees, and the front entrance was covered by a huge bamboo screen against which a coolie was splashing large buckets of water. He pulled aside the screen and I entered the dark exterior. To my right was a large desk behind which sat three elegantly dressed Sikhs, with great white, cloudlike turbans resting or perhaps floating on their heads. They wore broad red bands of silk across their chests.

"You will take your seat," a light-skinned receptionist told me after I announced myself. Soon a turbanned attendant appeared, motioning for me to follow him. As we walked through the halls and up a large stairway with magnificently carved teakwood banisters, I was reminded of a medieval castle. The floors were bare stone, the walls seemed to be granite, and the furnishings were sparse and impersonal.

On the second floor, attendants padded to and fro, swiftly and noiselessly. I was ushered into a large room dominated by a huge window stretching to the ceiling and looking out on to the broad avenue on both sides of which were the apartment houses for members of the Lok Sabha, India's parliament.

"Please come in, Mr. Davis," said a smiling chap behind a large desk. "The Prime Minister will see you presently. He's a little behind in his schedule." I took his proffered hand, almost tripping over my dhoti robe.

"I see you have adopted our dress," the Prime Minister's secretary said, smiling.

"Let's say it adopted me," I replied, wondering why I hadn't cheated by using a belt or at least a string to hold up the mass of material. It certainly would never do to have my dhoti slip away right in front of the Prime Minister of India!

One of the telephones rang. "Yes, sir," said the secretary. Then, looking past me, he said, "You may go in now, Admiral."

An elderly gentleman in resplendent uniform, sporting four inches of gold braid on the sleeves of his bemedalled coat, walked stiffly to the door at the right and disappeared inside. He charged out after several minutes, looking grim. Advancing to the chair at my left, the admiral plunged into it and started speaking in staccato Hindi to the secretary. The telephone rang again.

"Yes, sir . . ." Then he turned to me. "You may go in now."

The Prime Minister was standing behind a great curved desk of tan polished wood, which, though with many things on it, remained uncluttered and businesslike.

"Do come in, please," he said. His face for an instant surprised me. It seemed careworn, not as young as I had imagined from the strength and authority of his writings and speeches. His eyes were warm, friendly, and penetrating.

Not knowing quite how to present my offering, I held it up like an auctioneer showing a vase, and said in a strained voice, "I have brought you some fruit and nuts."

"Oh, how very nice," he said gently as I put it on the edge of the desk. Sensing my nervousness, he motioned to the leather chair in front of his desk. I sank into it gratefully. He looked at me inquiringly, waiting for me to say something. I looked at him, wondering what to say.

"Do you know," I heard myself saying, "I don't have the feeling we are meeting for the first time. I've read so much of your writing and know so many of your thoughts, I feel as if I am meeting an old friend." I stopped.

"How long have you been in India?" he asked quietly.

"I arrived April 4th," I told him, wondering whether I should bring up the World Passport at this point.

"I see. And where have you been since then?"

"First, I went straight to Bangalore, then up to Fernhill in the Nilgiris to visit Dr. Natarajan who is my guru."

"Your guru!"

"Yes, I first met Dr. Natarajan in 1950 when returning to the United States from Europe. I've been studying with him ever since."

"I see." He put his finger tips together. "And what does your ... uh, guru, teach you?"

"He revealed to me why I was a world citizen," I said slowly.

"Ah ha ... but didn't you know already?" he asked.

I laughed. "I thought I did, but it was more instinctive than reasoned ... a feeling rather than a moral awareness. I gave that feeling all sorts of rationalizations: a sentimentalized brotherhood of man, world federal government, fear of World War III, and others. But I didn't really understand it from the contemplative point of view."

"And now you do?"

"Let me say I am on the right path."

We fell silent. He seemed absorbed in some thought.

I took the World Passport from my briefcase. My heart pounding, I said, "Do you know, Mr. Nehru, that I travelled to India on a world passport?"

"A world passport? Really?"

"Yes." I handed it across the desk. He took it curiously and studied the cover.

"I see you have Hindi here." He opened the booklet, read the notice "Important" on page one, turned to page two where

Guru Natarajan had signed "In the Name of the Absolute" with his signature in place of Dag Hammarskjöld's.

"Very interesting," the Prime Minister said.

"This passport identifies the bearer as a world citizen," I offered hesitantly.

"Uh, yes, I noticed that," he replied. Suddenly he laughed. "Well, well, well, what have we here?"

"What page are you on, sir?"

"Seven."

I smiled weakly. It was the photostated Indian visa. "Yes, well you see, Mr. Nehru, I waited some time for authorization from here to have your New York consul put the visa on properly, but... well, it never came."

"And so you pasted it on yourself?"

"Yes, sir."

"I see. Very ingenious."

"You note near the bottom, sir, the entry stamp of the Bombay authorities?"

"This isn't your work also, is it?" he asked, his eyes twinkling.

"No, sir—not that I would have any compunction about doing it, but in the case of a rubber stamp it is easier to innovate than to forge, and besides, one keeps out of trouble."

"I quite understand. But tell me, Mr. Davis, how did such a passport come into being?"

"You see, sir," I replied, gathering my thoughts, "I am a stateless person and have been so for eight years. For the first five years, I found myself bouncing from jail to jail..."

"You've been in prison?" he asked in surprise.

"I've had a taste, sir," I replied, "though not as much as you have, of course."

"But how could you go to prison simply for being a stateless person?"

"Because a stateless person continually finds himself bumping against laws which don't protect him... especially as regards papers. If he is discovered without papers or can't get them for one reason or another, he simply languishes in jail under the polite term 'custody' until either he is given refuge—a degrading status—or sent to another nation to face the same idiocy."

"But surely the United Nations is taking care of this situation."

"The problem is too big for the U.N.," I replied. "It is a global problem and the U.N. is, after all, simply a club for states with a glorified clubhouse. What can the U.N. do? It is still restricted by national laws."

He skirted this delicate point. "But where have you actually been in jail?"

"Well, I was in Brixton Prison in London..."

"In London!" he exclaimed laughing. "Well, and what did the British imprison you for?"

"I was on my way to India in 1953," I replied, and then told him briefly of my adventures in England.

"I decided when I was returned to the States," I finished, "that I wouldn't leave again without a paper that at least identified me. Besides, I met dozens of people from all over in Brixton whose only crime was that they didn't have a paper from a so-called proper authority stating who they were. In fact, my entire eight years as a stateless person are a personal protest against this strangling bureaucracy."

"So you decided to make a *world* passport? Doesn't this add one more paper to an already overburdened world?" he asked.

"But it's a universal paper while the others are all restrictive," I answered. "I agree that no paper should be necessary ideally. What right does one man have to tell another whether he can travel on God's green earth? But stateless people feel this injustice more than others. We are a worldly people whether we like it or not and every moment of our lives we stand smack in the middle of the world anarchy...."

"Aren't you a bit of an anarchist yourself?" he asked quietly.

"Anarchist?" I echoed, looking at him in surprise. "Well, I suppose if you mean on the philosophical or spiritual level, perhaps I am. I certainly don't want anyone dictating what I should think or believe... though there is plenty of that today. But if you mean it on the political level, I am just the opposite. I insist on world law and order. That's my whole stand as a world citizen."

"I see," he said. There was another moment of silence. I heard the hum of the air conditioner for the first time. I wondered what was going on in his mind. I hadn't brought up any of the usual subjects: Bandung, Kashmir, disarmament, Goa. The interview seemed aimless, without tangible result... so far.

"May I present an Honorary World Passport to you, sir?" I asked. He nodded diffidently. As I delivered the presentation speech referring to his personal courage and dedication to freedom, he began to take some interest. When I read that President Eisenhower was the first recipient of an Honorary World Passport, he leaned forward slightly. And when I declared that from this moment on he was to be considered a "Sovereign Citizen of the World," he broke into a smile.

As I handed him the passport with the typewritten speech on top, I told him I was embarrassed because though it finished, "In witness whereof, we have set our hand and seal," I had left my seal in Bangalore!

"Quite all right," he assured me, opening his new passport. "No need for such formalities. Oh, here's my picture! Where on earth did you get this one?"

It had been taken during a *Satyagraha* campaign where he wore a simple white shirt, front open, and had a particularly vivacious glint in his eyes. He looked at it a long time.

"Well, this is very nice. I accept with pleasure."

I said, "I'm very glad, sir. Your moral support adds a great deal to my humble efforts."

"But I would like to hear a bit more of these efforts. What exactly do you do?"

I took out the latest issue of *Values* magazine and passed it across to him.

"This is our monthly magazine, sir, that is, the organ of the Gurukula Movement of which Dr. Natarajan is the founder and head. It explains our activity and the principles underlying it."

He took it cautiously.

"Our basic principles, of course, are yours," I added, "one world and one mankind."

He looked up. "One world, yes, and even one mankind... but it is a difficult jub. Look at the immense task we have right here in uniting India."

"Oh, we don't do any uniting, sir," I said hurriedly. "We start from the premise that mankind is already united and the world is already one. We merely advertise the fact, and when necessity arises, act upon it."

"Yes, as a world citizen, I dare say you would," he returned mildly.

"What I mean is, we try to represent the conscience of humanity in the face of absurdities and injustices. We contend that once men realize they are all members of the same species here and now, not in some vague future, then the details of world reorganization will fall into place naturally and spontaneously. That's what our world government does, simply represents man's moral value."

"Your world government!" he exclaimed, his eyes widening.

"You see, Mr. Nehru, as world citizens we had to be represented by our own government," I continued rapidly. "So we declared a world government in 1953."

"Oh, I see. And what does your guru have to say about all this?"

"Oh, he supports it. He says this is the political corollary of the ancient Advaita Vedanta since it's founded on unitive and universal principles."

"Well, this is all most interesting."

With Dr. Natarajan's words in my ears, I took a deep breath and said, "We would like your blessing, sir, for our work."

He looked at me sharply. "Well, I really don't know your work too well..."

"It is simply humanitarian work, sir, and we are fully dedicated and serious men. And, as I am in India for the present, it is necessary that I have your personal blessing in order to continue."

"Yes, well, you have my good wishes, certainly," he said.

I gritted my teeth. "I truly appreciate that, sir, but as this work is grounded in the highest idealism, your blessing is required also. May I have it?"

He looked at me judiciously. I held my breath. He lowered his eyes and stared at his finger tips. The hum of the air conditioner seemed loud in my ears. After what seemed an interminable time, a tiny sigh escaped him and a soft smile curled his lips. He looked up.

"Yes, of course," Pandit Jawaharlal Nehru said, "you have my blessing."

A news story about my interview with Nehru in the *Statesman*, a leading Indian daily newspaper, brought an abrupt end to my life of contemplation. I was immediately sought out by Indians of all rank—from Princess Brinda, the Maharani of Kapurthala, who invited me to her summer palace at Mussoorie to discuss world citizen education, to shopkeepers who recognized me from my picture. I was invited to tea with Madame Indira Gandhi, Mr. Nehru's daughter; wined and dined by Mr. J. C. Mathur,

I.B. 37.

DOCUMENT OF IDENTITY ISSUED TO AN APPLICANT WHO CANNOT OBTAIN A NATIONAL PASSPORT.

SOL GARETH DAVIS

London

Stateless (formerly American)

America

Garry Davis

20 JUL 1953

Here is a photostat of the British "official" document, used with the collusion of U.S. Immigration in my forced entry of July 27th, 1952 from the R.M.S. *Queen Mary*. Note that my signature has been taken from another document. (Actually it was taken from a piece of prison stationery.)

EMBAJADA DEL ECUADOR
WASHINGTON

August 5, 1954.

United World Service Authority
270 Park Avenue, Suite C-1315
New York 17, N. Y.

<u>Mr. Garry Davis, Director</u>

Gentlemen,

   Further to your letter of July 15, regarding passports to be used by refugees and stateless persons, we are now in receipt of the views of my Government on your ideas about the use of the proposed document for international identification.

   Ecuador has always given cooperation and assistance to refugees and stateless persons, by giving them special travel documents which have been accepted by other countries. My Government believes that your idea is interesting and, providing all requirements are complied with and security maintained, Ecuador would accept such documents for purposes of being used instead of a passport.

   Furthermore, my Government believes that if your office decides to open an office in Ecuador for legal and security reasons, you must include among the Directors of said office a Representative of the Ecuadorean Government from the Ministry of Foreign Affairs.

   In summary, Ecuador accepts your world passport as travel document for personal identification.

        Yours very sincerely,

        Dr. José R. Chiriboga V.
        Ambassador of Ecuador.

This letter was confirmation of my basic theory that individuals outside of states could legitimately identify themselves and then be recognized by states.

Director-General of All-India Radio; and taken to a fire ceremony to invoke the monkey-god, Subramanian, by Swami Nityaananda Kawishwar, a cosmologist and prophet. These activities were attended, as in France, by publicity and a growth of interest in world government.

In order to consolidate the ground won, I returned to Bangalore to collaborate with Guru Natarajan on a paper which would first ". . . arrive at axiomatic definitions as to what causes war and what creates peace in human society,"—as Emery Reves has written in *Anatomy of Peace*—and then set forth the principles on which a world government can be legitimately based.

The boldness of the project did not deter us. In our area, wisdom and politics have no common meeting-ground. "Practical" men deal only with the mechanics of power, while idealists abhor power as such concentrating only on the abstract world of values. Yet how are society's common problems—war and poverty for example—to be resolved without the application of wisdom, the highest of human values, the "pearl of great price"? In fact, does not the absence of wisdom inevitably lead to *all* social and private ills?

Here was an opportunity, I felt, to bridge the gulf between the pure knowledge of a sage and the techniques of power usage, in the context of world organization. The result, worked out in draft in my room at the Bangalore YMCA and polished by Guru Natarajan, we entitled *The Memorandum on World Government*.

The Memorandum on World Government was first published in *Values*, a magazine edited by John Spiers, Guru Natarajan's closest disciple, himself the head of a Gurukula outside of Bangalore. Shortly thereafter, the Guru departed for Singapore on a speaking tour with John Spiers, leaving the editorship of *Values* in my hands for two months. I rented a small two-room bungalow which I dubbed United World Government Headquarters. There, as I worked away on the next issue, it occurred to me that I might justifiably stake my claim as it were, or declare the bungalow in which I lived world territory.

Not long after so declaring, I received a letter from the District Superintendent of Police of Bangalore, addressed to *Mr. Garry Davis, American National, Narayana Gurukula, Bangalore*. I had failed to report either my arrival or my departure to the Registration Officer at Nilgiris, the letter stated, and therefore I was "hereby required to show cause within a week... as to why action should not be taken against you for your said failure, under the Registration of Foreigners Rules."

Instinctively, I dashed off a letter to the District Superintendent challenging every last premise in his notification to me. By mid-September I was visited by a representative of the superintendent. A mild-mannered gentleman, he reminded me pleasantly that my six-month visa would expire on October 4th and that I would have to apply for an extension if I wished to remain in India. I gave him tea and reminded him with equal gentleness that I was on my own territory, which was sovereign and global, and that national laws applied only as they were consistent with global laws. A code of behaviour, I added, predicated on the assumption that men were "foreigners", was incompatible with the second principle of United World Government: "One mankind." I showed him a copy of my letter to the District Superintendent. He left for further instructions.

Shortly thereafter, a three-man delegation from the same office appeared at my bungalow and, with a good deal less gentleness than their predecessor, demanded to be admitted. Not appreciating this cavalier attitude, I made them produce their badges—one poor fellow had forgotten his and had to drop out of the party—and then when I had ascertained that they were from the Alien Police, I refused them entry on the ground that "world territory" could not entertain Alien Police unless they were from another planet. Thinking they might try to arrest me at this point, I became indignant, telling them that I had the blessing of the Prime Minister and that I should let him know of this intrusion forthwith. They retreated rather piqued.

This of course was only a minor victory, for I really knew then that my sojourn in India was coming to a close. I had, after all, achieved my purpose in India, which had been to study with Dr. Natarajan. I had also managed to test the World Passport successfully, and what was more, I had been befriended by India's greatly loved Prime Minister Nehru. I did not wish to injure this trust, especially since I was convinced that a new nation such as India did not provide an especially fertile soil for an antinationalistic idea like world government. In any case, I had to do something—whether it was fighting the Indian Government or leaving India—and thus I took Dr. Natarajan's advice. "The answer is in the Dragon's Mouth," he said to me. So I packed my belongings—all of them this time, for I had the premonition that I would be leaving India for good—and returned to New Delhi.

There I repaired immediately to the Birla Mandir temple and asked for refuge. I was given a room in the hostel section, usually reserved for itinerant Hindu and Moslem holy men. My dress was still the dhoti, ochre-coloured juba, sandals and wooden beads.

Then I wrote. I addressed a letter "To All Ambassadors and/or Representatives of States, All Embassies and/or Consulates, and to the Prime Minister of India, New Delhi," to advise them "that as of October 5, 1956, World Government, founded 4th September, 1953, at Ellsworth, Maine, U.S.A., will be declared *de juris*." From that date, I continued, "all human beings will be represented as World Citizens by World Government according to the principles of *jus soli* and *jus sanguinis* which prescribe the legal bases for one world and one human race..." adding that "due to the termination of the 'Alien' status temporarily imposed on us personally under the Indian Foreigners' Act, we shall be represented legally only by World Government..."

The Legation of Switzerland wrote for a copy of the letter to send on to Geneva "for their information," and from the other eighty-one governments there came tacit acknowledgments.

When the press men asked Mr. Nehru a few days later whether it was true that the Indian Union recognized Garry Davis' World Government as of October 5th, Mr. Nehru informed them that he had extended my visa personally for another six months! Then he had his Secretary-General, Mr. Pilai, write to me asking if I would be good enough to relinquish my sanctuary at the temple at 4:00 P.M. the next day for a short visit with him.

When I entered his office next to the Prime Minister's in the Foreign Ministry building, he had in his hand the printed proclamation of World Government.

He came directly to the point. "Really, Mr. Davis, the Prime Minister is quite upset over this . . . this"—he rattled the paper distastefully—"way of doing things."

"Yes, I am sorry it is such a poor job," I said. "But we really are operating on a shoestring, you know. Perhaps if the Indian Government could advance us a few crore . . . ?"

"Now see here, Mr. Davis, Mr. Nehru has been quite decent to you . . . extending your visa for another six months . . ."

"But I didn't ask him to extend it, Mr. Pilai," I returned, "and frankly, I don't see how it can be extended without my consent. And since I still have my passport, I don't know what it was extended on."

He became all official. "I am obliged to inform you, Mr. Davis, that the Prime Minister does not look with favour on your present activity and he has asked me to request that you discontinue it while you remain in India."

"And if I refuse?" I asked.

"Steps will be taken."

"What steps, Mr. Pilai?" I asked.

"That remains to be seen. Now, I bid you good day, sir."

Back at the Birla Mandir, I finally chose the "press on" alternative. I was going to leave. I had won many friends in India and I did not want to lose them now by pitting myself against their new and hard-won independent nationalism.

Accordingly, the next day I obtained a valid seven-day transit visa on my World Passport from the High Commissioner of Pakistan. Then I began to pack. When I had finished, I stood up with a thirty-five-pound pack on my back, a nine-pound typewriter in one hand and a five-pound sack of papers in the other. I had absolutely no money in my pocket, the nails were already beginning to creep through my secondhand boots, and my destination—I had decided on Berlin—lay some 9,000 miles to the west. It was a fantastic predicament, but there were no alternatives.

I clanked out of the temple like a juggernaut. My slight frame was already beginning to buckle under the load. Outside, I set down my typewriter, mopped my brow and gazed out over New Delhi.

"Farewell, India!" I blurted out, half to myself, half to the beggars outside the temple. "I'm hoofing it to Berlin!"

I picked up my typewriter and started walking. I could never have dreamed then, as I trudged down the dusty road, that less than three months later I would be flying into New York's Idlewild Airport, first-class, aboard a KLM "Flying Dutchman", with the World Passport in one hand and a glass of champagne in the other.

I I

Dr. Natarajan had given me two precepts for travelling. "Look for signs," he said, "and do not insult money."

The first of these meant that I should not only keep an eye out for route markers, but for hidden clues or perhaps even omens as well. "Attend to details," the Guru elaborated, "and you will find guidance and replenishment where you least expect it." The second precept meant that while I should not beg, I should always accept gifts of money if freely offered.

I put both pieces of advice into action almost immediately and before I had taken as many as a hundred steps. For whom should I meet but an old friend from my first visit to New Delhi, the wife of a wealthy government official.

"Garry, where on earth are you going?"

"To Europe."

"But you cannot *walk* to Europe!" she said with a mixture of concern and exasperation. "How will you eat? Where will you sleep? Garry, really, you must be more practical!"

I laughed. "But how can I be more practical? I have no money and two good legs and I want to get some place. What else can I do but simply start walking? I don't mind walking. I can see more of the country that way."

The conversation continued, with her becoming progressively alarmed and my becoming progressively chipper, until she virtually forced upon me the train fare to Amritsar, the closest rail town to the Pakistan border, sixteen miles distant. I blushed, but accepted her generosity and thanked her as kindly as I could. On the train that night I began to wonder to myself about Dr. Natarajan's precepts. So far it had all seemed too easy. I had simply met a friend in a city where I had many friends. The real test lay ahead in parts of the world totally unknown to me. I fell asleep on the train that night to the monotonous tune of fear and loneliness played out by the click of the wheels over the endlessly slapping rails.

Next morning, from the frontier town of Amritsar, I struck

out on foot. Once again I was accosted after only a few steps and this time it was by a complete stranger.

"Pardon me, but may I ask your name?"

I turned. Walking beside me was a short, solidly built man of about my age with a round, dark face, jet black eyebrows and hair, and wearing coveralls.

"My name is Garry Davis," I replied. "And yours?"

"I am Rama Gupta Singh, but tell me, where are you going with all this?"

"Berlin."

"No, I mean where are you going on your way now?"

"Berlin."

"Berlin?"

"Berlin."

"I see." We walked along in silence a moment. Then, "But you are walking."

"That is correct."

He thought. Then he remarked matter-of-factly, "Do you know, we seldom see a white-faced man with a pack on his back walking along this road to Berlin?"

"That's odd," I returned solemnly. By now the nails in my hand-me-down boots were jabbing through my socks and I was limping a bit.

"Are you lame?" he asked. I explained. "Well, if you are walking to Berlin," he said, "you must have proper shoes. Come, I have a friend close by who is a shoemaker. We will have a cup of tea while your shoe is being fixed."

When we were seated in his friend's tiny shop by the side of the road and the aggravating shoe was under diligent repair, with tea and cookies served, Rama Singh wanted to know all about my strange odyssey. When I explained to him that I had no money, he wanted to know how I could manage.

"You know, it is not so difficult," I said munching a cookie. "In the first five minutes of my journey, I was given a train ticket. Now I am offered tea and biscuits by a total stranger."

"But that is nothing," Singh replied. "It gives me pleasure to have you as my guest."

"Perhaps you have answered your own questions," I said.

"What a strange thing," his friend the shoemaker said. "You talk more like one of our sannyasins than an American. You are an American, aren't you?"

I hesitated. "That depends on what you mean by 'American', " I replied.

"An American. A citizen of America."

"No one is a citizen in America," I said, "because America doesn't exist. There is North America, Central America, and South America, and together they make the Americas. In that sense, everyone who lives in the Western Hemisphere is an American. But there is no common law for all the different citizens of all the nations there, so there cannot be an American citizenship."

"But here in India," Singh said, puzzled, "we think that all people born in the United States are Americans."

"That's true," I replied, "but all Americans are not born in the United States. Canadians, Mexicans, Colombians, Brazilians, and many millions who immigrated to the United States from Europe and elsewhere are Americans."

"But then are you not an American?" Singh asked.

"Yes, I guess I am."

"You're not sure?"

I wiped my forehead. "If you mean 'American' in the sense of a state of mind, or a person who loves freedom, justice, equality and so forth, then I would say I'm an American."

"Then you are not an American in a practical sense?"

I laughed. "I am not an American in the sense of exclusive national citizenship."

He paused to think. I sipped my tea. The shoemaker's hammer sounded loud in the small shop. I looked out and could see heat waves shimmering off the asphalt road.

"I have heard of some American who was in New Delhi not long ago," he said finally, "and he called himself a world citizen." He looked at me sharply. "Could that have been you?"

"Yes, that was me."

"Well, I am so happy to meet you. This is a grand and noble idea. We Sikhs have such an idea in our holy books . . . that mankind is one and we are all brothers."

"That is right," his friend said, handing back my mended shoe.

"Many thanks," I said, putting it on.

"No thanks, no thanks for such a thing," he said. "It is my duty."

I rose. "Well, I must be getting along. I hope to make the border by nightfall."

"I will walk with you a little way," Singh said.

We took the road once more and continued in silence.

"Do you know," he said finally, "I believe the professors at our University would be interested in hearing from you. The Punjab University, largest Sikh University in India. It is just on the way. Perhaps you can address the students."

The professors seemed fascinated as I began to talk in their ready room after being introduced by Rama Singh. One went bustling off after a bit to find the dean to arrange a lecture for the students in the main auditorium for the next Monday, the day being Friday. A physics professor offered me bed and board for the weekend and a history professor wanted to know whether I had eaten that day.

I could not help but marvel at the cascading nature of events, even on this second day of my journey. It will be a rich experience indeed, I thought to myself as I lay in bed that evening, if these two days are any indication.

Directly after the Monday meeting with about five hundred serious-looking, turbanned Sikh students, I boarded a bus to Waga in front of the University, the ticket purchased by an *ad hoc* committee of the new Punjab University Students' Citizens of World Government.

Reaching Waga after the border had closed for the night, I stayed at the guardhouse, and crossed the next morning, October 24th, into Pakistan. My first stop was Lahore, 12 miles from Waga. At the station, I was suddenly overcome with exhaustion and barely dragged myself to a room where I composed a short article about travelling on a World Passport for the *Pakistan Times*.

The next day, after lunching with the American head of the local Y.M.C.A., I was taken to a hospital. My temperature was 104°. I had malaria. Three days later, after suffering through the "quick cure" of massive shots of paladrin, I left to discover myself locally famous. The *Pakistan Times* had featured my article in its Sunday edition, and I was invited to speak at the Y.M.C.A., the Rotary Club, and the F. C. College, the largest college in the area.

Pakistan then was spending 85 per cent of its national budget for arms and "defence," yet beggars were everywhere, pathetic bags of flesh and bone with dirty, running sores. In such countries as Pakistan—the slum areas of the world—expenditures of national income on weapons reveal starkly the blight of nationalism. I registered twenty World Citizens, set up a provisional regional office with a local citizen in charge, had luncheon one day with Governor Gurmani, to whom I presented an Honorary World Passport and a copy of the "Memorandum on World Government," and then pushed on to Peshawar, on the Pakistan-Afghanistan border.

Here I obtained an Afghanistan transit visa from the local consulate and at the same time arranged a ride through the Khyber Pass in a Chevrolet station wagon transporting an Afghanistan diplomat and his family home from a post in Washington. It was this diplomat who assured the local viceconsul, who did not speak or read English, that my passport was evidently valid as it was issued from New York City and carried a Notary Public seal of New York State. Afghanistan thus became the fourth nation to visa the World Passport.

As we drove up to the Khyber Pass, we found the border closed. A large group of fierce Pathan tribesmen, each with a rifle slung across his shoulder, was arguing with border guards. Our chauffeur stopped about fifty yards off while the diplomat went ahead to see what the trouble was.

"It is a dispute over papers," the chauffeur told us casually. "The Pathans see no need for papers since their ancestors owned these hills. Besides, they can't read anyway."

The diplomat was in the thick of the argument, listening first to the border guards, then to the tribesmen. As the debate went on, the argument becoming more and more heated, we noticed, on the fringes of the tribe, men unslinging their guns. The wife of the diplomat became agitated and urged the chauffeur to honk his horn. But the diplomat, obviously feeling in his element, continued to argue. Additional border guards with side arms were coming from the garrison house just beyond the road gate. This provoked the tribesmen further and more guns were unslung. The diplomat's wife, now beside herself, implored the chauffeur to lean on the horn, which he did, and the diplomat finally turned to us, annoyed. His wife pointed to the gunmen. He took in the situation at a glance, began to beam broadly at one and all, turned to the nearest border guard, spoke to him, then turned, beaming and bowing, and walked hastily to the car. When he was safely in, he barked orders to the chauffeur. Our car shot forward, hillsmen and guards scattering. The road gate popped up just as we came to it and slammed down as soon as we had roared through.

When we arrived in Kabul that evening, I could not have felt more alone and friendless. Besides the feeling of having moved six hundred years into the past, I was numbed by the long and bumpy car ride through the Khyber Pass, with numerous police checkpoints along the way. It was only the presence of the Afghan diplomat which overcame the suspicions of the various officials we encountered along the tortuous route. I trudged to the only hotel in Kabul, checked in and immediately clambered into bed. My head had hardly touched the pillow when there was a knock on the door.

"Welcome to Afghanistan, Davis. They just told me downstairs you popped in. My name's Hunter, Ed Hunter. I'm doing a book on Afghanistan. Come on over to my room and have a cup of tea. I have two girls along and we need a fourth!"

Ed Hunter had written *Brainwashing in Red China* and *Brainwashing—The Story of Men Who Defied it*. He was a U.S. journalist who had been in the Far East for twenty-five years. Fascinated with my trip, he gladly accepted a world passport and gave me twenty dollars for a plane ride to Herat, due west of Kabul and the closest town to the Iranian border. The next day I obtained an Iranian visa from the Ambassador himself in Kabul, and we chatted for several hours about Indian philosophy and world government. I then flew to Herat and proceeded by bus to Meshad, Iran—where, of all people, I happened to meet a twenty-five-year-old American-Swiss going to India to visit me! We embraced like old buddies. I continued by bus for Teheran. I had just enough money left from Ed Hunter's $20 for the ticket. Arriving in Teheran on November 29, penniless, I decided I had nothing to lose by checking in at the best hotel in town, the Hotel Park. So with a two days' growth of beard, my clothes heavy with dust, and my various sacks sticking out all over me, I strolled into the lobby just as if I owned Texas. The magnificently outfitted clerk sniffed at me a bit, then swung the great register around and I wrote my name, passport number, date issued, date of expiration, and for my occupation put *Co-ordinator, World Government*. He swung it back and started reading. Without batting an eyelash he rang for a bellboy, took a key from the rack and said in French, "Suite A."

Suite A was a collection of six rooms and two baths! In fact, it was the Presidential, or I suppose the Shah's suite. I decided it was a bit too much space for one man and asked on the phone whether there wasn't something smaller available. I ended up in the smallest nook in the hotel.

The next day I told the now sceptical Mr. Mack, the manager, that I would like to hire a room to hold a press conference. He brightened visibly. Then I discovered, to my consternation, that there was only one newspaper of any consequence in Teheran. *Eetalat*, which printed Parsi, French and English editions. It would be simpler to go down to the editorial offices to give my story and then to cover the wire services separately, so I cancelled the room I had hired and went to the *Eetalat* offices. There I met the editor, who ran a story about my trip on the front page the next morning.

The Hotel Park was the gathering spot for Iran's top society, the diplomatic bigwigs, leading businessmen and first-class tourists. Now that the press had given me attention, I began to meet some of Iran's first citizens . . . in the cocktail lounge. I was usually asked who was "behind" me. The Hotel Park was not noted for handling charity cases. When I replied that I travelled without national moneys, the reactions were spectacular. One businessman thought this proved me a complete charlatan; a French rug manufacturer regarded me as a foolish Utopist; his young American wife considered me bravely idealistic; a revolutionary former government official regarded me as the logical person to smuggle documents out of Iran "for the world to know the truth"; and Stanley Carter, the Negro pianist, and his lovely Swiss wife, who tended bar, thought the whole adventure "a gasser".

With only a ten-day transit visa, I was due to leave on December 10th. The Iraqian Embassy referred to my request for a visa by cable to Baghdad. There was no immediate answer. Accordingly I checked elsewhere. But the Syrian and Turkish consulates refused even to consider a visa on my World Passport, and the Egyptian Second Secretary couldn't possibly see any use in contacting Cairo since all foreigners, in the aftermath of the Suez War, were being rigidly excluded. Sensing another crisis, I requested an audience with the Shah in order to present him with a world passport and ask for his "indulgence". Two days later, the audience was refused by the Minister of the Court. Then I checked back with the Iraqi and Egyptian consulates. No reply either from Baghdad or Cairo. Time was running out . . . only two more days left to be in Iran. By this time, Mr. Mack and I were good friends, having had many discussions about world citizenship in which he agreed with me on all points, including allowing the hotel management to absorb my bill. "After all," he told me grandly, "how could you stay anywhere else, considering your position."

Over the weekend I prepared my next move carefully. According to my visa, I had to be out of Iran on Monday. This time, however, I had no continuing visa. The harassed police captain of the Foreigner's Division at police headquarters had refused to extend my transit visa on the World Passport, claiming that the Ambassador in Kabul had made a dreadful mistake in the first place by issuing it on the document. I must definitely be out of Iran by December 10th, he warned me.

By means of a generous donation by the once-sceptical French rug manufacturer, I had some "World Government Press Release" stationery printed, and on this I typed a statement outlining my new plight. I would be holding a press conference, I added, in the Egyptian Embassy at 11:00 A.M. on Monday, December 10th, to which all newsmen were invited. After delivering this to the editor of *Eetalat*, and to the correspondents for Associated Press, United Press, Reuters, and Agence France Presse, I returned to the Hotel Park, packed my papers and my sack, and bedded down for my last legal night in Iran.

At 9:15 in the morning, I swung my rucksack to my back, picked up my portable typewriter and small case for papers, "cheerio'd" Mr. Mack, who was standing at the front desk at elegant attention, and moved out, looking for all the world like a combination postman-general-journalist on a secret mission to the "interior".

It was a grimy day, overcast and a little chilly. I walked around the block to the Egyptian Embassy, "casing" the front entrance. There were three bored-looking policemen in front of the gate and one little fellow in a tiny guardhouse directly inside. I walked purposefully through the ornate grillework gates of the Embassy without a look at the policemen or the guard. Since the Embassy grounds were theoretically Egyptian territory, according to over two hundred years of international precedent, I had "left" Iran.

Walking quietly through the small park, I approached the consulate building, a sombre, square, tomb-like edifice. I entered the outer hallway. It was dark and cold. Except for two wooden chairs on either side of the small stove, it was barren of furniture. Ugly ceiling frescoes alone broke the monotony. The Iranian oil stove was valiantly trying to heat the empty hall, but no amount of heat could take off the chill. I shivered involuntarily.

Putting down my sack and typewriter, I handed my card to an attendant and went to the stove to warm my hands. The Second Secretary, to whom I had talked about my Egyptian visa two days before, came from his office. He asked me to come in. I sat down in the chair indicated. He was drinking some Turkish coffee in a tiny cup but did not offer any to me.

"What may I do for you, Mr Davis?" he asked.

"I would like to see the Chargé d'Affaires," I replied.

"I see," he ruminated, eying me narrowly. "He will not be in till ten o'clock."

"In that case," I said, "I will see the First Secretary."

His eyes glinted. "He will not be in till ten o'clock either."

I smiled. "I'll just wait outside," I told him. "You must be very busy." His desk top was empty.

I went into the cold hall, took out my portable and began typing the above details. At ten o'clock I was admitted to the office of the Chargé d'Affaires, the senior officer in the consulate. Motioning me toward a chair in front of his desk, he said, "Please sit down, Mr. Davis." A smile played around his eyes. "Will you have coffee or tea?"

"Coffee, thank you." I paused, wondering how to begin. Then, screwing up my courage: "I have come to your embassy because of a rather unique situation in which I find myself involved."

"I see," he said, his eyes unwaveringly fixed on mine.

"I was given a fifteen-day transit visa by the Iranian Government in Kabul. My intention was to leave Iran within the prescribed period, but I have been unable to do so. The visa expired last night at midnight." He leaned back in his chair and put his finger tips together. "As you know," I continued, "if I were not to leave Iran at the expiration of my visa, I would be faced with either jail or deportation."

"But, Mr. Davis," he said, "I don't understand what all this has to do with us."

"I have been obliged to seek refuge here until my visa from Egypt comes through."

He came forward with a bound. "Refuge! Here! Quite impossible! Out of the question! Why, why, we have no facilities for such things." His tone changed abruptly. "You seemed like such a reasonable man . . . at first. Frankly I had expected something quite different."

"What did you expect?" I asked curiously.

"Oh, I don't know, some sort of California mystic."

I laughed. "I'm from Maine and more of a hard-boiled Yankee," I told him.

The tension broke. He became confidential. "But tell me, Mr. Davis, between you and me, how did you manage to get those visas on your world passport?"

"Well, it's quite interesting," I said, "but first may I show you the statement I released last night?"

"Statement?" he asked in surprise, taking the sheet. He read and started laughing. "You were rather sure of being here, I see."

"Yes, of course. Why shouldn't I be here?" I replied. "Where else can I be?"

"*Hmmm.* Yes," he murmured reading on. "What's this! A press conference in the Embassy!" He stared at the sheet, his fingers almost ripping it.

"I don't understand, sir," I said. "What's wrong?"

"Wrong!" he exclaimed. "WRONG! But you have no authority to call a press conference in my Embassy."

"Egypt's Embassy," I corrected.

"Egypt's Embassy!" he roared.

"But I don't understand what authority is needed," I said, "other than Egypt's traditional hospitality to the persecuted and President Nasser's endorsement of international law."

"President Nasser's endorse——" He stared at me, his mouth open and moving, but nothing was coming out.

"Please understand my extremely precarious position in this matter, sir," I went on. "I have no army to back me up. I have no police force to guarantee that my rights are going to be recognized. I am one single, lone man, a stateless person. I must speak for myself. I must claim my rights as a human being . . ."

"Yes, yes, I know all about that," he said impatiently.

"I'm glad you do because then you can understand why I

asked the press to come around to the Embassy at eleven. The public are my only fellow citizens; the press is my only ambassador. I simply want to report to my fellow citizens through my ambassador that I have been granted refuge by Egypt in accordance with its sacred international—"

"Out of the question, out of the question," he said, looking at me accusingly, "and I want to add, Mr. Davis, that I was favourably impressed at first, but now I must think, well, your methods are . . . well, I'd rather not say."

He eyed me darkly. I returned his stare. Finally he said, "Now, Mr. Davis, really . . . put yourself in my place. I am in charge of this embassy. You come in"—he rolled his eyes—"you ask asylum. You say you are a World Citizen. You have called a press conference. You have no papers, that is, proper papers. What am I to do with you?"

"But is it my fault I am forced into this absurd position?" I asked. "If you consider yourself a victim of circumstances, how much more so am I? And since you ask me what you should do, you give me the right to advise you to ask your own government for advice."

"And in the meantime?"

"In the meantime, wait."

"But what about you?"

"I'll wait too."

"Where?"

"Here. Where else?"

He popped up to his full five-foot-four height. I stood, too. "Now see here, Mr. Davis, this comedy has gone far enough. I have a lot of important work to do, and if you will excuse me . . ." A frozen diplomatic smile stiffened his features.

I didn't move.

"You cannot stay here."

"Legally I can't move."

"That is not our concern."

"I'm afraid it is, according to Article 24, Section 1 of the *Universal Declaration of Human Rights* to which Egypt is a signatory nation. I have asked for the right of asylum according to international law. Does Egypt refuse this to me?"

"But you present a passport you have made yourself," he said in exasperation. "Why, I could make such a passport tomorrow. It has the backing of no government."

"It has the backing of World Government," I said.

"And World Government has the backing of no government."

"On the contrary, it has the official recognition of five governments," I returned. "You have seen the visas on my passport."

"Perhaps," he said testily, "but we have our own rules and regulations and we must abide by them. Personally, Mr. Davis, I have great sympathy for this . . . this dream of yours, but your document is simply not valid."

"Are you now refusing me entry before receiving instructions from your government?" I asked.

"No, no, I didn't say that."

"Then do I understand that you refuse me asylum?"

"That is correct."

"Why?"

"Mr. Davis . . ." He was near the breaking point. "I have said all I am going to say on the subject. We have no facilities for you here. We leave the rest up to your good judgment." He sat down and started scribbling furiously.

"In that case, I will remain," I said, sitting down.

"Now really, Mr. Davis." He looked up menacingly, his hand reaching for the pushbutton on his desk. "I have lost what little respect I had for you . . ."

"No need to get personal, sir," I said. "I assure you I am your personal good friend in spite of your un-cooperative official attitude."

"And I yours," he returned through clenched teeth. "But now, you oblige me to ask the guards to expel you if you do not leave immediately."

I eyed his finger poised above the button. I got up.

"What are your intentions?" he asked nervously.

"I will wait outside."

"You will have to wait outside the building."

"Does that mean that you give me asylum on the grounds?"

"Certainly not." He paused. "Come, sit down. We might as well finish this. Tell me, under what conditions would you, uh, re-enter Iran?"

"That's an interesting question," I said thinking rapidly. "Let's see, I could only re-enter if the Iranian Government legally recognized my rights as a World Citizen, which of course include the right to be represented by World Government."

I am administered the Oath of Allegiance to World Government at the Birla Mandir temple in New Delhi by a disciple of Nataraja Guru on October 5th, 1956, the day after my Indian visa expired.

January 9th, 1957. The K.L.M. ticket from Amsterdam to New York is torn up at Amsterdam's Skipholt Airport.

"But that is ridiculous!" he exclaimed. "How could they do such a thing?" I shrugged. We stared at each other. The telephone rang. I glanced at my watch. It was just eleven. He picked up the phone, barked into it, listened; his eyes grew wide, he looked at me, barked some more, and hung up.

Then he turned to me slowly and grimly. "So you are obliging me to use force with you, is that it?"

"I am obliging you to do nothing, sir. I think it would be a very unwise move on your part to use force."

"Yes, well, Mr. Davis, please wait out in the hall."

I got up, smiled at him and left his office.

Once out in the hall, I took out pen and paper and began jotting down the above conversation. After half an hour, the Chargé d'Affaires came bustling out of his office and said, "Mr. Davis, will you come out please? I myself will be happy to escort you personally." He went to the front door through the short vestibule. The three attendants as well as the First and Second Secretaries were in the hallway watching.

I got up, took my coat from the hook, put on my scarf, put on my coat, and then promptly sat down again near the warm stove. He came charging back into the hallway.

"Now, you get out of here!" he bellowed at me. "I am tired of this nonsense!"

"No need to get angry, sir," I said, regarding him calmly. "As a matter of fact, I don't like people raising their voices to me."

"You don't like! You don't like . . ." His voice trailed off in popping noises. Then he turned to the porter and gave an order in Arabic. The porter saluted and went dashing out the door. There was an ominous silence in the hall as we waited for "La Force" to arrive. It arrived in the form of the Iranian gate guard, his sad face and unpressed uniform pathetically belying his authority. He entered the hall timidly and stopped short as he took in the tableau. The Chargé d'Affaires drew himself up and pointed to me. The guard moved forward, eyeing my uniform apprehensively.

I held up my left hand before him like a traffic cop while I reached into my pocket with my right hand. He stopped, bewildered. Out came my World Guard badge, newly gold-plated and flashing like a thousand Mogul swords. I shoved it before him. He shrank back. The Chargé d'Affaires was looking at my badge with a mixture of consternation and awe. Recovering, he barked an order at the retreating guard, his finger remaining pointed at me accusingly. My gaze was on the guard, straight in his eye, while I held the gleaming badge before him. Slowly I smiled. Caught in this crossfire, the guard withered, all pretence of authority oozing from him like water on sand. He turned and fled rapidly out the front door, leaving the Chargé d'Affaires surrounded by a giggling staff. He turned and stamped back to his office, while the others quickly returned to theirs.

I remained in the hall writing for about an hour when the First Secretary called me into his office. An Iranian police officer with one star on each shoulder was standing near his desk. The Secretary informed me with relish that the officer had come to "escort" me away.

"I want you to understand before you take any overt action that my Iranian visa expired last night," I said to the Iranian officer.

He looked at me, smiling.

"Maybe you'd better show him your passport," suggested the Secretary helpfully.

"Good idea," I said and pulled it from my coat pocket, opening it to the page where the Iranian visa was stamped. The policeman looked at it, still smiling vapidly.

"You see," I said, pointing, "Iranian visa finish yesterday. Here . . . Egypt"—I pointed to the floor—"there . . . Iran." I pointed out the window to the street. He just gaped happily. I turned to another Secretary sitting near by who had been rattling in French to the First Secretary.

"Please tell him that if he removes me by force, he will be breaking an Iranian law." This was gleefully translated for me. The officer nodded happily. He was the happiest officer I ever saw. I turned to the Secretary deperately.

"If you have called the Iranian police, what is the charge against me?"

"But there is no charge," he replied. "We simply cannot have you here."

"But this is not a police matter," I said. "This is a diplomatic matter. I have asked asylum. Now you call in the very police from whom I have fled."

"Monsieur Davis, you are very amiable and we have all

enjoyed your company, but we have asked you very cordially to leave and you have refused. There is nothing more to do. It is now 1:45 and you have wasted our time all morning."

"I have wasted *your* time!" I exclaimed. "This is the first time I have spoken to you this morning. If anything, it is my time that has been wasted."

He nodded to the policeman, who went to the phone and rasped some orders, and then came back and sat down, smiling vacuously.

There was a general silence while we waited. I felt hungry and apprehensive, in that order. To break the silence, I told the three Egyptians that they were making a mistake by expelling me, that it might appear as a rejection of world citizenship and the principle of world government. They smiled patronizingly.

"Then there's the question of Egypt's delicate geopolitical position," I said.

The Secretary leaned forward. "Just what do you mean?" he asked, his eyes narrowing.

"The removal of British and French troops from Egypt, and Egypt's need of outside help to solve its economic problems, leave a power vacuum in the Near East," I replied. "You certainly aren't interested in becoming a Communist satellite, are you?"

"No," he replied hesitantly.

"Well then, Egypt must turn in the other direction, that is, toward the United States, right?"

"That is possible," he admitted.

"But in a way that's just as dangerous, since it will appear to the Soviet bloc that Egypt is on the Western side," I continued.

He said nothing. The room was quiet. I could hear the ticking of the mantelpiece clock and the faint sound of street traffic outside . . . in Iran.

I persevered: "Egypt therefore is in an extremely advantageous position, but only if it accepts an ideology that considers Egypt part of a total world community where it relates itself to the rest of the world community just as one section of an orange is related to all other sections. That means Egypt will be better off adopting in down-to-earth, realistic terms the global principles of world citizenship and world government."

The First Secretary smiled ingratiatingly. "Personally, Mr. Davis, we all agree with you. But we are not the Government."

"That's the excuse everybody makes," I shot back. "But just who is the Government? We boast that the people are sovereign. We talk grandly about democracy and freedom, saying it is our way of life. Then when it comes to independent thinking and action, we lie down like beaten dogs and whine that we aren't the Government and therefore it isn't our fault that the bombs fall. What colossal nonsense! We *are* the Government, each one of us. And now we've had two world wars to prove our lack of moral guts to claim it. Do we have to have World War III before we wake up to the realization that, after all, *we* had the power and intelligence to prevent it if we had acted in time? What a mockery our understanding would be then!"

I was steamed up and found myself on my feet. All three were staring at me wide-eyed. But just then the door burst open and four burly Iranian policemen entered. The officer jumped to life, pointed his finger at me, and the men moved in. I didn't budge. They stopped short. I raised my hand dramatically. "I protest in the name of human rights, international sanctions, Iranian and Egyptian law... and, oh, what the hell!" I sat down.

They grabbed me where I sat and jerked me to my feet. I shook them off and walked disdainfully to the hall for my coat. Taking my time putting on my scarf, coat and gloves as if going for a stroll, I took a look at the rucksack leaning against the wall, decided to let one of them carry it, and then walked nonchalantly out of the door.

Two photographers tried to take our pictures on the way out but only got their equipment smashed for their trouble by the irate policemen.

I was "imported" into Iran at precisely 2:17 p.m. under the escort of four Iranian policemen.

The date, December 10th, was the eighth anniversary of the proclamation of the *Universal Declaration of Human Rights* by the United Nations: "Everyone has the right to seek and to enjoy in other countries asylum from persecution" (Article 14).

12

"Good afternoon, Mr. Davis. Will you have coffee or tea?"

"Coffee, thank you."

My host this time was a hulking, black-uniformed and medal-bedecked General of Iranian police who received me in his posh office in the main police station to which I had been taken by the four policemen.

"Now, Mr. Davis," he began, arching his back and pressing the palms of his hands against the top of his desk, "you really must leave Iran, you know." He smiled as if his words had summed up the situation more quickly than he had believed possible.

"But I left Iran this morning," I said. "I was on Egyptian territory when you imported me into Iran quite against my wishes."

"Yes, yes, I know all about that," he said, "but let us be serious."

"Oh, I am quite serious," I said. "I have complied fully with your laws, but now I find that you yourself have abrogated them by bringing me back into Iran after I had legitimately left."

"We have abrogated our own laws!" he exploded. "Now see here, I don't think you realize to whom you are talking."

"Well, that's possibly correct since no one yet has had the kindness to answer any of my questions since I have been in the hands of the police."

"Well," he said, "you will then be pleased to know that you are talking to General Darakhshan, Chief of the Iranian police."

"In that case, it is my duty to ask you what I am doing here."

"It is because you are illegally in Iran," he said, somewhat taken aback.

"One moment!" I exclaimed. "You who forced me into Iran from the Egyptian Embassy are charging me with being here illegally?" I stood up. "I demand to be taken back to the sovereign territory from which you brought me."

He blinked. "Sovereign territory?"

"Egypt!" I said triumphantly.

"Now Mr. Davis, please be reasonable," he said. "They don't want you in Egypt . . . I mean, in the Egyptian Embassy. . . ."

"Oh, then you *do* want me in Iran?"

"No, no, that's not what I meant."

"Then why did you bring me here?" I asked.

"This is getting us nowhere," he said impatiently. "You simply must leave Iran. Aren't you an American citizen?"

"No."

"Well, then, where would you like to go?"

"Egypt."

"Impossible. What about Syria? Would you settle for Syria?"

I thought for a moment. "Yes of course," I said, "but I have already been to the Syrian Embassy and they have refused my request for a visa. I would take a visa from Turkey, Iraq, Lebanon or any country west of Iran through to Europe."

He leaned back and said, "Well, we will see what we can do."

"But where am I to stay in the meantime?" I asked him.

"Stay? You may stay wherever you like."

"Oh, fine, and to whom shall I send the bill?"

"What bill?"

"Why the hotel and food bill."

He looked blank.

"I have no money," I told him, "and since the Iranian Government is now responsible for me, naturally it will take care of my living needs."

He looked as if he had been shot. "But, Mr. Davis, surely you can't expect us to . . . to keep you?"

"What else can I expect after your concern so far?"

"But . . . but we have no funds for this sort of thing."

"Then I will go back to the Egyptian Embassy," I replied.

"Oh, no!" he shouted, almost jumping to his feet. "We will arrange something." He pressed a button on his desk. An attendant came in and I was escorted to a second-class hotel on a main street where the police arranged accommodation.

I wrote out a statement the next day describing the recent events and took it down to the editor of *Eetalat*. He was delighted with the story and assured me of front-page coverage. During the next three days, I was visited by many local citizens interested in world affairs, including a delegation of four bearded men from the ancient religious Dervish cult. There were visits also from reporters for Iran's national weeklies.

On December 21st, I was asked to present myself at police headquarters with the World Passport. The Chief of the Foreigners' Office asked to see the document.

"Why?" I asked suspiciously.

"We want to examine it to see if something cannot be done for you," he replied.

"All right, but with the understanding that nothing is stamped inside without my express agreement." I did not want to receive a visa from Lower Transylvania, for example, and then be dumped on a freighter for Rangoon. Three days later I obtained an appointment with Prime Minister Ali's private secretary and learned through him that General Alavie, General Darakhshan's chief, together with the Prime Minister, had decided that I was to be shipped to New York by air.

"Your home address is clearly marked on your passport," the secretary said. "It is New York City, I believe."

"Yes, it is," I answered, "but what about a re-entry permit? I am not a U.S. citizen, you know."

"For us, Mr. Davis, you are an American," he replied. "One cannot give up one's birthright."

The day after Christmas, I was told by a police officer to prepare myself for immediate departure. We were going to the train station within the hour!

"The train station!" I exclaimed. "What for?"

"Why, to take you to Abadan, of course," he replied. "From there you will fly to New York."

I was powerless to do anything but register a futile protest. Within the hour I was taken to the station and forcibly transported to Abadan, the oil metropolis situated at the head of the Persian Gulf. There I was billeted in a hotel to await my flight. One morning when I attempted to leave the hotel, I was suddenly accosted by two husky policemen. A scuffle ensued. Then, as the police pounded me with their billies, a passer-by with a small child stepped up to the scene and barked at the policemen. They stopped, looked at him and stepped back, bringing their hands up in a salute. The stranger approached me.

"Please, I am Karkhairan," he said. "Can I be of any assistance?" His English was faultless. The little girl in his arms was regarding me wide-eyed, one small finger in her mouth.

"This is very kind of you, Mr. Karkhairan, to offer your assistance," I replied, getting up off the ground. "These gentlemen here apparently have orders to keep me in this hotel. I have no way to protest the injustice of those orders other than by disobeying them."

He turned to the police and asked several questions.

"I think I understand the situation," he said finally. "If you will permit me, I would be happy to receive you in my home while you are here in Abadan. I will speak for you. It so happens that I am a personal friend of the Chief of Police and there will be no difficulty. Will you agree to be my guest?"

"Gladly," I said. "I am honoured."

"Fine, I will make all arrangements." He turned to the policemen and spoke to them again. They nodded and with salutes to him and me got into their car and drove off.

"Now if you will gather your things, we will be off," he told me, smiling.

We drove off in his chauffeured car to Mr. Karkhairan's beautiful home. On the way he told me the police did not want me wandering around the street, because there was the danger of theft.

"Do you believe that?" I asked him.

"No, of course not," he replied without hesitation. "We can be frank. They are annoyed at their orders from Teheran concerning you. And like everyone who has authority but no responsibility, they abuse common sense and knock others about."

"Why did they salute you, may I ask?"

"I am chief security officer for your American oil company here," he replied.

For the next three days I slept on Mr. Karkhairan's living room sofa and ate at his table. His large family, including his wife, three sons and several daughters, treated me as one of the family.

On December 30th, I was driven to the airport by the police captain. In the little K.L.M. office, I asked the agent whether he knew he was transporting an unwilling passenger.

"But I have your ticket right here, Mr. Davis," he protested.

"Please let me see," I said. The police captain tried to intervene but it was too late. The ticket was made out in my name. Its destination was Dhahran, Saudi Arabia! I took a deep breath.

"To begin with you have not my consent to use my name on a commercial ticket," I told him. "Secondly, as a private carrier bound by the rules and regulations of the International Air Transport Association, you cannot transport anyone without his consent, especially across national frontiers. Thirdly, should you do so, you become an aid and accomplice in an act of flagrant violation of my rights as a human being, and subject yourself to a lawsuit."

"But I do not understand," he demurred. "Don't you want to leave Iran, Mr. Davis?"

"All this is unnecessary," the captain interrupted. "This man will be put aboard the 10:30 plane for Dhahran. Those are my orders and they will be carried out."

"May I use your typewriter?" I asked the agent.

"Of course," he replied.

I typed out a formal protest, giving one copy to the agent, one to the captain, and keeping a copy for myself.

The agent read it, and turned to me. "Mr. Davis, please, I am in a crossfire here. Put yourself in my place. What would you do? If we do not take you aboard Flight 602, K.L.M. will lose its franchise in Iran!"

"If Iran has given you a franchise to commit crime," I replied tautly, "then you will be better off without the franchise."

To be sure, I got in the last word, but the police captain won the day. I was led aboard the big airliner, buckled into my seat and given what I suppose one might call a "flying start" on my way out of Iran.

"This is Dhahran, Mr. Davis," said the hostess after the plane had landed in Saudi Arabia.

"Yes, I know," I replied not moving.

"But . . . isn't this your stop?"

"No, ma'am."

"But I believe your ticket . . ."

"My ticket? I have no ticket. There must be some mistake."

"Everyone has a ticket, Mr. Davis. I have yours right here. It is marked for Dhahran."

"Did I give it you?"

"Well, no."

"Then what makes you think it is my ticket?"

"It has your name on it."

"I can't help that."

"Aren't you getting off here, Mr. Davis?"

"I'm sorry, miss, but I really have absolutely nothing to do in Dhahran."

She went back up the aisle and spoke to a K.L.M. official at the open door. He came to my seat.

"Mr. Davis, we are obliged to ask you to leave the ship," he said.

"I have no doubt you are," I replied, returning my gaze to the busy airport where rows of U.S. Air Force DC-7's were lined up along one side.

"Are you going to leave this ship or not?" he asked sharply.

I turned to him slowly. "Only a half hour ago," I said smiling, "one of your fellow employees at Abadan was equally concerned with my boarding her."

"Mr. Davis, I know nothing of what happened a half hour ago. I only know that your ticket reads Dhahran and you must get off here."

"Are you prepared to put me off?" I asked quietly.

"We can arrange that," he warned.

"If a K.L.M. employee touches me . . ."

He looked shocked. "No, no, we have no intention of touching you, Mr. Davis. But the Saudi Arabian police . . ."

"Oh? I didn't know they were so anxious to have me here as all that," I said. He hastened up the aisle and out the door.

Ten minutes later, a few passengers for the plane's next hop came aboard with the official behind them. He spoke in low tones to the hostess, then came forward to my seat.

"Well, it seems, Mr. Davis, that Saudi Arabia doesn't want you either," he said, smiling and winking.

Five minutes later, we were in the air winging east to Pakistan, which I had left a month and a half ago.

We arrived at the Karachi airport at ten o'clock in the evening. The date was December 30th. There, once again, all the passengers debarked with the exception of myself. A K.L.M. official explained to me that the plane could not be moved while I remained in it, that it remained at Karachi overnight for servicing and that I was expected to step into the airport for a chat with Pakistan Immigration.

"What on earth do I want to talk with Pakistan Immigration for?" I asked. "I just came from there. My destination is Berlin, not Karachi."

154

"Yes, we know, Mr. Davis, but . . . well, we have no authority to carry you any further."

"No authority!" I said laughing. "And what was your authority to carry me this far? No, I'm not leaving this plane."

"But you must! You simply must!" he pleaded. "Our schedule. . . . We have crews standing by. We need the parking space for incoming planes. Don't you see?"

I could visualize more and more planes circling over Karachi, waiting to land with other planes getting shunted off to alternate airports and so on, so at length I went along to the deserted transit lounge. After some minutes, another K.L.M. man asked whether I wouldn't "just step into the next section" where the Pakistan police had a few questions.

"No thanks," I told him. "I'm quite comfortable here."

He left and returned moments later. "You cannot remain in Pakistan, Mr. Davis," he informed me stiffly. "A first-class Flying Dutchman will be along in an hour, westbound, and a ticket will be blocked through to Frankfurt for you." I asked him what the Bonn Government had to say

"There is no Bonn Government here," he replied. "Besides, for Americans, no visa is required for Germany."

Sure enough, after an hour's wait I was escorted aboard a huge Flying Dutchman and lifted gently on my way. With stops at Cairo, Athens and Rome, it was difficult during the next thirteen hours to get much sleep. Austria was blanketed with snow, and Germany looked much as I had seen it years ago from the cockpit of Calamity Jane. My mind's eye saw alongside us the ghosts of ships in tight formation, their bomb-bay doors opening slowly . . .

"Fasten your seat belts, please."

It was five o'clock as we glided in on the long runway of the Frankfurt-am-Main Airport where the United States Air Force has its largest base in Europe.

The Passkontrolle police at the airport pored over my passport like ants at a picnic.

"See, here is another visa!" one exclaimed as the chief turned the pages.

"*Ach, und* another yet! *Wunderbar!*"

When the fun was over, the chief handed it back. "I am sorry, Herr Davis, but ve do not recognize this as a valid travel document. We cannot allow you to enter Germany."

"About three hundred refugees come stumbling into West Germany every week," I said. "Do they all have 'valid' travel documents?"

"Ah, but that is different. They are refugees. You are not. And you have not exactly stumbled in."

"Before you make a final decision, will you at least ask higher authority in Bonn?" I asked.

He shrugged. "As you wish."

While he was telephoning to Bonn, I wandered around the great airport building unmolested. Exchanging some leftover rials for Pfennigs, I called both Associated Press and United Press, telling them I would probably be sent on to Amsterdam but had requested permission to remain in Germany. Both said they would try to have men on hand at Skipholt Airport in Amsterdam.

The chief returned with the news that he could not reach anyone of authority in Bonn as it was past five o'clock; besides, that day marked the transfer of the Saar region to German sovereignty, an event with which all officialdom was engaged.

He then asked for my "invalid" passport, opened it to an empty visa page, and stamped it *Zurückgewiesen* (sent back). When I pointed out that he had just recognized it, he replied, "*Ja*, but only as a document of identity; not for travel!"

It was snowing when we landed at the Skipholt Airport outside of Amsterdam. Being at their home base, K.L.M. officials perfunctorily turned me over to the Dutch police. I was taken into a small guardroom by four border guards in military uniform. There, behind the desk, sat a red-faced sergeant.

"Your passport, please," he asked brusquely.

"I have a passport," I said wearily, "but you will not consider it valid."

"We will be the judge of that," he said. "May I see it please?" I turned it over to him. He glanced through it as if he had seen it many times before.

"This is not a valid passport," he said, handing it back. "You cannot stay in Holland."

"But it is you who brought me to Holland. Do you think I want to be here? Did I *ask* to come here?"

He was smiling as if humouring a child. "That is of no consequence, Mr. Davis. The fact is that you have entered Holland illegally and will either have to leave immediately or be taken into custody."

The drama of the state versus the individual without "valid papers" was again about to be enacted, I thought dully. Did I have any legal rights? I should have to find out.

"I would like to make a telephone call," I told the sergeant.

"I'm sorry. That is forbidden. Besides, who do you know in Amsterdam to call?"

"Are you refusing me permission to telephone?" I asked tightly.

He looked at me warily. "Who do you wish to call?"

"My counsel."

"Your counsel! That is good. More probably the newspapers. Mr. Davis, why do you trouble us in Holland?"

I felt my patience leave me. It had been two days since I had had any real sleep. And I had been flown a quarter of the way around the world against my will like an empty bottle no one cared to claim. Now, I was about to be sucked under by a Dutch whirlpool only to find myself resting on the "bottom" surrounded by four bare walls.

"Are you holding me incommunicado?" I asked.

"That is right," he replied with a crooked smile.

"I will give you five minutes to change your mind," I said. "If you refuse, I will not be held responsible for the consequences." His eyes tightened imperceptibly. He shrugged. I set the stop watch on my chronometer moving.

As the hand circled once, I called out "One minute." He remained silent reading a Dutch newspaper. The other guards had gone out and were standing around the door. The hum of airport noises filtered into the cubicle of the room. I looked at my watch.

"Two minutes."

He looked up slowly to the door, motioning to his fellow guards to come in. They did so and ranged themselves around the small room. He turned the pages of his newspaper with exaggerated nonchalance.

"Three minutes."

He laughed uneasily. "What can you do? There is nothing you can do." The other police glanced from one to another and shifted their weight aimlessly from foot to foot. Indeed, what *could* I do? I wasn't a judo expert ... or a hypnotist ... or a millionaire. I got up and started pacing the floor. I had noticed the small room was lined with light curtains hung on rods. It would undoubtedly prove a useless gesture but my anger plus fatigue blinded me to reason.

"Four minutes."

If I had nothing else left, I at least had my sense of drama. The sergeant said something in a low voice to the guards. They tensed. Four pairs of eyes followed me.

Finally, the five clicked over as the sweep second hand crossed "12". I stopped by the window.

"May I make a telephone call?" I asked quietly.

"No, you may not," the sergeant barked.

My hand reached up and, before they knew what was happening, half the curtain was ripped down. For a second they hesitated, then the three came for me. I remained absolutely still.

Addressing myself to the sergeant, who had risen to his feet, face blustering and more red than ever, I said, "You have forced me, Sergeant, to make this protest in view of your refusal to allow me communication to the outside." The guards, confused, did not touch me. "Now may I make a telephone call to my counsel?"

"No, by God, you cannot! No, you cannot!" he bellowed, his fist coming down on the desk.

I reached up quickly and ripped down the other half of the curtains. A crowd had gathered outside to watch. There was some laughter as the curtains came down completely. The three guards then grabbed me, their faces grim, and forced me down into a chair. Two of them bent my arms over the back of the chair while the third stood directly over me, his hands on my shoulders. One guard had gotten hold of the middle finger of my left hand and bent it back until I could hear it crack. The sergeant was dialling. I tried to shake loose but the guards were now determined.

"For God's sake, let go of my finger!" I said between clenched teeth. The sergeant looked up quickly from the phone and commanded the guard to ease his grip. Thus we waited in silence for about ten minutes. I relaxed completely although the guards never moved. Finally, four more guards burst into the room. I was hustled out and into a waiting police van, my gear thrown aboard with me. Fifteen minutes later I found myself in the Amsterdam city prison, emptying my pockets and being frisked for hidden weapons. I was only half aware of what went on, despite the pain in my finger, and I found it difficult to keep my eyes open.

"What's the charge, Captain?" I asked sleepily.

"We make no charge for the moment," he said. "You are just in our custody... a guest of the Queen, so to speak." The others laughed.

"Okay, Davis, step through that door," said the desk sergeant, indicating a door of steel bars which had just clicked open.

When I didn't move, my guards gave me a slight push toward the door. I went through. It closed with a metallic snap behind me as another door ahead clicked open.

"Just turn left and go up the stairs," called the man at the desk. "The guard will take care of you there."

On the floor above, an elderly guard in a grey smock, smoking a cigar, waited at the great barred door behind which were rows of cells. After carefully locking his door behind us with a large screw key, he led me to a cell at the end of the corridor in which were stacked bedding and miscellaneous equipment. I took two blankets, two cotton sheets, a pillow, and a straw-stuffed mattress to the cell he indicated.

In the four-by-eight cell was an iron bed fixed to the wall, a wooden table with a round stool behind it, and an open bowl with a spigot directly above. I made the bed, undressed to my undershirt and shorts, and crawled in gratefully.

The guard came shuffling along, saw I was in bed, and clicked off the light from the switch outside.

"Good night, Mr. Davis... and Happy New Year," he said as the door clanged shut.

It was December 31st, New Year's Eve.

13

I awoke with a start, my eyes trying to shut out the light which had just flashed on. A key sounded in the door somewhere. Foggily I tried to recall where I was, but to no avail. Turning away from the light toward the wall, I was dozing off again when someone spoke.

"Mr. Davis, here is the American Consul. He is here to help you."

I rolled over to see, standing in the middle of the cell, a well-dressed, middle-aged man in a black top coat and Homburg. He introduced himself and asked whether he could be of any assistance. Shaking myself awake, I asked him if he knew that I was not a U.S. citizen. He said he was aware of that, but he thought he might be able to help me anyway. The first way he might help me, I told him, would be to help me out of jail. That he could not do, he said emphatically. What did he mean by "help"? I asked. He said he thought I might have some suggestions. I thought a moment, then said that he might send me some magazines and perhaps a bar of chocolate.

"Well, if you do not wish to co-operate," he replied.

"I am in jail, sir," I told him, "only because I have no piece of paper which the Dutch Government calls 'proper.' Furthermore, it was a Dutch carrier that brought me here. My own wishes have been utterly disregarded and now I am here. If you cannot see the injustice in all this, obviously you cannot help me. Good night." I turned around and was asleep in minutes.

When friends in Holland found out the next day from the newspapers that I was in prison, various attempts were made to see me, all unsuccessful. The world federalist organizations in Rotterdam and Amsterdam then took advertising space in the local papers, protesting my imprisonment. They based their protest on the *Universal Declaration of Human Rights*, Article 9, which said: "No one shall be subjected to arbitrary arrest, detention or exile"; various provisions of the Dutch Constitution; and excerpts from statements of leaders on human rights.

On January 3rd, I was allowed to see Peter Troost and Hans Holzhaus, two longtime one-world advocates.

"What do you want us to do, Garry?" asked Peter. "Shall we picket the prison? Shall we have a meeting? What?"

"I really don't think there's much to do," I told him.

"That's what I thought," he said cryptically and fell silent. Hans then told me two lawyers had volunteered to do whatever legal work I required.

On January 4th I met my volunteer legal staff—Mr. Veth, young, with full red cheeks and bright eyes, and Mr. Conneger, small eyes, heavy eyebrows, a sallow complexion and greyish teeth. The lawyers had spoken to Mr. Temkink, Deputy Minister of the Department of Legal Affairs. He told them that there was no possibility of my remaining in Holland.

"Did he give you a reason?" I asked.

Veth hesitated. "Not exactly, but he did say there couldn't be a precedent..."

"He mentioned national security," Conneger said.

"He explained that if you were allowed to remain in Holland everyone could do the same," continued Veth.

"But did you point out that I was brought into Holland against my will?" I asked.

"Yes," answered Conneger, "but he insisted you're here without papers. That is true, is it not?"

I looked at him squarely. "First, I *have* papers, but the Dutch Government doesn't choose to recognize them. Second, *I* am the injured party, not the Government. If I put a gun to your head, order you across the border of another state, and then, still pointing the gun at you, I call the authorities of that state and they accuse you of not having proper entry papers, who is the real culprit?"

They both considered the point. "Incidentally, what is the real reason the Government doesn't want me here?" I asked. "Certainly there are thousands and even hundreds of thousands of precedents for people being admitted to countries without papers. How about the Hungarian refugees and the almost ten million refugees in Germany?"

"Yes," admitted Veth, "but you are not a refugee."

"That may be true, but is the Government then afraid of my world citizenship claim?"

"Afraid? I don't think so," Connegar said. "It just doesn't

want demonstrations and people travelling around on world passports."

"Yes, that would be a shame if freedom of travel were a reality," I said. "I think you've put your finger on it. Let's be frank. The Dutch Government doesn't want a world citizen running around loose. Isn't that true?"

Veth shrugged. "Perhaps. Though I don't see——"

"This is an old story with me," I broke in. "A man who claims to be a citizen of the entire world denies the exclusive sovereignty of the state."

"I see what you mean," Veth said. "But rules...."

"Yes, there are rules and regulations and resolutions and reports and dogmas and dictums," I shot back, "but where is justice and humanity? This is the hypocrisy that will lead to World War III: palm leaf in one hand, H-bomb in the other; subscribing to the U.N.'s Bill of Rights on the one hand, then denying it in practice on the other. And yet we condone it in the name of nationalism. Condone it? We worship it, bleed for it and even die for it."

Both lawyers were silent. Just then a guard poked his head in and spoke to Veth.

"The chief wants to speak with me," he said and left the room. A moment later he was back. "The American consul says you can have an immigration visa."

"I can't accept it," I told him.

He looked dismayed. "You won't take an immigration visa?"

"Of course not," I said. "How can I immigrate to my own home?"

I looked out of the window at the grey buildings opposite, the sun's lengthening shadows cutting diagonally across the walls. A canal barge was taking on large drums at a small dock fifty yards below. The streets were bustling with traffic—tiny buzzing cars, motor scooters whizzing along and vying with many bicycles for space.

"Well, we go down to see the chief now," Veth said, "and we will be back tomorrow."

At about 4 P.M. the next day, a constable told me that a Mr. Fonteyn, Chief of State Police, would "see vat you vill".

"Come," he said. I followed him down the long hall with the silent iron doors on each side. Standing nervously by the door to an inner office was a small man with extremely thick glasses perched on a round pink nose. He extended his hand.

"Mr. Davis, I'm Mr. Fonteyn. Won't you come into this office? First, I want to apologize for having to keep you here for the moment." He had a slight accent. "I can understand that this is a disagreeable situation for you," he continued hurriedly, "and we hope to be able to give you your freedom very shortly."

"I'm glad of that," I volunteered.

"Well, you did come to Holland without papers, and——"

"Forgive me, Mr. Fonteyn, but I was brought to Holland, and I had papers, though you didn't see fit to recognize them." I was beginning to sound like a broken record.

"Yes, yes, of course, your World Passport," he returned impatiently. "But the fact remains that you are here and the situation is very difficult for the Dutch Government. We could not very well recognize your World Passport."

"All right," I replied, "but is that any reason to jail me? I'm not a criminal because you won't recognize my World Passport."

"No, no, of course not," he said hastily, "and you mustn't consider that you are in jail . . . just in custody."

"Just custody? I will remember that tonight when the guard locks the cell."

"Well, Mr. Davis, you did catch us unawares, coming in on New Year's Eve like that with no papers . . . pardon, your own papers . . . and no money. When the call came in that Garry Davis was at the airport under those conditions, we did the best thing we could under the circumstances."

"But the next day, you had time to reconsider," I said quietly, "yet I remained in prison . . . and the next day, and the next."

"Yes, I know," he said and took out a handkerchief for a mop at his forehead. "But tell me, Mr. Davis, what would you have done in our case?"

"I would have found out who paid for Davis's ticket, since he had no money."

His eyes blinked at me through the thick glasses. "What good would that have done?"

"If a man is stone broke," I replied, "he usually is not flying here from Pakistan on a K.L.M. Flying Dutchman."

"But we knew K.L.M. brought you here," he said warily.

I smiled. "Then why isn't the K.L.M. pilot in jail instead of me?"

He pursed his lips disapprovingly. "Tell me, how did you get to Iran?"

I told him the story of my trip, starting from New York on April 2, 1956. After I had finished, he asked, "Mr. Davis, on what conditions will you return to the United States?"

I looked at him sharply. So that was it! I had been wondering what was behind the interview in the first place. "You imply of course that I have a choice in the matter," I said.

"But of course you do," he assured me.

"The choice of a prisoner is highly prejudiced," I reminded him.

"Please, Mr. Davis," he pleaded, "forget that you are a prisoner for a moment if only to help me out of my unfortunate task."

"Well, your question first assumes that I want to go to the United States."

"Yes, don't you?"

"That's not the issue for the moment, whether I do or not. Why do you assume I *do*?"

"Well, we assumed . . . we naturally thought. . . ."

"All without asking me personally. First you jail me with no charge. Then you ask me what I want. Then before I tell you what I want or that I want anything, you tell me what you want for me, then ask me a question which assumes I want it too!"

He looked at me and shrugged. "Well, if you won't co-operate, Mr. Davis . . ." He started to rise, then changed his mind and sank down. "I am not so sure who is in prison, you or me!"

I burst out laughing. "Well, let us assume for now that I desire to return to the United States," I said, feeling almost sorry for him. He leaned forward. "Just assuming, of course," I added.

"Of course."

"First, I should naturally have to have full protection of the law. To go from a Dutch prison to a U.S. prison would be absurd, would it not?"

"Naturally. But would you immigrate?"

"Immigrate! To my own home?"

"No, of course not," he said sadly. The light left his eyes.

"To ask me to immigrate to the United States is to deny my home, my family, my friends and all I stand for."

"Yes, yes, I quite understand," he clucked. "But would you return to the United States without papers of any kind, that is, without signing any statement?"

I thought for a moment. "Yes, I would," I told him, "providing I still would enjoy the full protection of U.S. laws." He scribbled furiously. "As a matter of fact," I went on, "I have already entered the United States since my renunciation of citizenship without signing any papers."

"You have!" he exclaimed. "When?"

I told him about my entry on July 27, 1953, from the *Queen Mary*, all the while wondering if I really did want to complete the trip by re-entering the United States armed with only my World Passport. But he seemed delighted.

"I think we have something now," he said, looking over his notes. "If they will only waive the re-entry permit...."

I took from my pocket my copy of the *Universal Declaration of Human Rights*, opening to Article 13, Section 2. "Here it says that everyone has the right to leave any country, including his own, and return to his country. Interesting statement, isn't it?" I passed it over. "Doesn't say anything about visas, passports, re-entry permits or even citizenship."

He made no comment.

I leaned over and pointed out Article 6: *Everyone has the right to recognition everywhere as a person before the law.*

"This might be relevant to our conversation, don't you think, Mr. Fonteyn?"

"Yes, of course, but this is only a declaration," he said impatiently. "It is not recognized."

"I recognize it," I told him flatly, "and, after all, I'm one of these human beings the declaration is talking about. Besides, Holland signed it back in December 1948." I glanced at the document again. "What about this: 'No one shall be subject to arbitrary arrest, detention, or exile'?"

"Do you consider your being here arbitrary?" he asked.

"Do you think this detention enjoys my approval?" I asked in return.

"Now listen here, Mr. Davis," he answered. "I was in a German prison camp for four years, and you have been here only seven days. I know what injustice is."

It was almost too easy to spring the trap he had set for himself.

"Are you comparing the Government of Germany at war with the Dutch Government at peace?"

He rose to his feet, laughing. "You're right. Good point. Very good." He seemed strangely pleased.

I rose also. "When are you going to release me?" I asked point-blank.

"We hope to release you tomorrow or the next day."

"Are you afraid to release me now?"

"No, of course not."

"Then release me."

"Well, there are the laws—"

"Laws? What laws? You yourself said there was no charge. Don't you realize the longer I am here, the more absurd your Government appears to the public?"

"That we know."

"Then what are you afraid of?" I insisted, hot on the trail of I knew not what. "You have been talking with me for forty-five minutes. Do I appear to you as a fanatic, or a wild-eyed propagandist?"

"No, most certainly not," he admitted calmly. "You seem to be a man of principle . . . and this can be a danger to organized society."

Ah, it was out! The naked truth.

I had never heard such honesty from a state official before. There was now no need for further talk between us. I could not help thinking of Thoreau's words: *I think that we should be men first, and subjects afterwards. It is not desirable to cultivate a respect for the law, so much as for the right.* . . .

The interview was over and Mr. Fonteyn accompanied me back to the reception room. "Thank you for answering my questions, Mr. Davis," he said, smiling tightly.

"And I appreciate your frankness, Mr. Fonteyn," I returned.

The iron door clicked open and I stepped through. He hesitated a moment, then said, "I'll see you to your cell." The men standing around stole glances at each other as we went slowly up the stairs.

"Be ready to leave in half an hour, Garry," sang out my friend with the keys and the long cigar as he hung up the wall phone in his small room. I had finished the nightly stew and was munching an apple while reading. It was January 9th, the tenth day of my imprisonment.

A half hour later, gear and "office" packed away and on my back, I was escorted downstairs to the sergeant's office where Mr. Fonteyn and two men in bulky black coats met me.

"So you are finally on your way, Mr. Davis," Mr. Fonteyn greeted me.

"Am I? And where am I going?"

"Why, to New York, as you wish," he replied.

"Wait a minute," I said. "What assurance have I that I will not be transferred to a U.S. prison once there?"

"Oh, I do not think they will put you in prison," he replied, "especially as you claim it is your home." Speaking in Dutch to his men, he turned and walked out the door. I was hustled into a waiting car and we wheeled out the prison gates. Several photographers tried to get pictures as we whizzed by.

Forty-five minutes later, we alighted from the car at the supermodern Skipholt Airport, as bright as Broadway in the night, with its red and yellow criss-crossing runway lights and glistening main buildings. Two policemen greeted us at the main gate, coming forward to take me by the arms. We moved through the door and down the long, glittering hallway at the end of which was a knot of photographers and newsmen. Seeing them, the guards released my arms. I turned immediately and started for the door. The police came pounding after me. Again we started down the long hallway, their grip firm on my arm. We came to within twenty feet of the newsmen when the photographers raised their cameras. The hands of the guards loosened from my arms once again. I spun around and galloped for the exit. Once more they came charging after me, catching me at the door. Mr. Fonteyn was grim as we came up for the third time, the guards' hold on me like iron.

"They didn't seem to know that I was your prisoner," I said to Mr. Fonteyn, "especially with the press around."

He said nothing and the police propelled me to the K.L.M. passenger desk where a vacantly smiling young man was waiting for me.

"Welcome to K.L.M., Mr. Davis!" he said brightly. I bit my tongue to keep from bursting into laughter. "Here is your ticket for New York." I looked at it in his hand. It was a first-class ticket made out in my name.

"What is the fare?" I asked mildly.

"Oh, the ticket is paid for," he said eagerly.

"That's not what I asked you," I told him.

"Oh, the fare. Yes, just a moment," he said, giving a quick glance at Mr. Fonteyn and the amused journalists. He consulted his book. "Four hundred and sixty dollars."

"Who paid for it?" I asked.

"Why . . . why, you are a guest of K.L.M.," he said, flustered.

"I see. Did I ask to be K.L.M.'s guest?"

"Well, you see . . ."

"And did I reserve space for New York?"

"Well, no, not exactly," he replied, looking at Mr. Fonteyn desperately, "but . . ."

"Then why is it made out in my name?" I persisted.

Mr. Fonteyn reached over and took the ticket. "I will hold it for you, Mr. Davis."

One of the newsmen came forward. "Mr. Davis, may we ask you a few questions?"

"Well, I'm in the custody of the Dutch police," I replied. "Ten days ago, in this same airport, I was held incommunicado by the police. Have they changed the rules since then?"

The reporter turned to Mr. Fonteyn who squirmed under the gaze of the journalists. "Well, you see, ten days ago the situation was somewhat different. . . ."

The newsmen took this for assent. "Please, Mr. Davis, we have arranged for a small press conference in the restaurant."

Our group moved to the large restaurant where one section had been blocked off by huge screens behind which dozens of chairs and a long conference table had been arranged. Giant floodlights stood at either side of three television cameras directed toward the table. Milling about were close to a hundred men and women, talking, laughing, drinking. Escorted by the newsmen, I made my way to the centre table as flashbulbs popped and cameras whirred. During a television interview, I was asked whether I had any resentment toward the Dutch Government for my imprisonment. I replied that as this was my eighth imprisonment in eight countries including two ships' brigs, all for the same offence, I found the Dutch Government's treatment perfectly in accord with her sister governments throughout the world.

Toward the end of the interview, Mr. Fonteyn eased toward

the table, holding in his hand the ticket for Idlewild Airport in New York.

"Here is your ticket, Mr. Davis," he said sweetly, handing it to me in front of the journalists.

I took it with a smile. "Thank you, Mr. Fonteyn. You say this is my ticket?"

"Yes, Mr. Davis. First-class, too."

"And naturally everyone who flies must have a ticket?" I asked gently.

"Er . . . naturally," he said, the smile leaving his face.

With that, I slowly tore the ticket into bits, dropping the pieces into the ashtray. The Chief of Police's face crimsoned while the journalists laughed.

A Flying Dutchman outside was being filled up and the flight was announced over the loudspeaker.

"This way, Mr. Davis," Mr. Fonteyn said.

"But I have no ticket," I protested.

A silence had fallen over the group, the noises from the restaurant and the flight line suddenly seemed loud. This is a futile protest, I thought to myself, much as at Abadan. Even if I have the right, they have the force. Whether I co-operate or not, in minutes I will be on a plane bound for New York. But something inside said, "Sit! Don't co-operate. Insist to the last that you stand for world law. You're only one, but at least you're that."

The captain gave an order and his men charged over to where I was sitting. They stopped ludicrously, not knowing how to tackle me behind a table with journalists on each side. I stared straight ahead. Suddenly, over the loudspeaker came the last call for the flight. The captain spat out his order and again the guards sprang into action, moving the table away and grabbing me under the arms.

As soon as I was deposited into my seat aboard the plane, great engines sprang into life and we taxied out on to the wide macadam runway. A few moments later, we were airborne, swinging away from the lights of Skipholt, Amsterdam and Europe, over the black Atlantic. It was exactly seventy-nine days since I had left Amritsar, penniless and armed with only the World Passport.

I followed my usual procedure at Idlewild and remained aboard the plane after everyone else had debarked. I wanted to know what U.S. Immigration might have in mind for me before I jumped into the lion's mouth.

Presently I was joined by a K.L.M. official.

"Mr. Davis, we must ask you to debark."

"But am I a free man?" I asked.

"Of course you are free," he said with surprise.

"Then I don't understand why I was forced aboard by the Dutch police," I said. "Obviously I was not a free man then. What has happened in these last twelve hours to change me from a prisoner to a free man?"

"I cannot answer you, Mr. Davis, but you must leave the plane anyway. It is regulations."

"Ah, regulations!" I sighed, and turned the other way.

He hesitated. "Well, I shall inform Immigration," and off he went.

Five minutes later, the plane began to fill with New York City policemen—"Trouble on 422!"—but when they saw one lone man sitting, just looking out of the window, they relaxed and sprawled in the seats, joking with each other. Two news photographers poked their heads in the cabin and asked me whether they could shoot some pictures. It wasn't my plane, I told them, so they clambered aboard. The policemen, happy to have something to do, obligingly posed near me.

The K.L.M. man returned in a half hour with the news that Immigration definitely wanted to talk with me, having been assured that there would be no trouble about my entry.

"I'm not so concerned about my entry as with what happens afterwards," I said. "The Dutch police also allowed me entry. No thanks."

"But they must examine your passport, Mr. Davis," he insisted, "before anything definite can be decided."

"Fine, let them examine it," I said.

He eyed the policemen, who were listening intently. "But how can they examine your passport if you don't bring it to them?" he asked plaintively.

"Let them come here," I replied.

"Oh, but Immigration never boards planes," he said. "It is against policy."

"In that case, you can take it to them," I said, pulling the World Passport out of my pocket and handing it to him. He took it with a grimace and left. The policemen gradually drifted out, leaving only two of their number. The K.L.M. man was back in five minutes. "They refuse to accept your passport," he said briskly, handing it back to me. "You will return to Skipholt."

My heart flipped over. "So be it," I said.

He left hurriedly. A police sergeant poked his head in the door and said, "Okay, boys, let's go. The party's over."

I paced up and down the narrow aisleway. What an extraordinary position I had gotten myself into! Halfway between nations, neither in one nor the other, but on a carrier in between. What if I refused to debark at Skipholt on the assumption that I would be thrown back into prison? I wondered. Perhaps the Dutch Government would compel K.L.M., the original carrier, to fly me back to Abadan, whereupon the horrified Iranian Government would bundle me across the Afghanistan border and the indignant Afghans would escort me through the Khyber Pass eastward to Pakistan where the exasperated Pakistanis would trundle me back into India where naturally the vexed Mr. Nehru would order my return to New York and thus in a month or so I might find myself at this very same airport, still on the international merry-go-round. I began to tremble, thinking of all the guardhouses I would pass through and all the robotized officials with whom I would come into contact. It could happen, I told myself. In this nation-crazy world, it could happen.

But how was I to leave the plane now after Immigration had refused to accept the World Passport? I could be charged with illegal entry and jailed all over again. This also could happen. There seemed no answer to the dilemma.

Then I heard heavy footsteps on the ship's ladder. In walked two men: the first, beefy and small-eyed, wearing a blue suit, brown derby and chewing on a big cigar; the other with a long, drooping face and sad eyes, in the uniform of a U.S. Immigration Inspector. They marched up to me and stopped as if I were about to have my chevrons ripped off.

The man in the derby chewed several times on his cigar, then said, "Okay, Davis, you're free."

"Yes, that's right," I returned.

"No, I mean you're free. You can go. He waved his cigar over one shoulder. The Inspector moved back a pace.

"That's fine," I said, "but I don't understand. Who are you?"

He looked at me in disgust. "Immigration, who else?"

"May I see your credentials?" I asked.

Grudgingly he reached into his pocket and produced his Department of Justice shield. I carefully took down his name and number.

"Now, you tell me I'm free?" I said.

"That's right."

"Why?"

He looked at the Inspector. "Why? Whaddya mean, why? Ain't it clear? Free's free. We're freein' ya."

"Oh, I see, you're freeing me. When did you jail me?"

"Listen, Davis, I'm not here to argue with you," he said glowering. "I'm here to tell you what's what."

"All right," I returned, "just what *is* what? For example, what is the law which permits you to 'free' me when I haven't even consented to enter the United States?"

"Law? Yeah, well, we're goin' ta parole ya," he said nervously.

"Parole me!" I exclaimed with a laugh.

"Yeah, like the Hungarians. Special law. We couldn't figure out nothing else."

I sat down on the edge of the seat, not knowing whether to laugh or to cry. So the Hungarian "freedom fighters" were "paroled" into the United States!

"And just what does it imply, to be a . . . parolee?" I asked.

"Oh, nothin' much," he replied casually. "Ya gotta report to us when you move and stuff like that."

"And how about the courts? Does a parolee have access to the courts?"

He looked at the Inspector, who shrugged. "Well, ya see, they're not like citizens, you know. We gotta be careful. . . ."

"I see. In other words, if Immigration or the F.B.I. or the State Department doesn't like what a . . . parolee is doing, alleyoop, back to where he came from. Is that it?"

"Yeah, well, I guess we got that right, but it don't often happen that way."

"I'm sorry, boys," I said, almost sick to my stomach, "I don't buy it. What else have you got?"

They both started. "What else—— Listen, Davis, we're not here to bargain with you. We came out here friendly——"

"So you're not here to bargain, eh? Then why was I told a half hour ago you refused to recognize my passport? Why was I told by a K.L.M. official I was going back to Holland and now you tell me you're willing to parole me? I agree that's no bargain;

in fact, it's an insult. Furthermore, what are you doing aboard a Dutch plane anyway? That's against policy, isn't it?"

He turned to the Inspector and motioned. They went forward to the pilot's section and closed the door. My lips were dry and I had a dull headache. What if I accepted him at his opening words: *"Okay, Davis, you're free"*? What if I entered the United States just like that . . . freely? Wouldn't I be returning either as a citizen, or, as in July 1953, as a sovereign? The front door was opening. I pulled my thoughts together. They were coming out.

"Gentlemen, I have a proposition for you," I said as they came down the aisle.

They stopped. The official chewed his cigar nervously. "Yeah?"

"I'll enter the United States on one condition."

"And what's that?"

"First, I want it understood that I do not accept to be considered a parolee. Is that clear?"

He looked at the Inspector, who stared back sadly. "Yeah. Okay. Now what?" he replied caustically.

"My condition on entering the United States is . . . no conditions."

He stared at me blankly. Then a look of supreme disdain crossed his face. He turned to the Inspector.

"Let him in anyway," he said and brushed past me and out the plane, the Inspector following.

I gathered up my things, walked out and down the portable stairway. The noises of the airport were loud in my ears: the roar of the planes taking off and landing, the fresh swish of the wind sweeping across the snowy runways, and the gabbling voices as I came to the main building. No one was at any of the numerous desks spread along the narrow aisleway which was the Immigration inspection section. I passed through like a wraith. A small group of newspapermen were gathered at the end to interview me. We went to the press room.

"Why did you agree to come in as a parolee, Garry?" the Associated Press man asked me.

"What!" I exclaimed. "Who told you that?"

"The Immigration Inspector," he said in surprise. "He said you even signed parolee papers."

"Has the story gone out?" I asked.

"Sure, we just passed it over the wires."

I told them precisely what had happened on the plane. Most of the European press carried both versions of the episode while the American press carried only Immigration's version.

"Let's have a look at the World Passport," the United Press man asked. I passed it around.

After leaving the press room, I suddenly realized I had no money for a bus to New York. Well, I had gotten halfway around the world without money, I remembered, so I should be able to get from Idlewild to New York City the same way. As I started to leave, a press photographer asked me to pose at the door with my gear.

"On one condition," I told him seriously.

He gave me a sharp look. "What's that?"

"That you give me a lift into town."

He laughed. "Sure, any time."

14

It was good to be home again, even if I had been tricked into entering the country. It was wonderful to be with family and friends again, however irksome the idea of being stamped with the artificial status of "parolee". It was good to enjoy a home-cooked meal, a hot shower, a comfortable bed—all the luxuries a practising world citizen often had to do without. And yet I was still quietly determined to get to Berlin.

Berlin had been my objective on leaving New Delhi; in fact, Berlin had been my destination on my very first trip abroad. But it had always eluded me. For years now the city had preyed on my mind. For no other city in the world so clearly exemplified the evils of nationalism nor seemed so obvious a place to plant the staff of World Government. As a victim of hysterical nationalism a decade before, Berlin became the decimated capital of an "aggressor" nation. And now, within the experience of a single generation, Berlin was in torture again—divided between the two great mutual aggressors of the Cold War and a focal point of the conflict in national interests of the Soviet Union and the United States.

Truly, if the people of any city in the world were ready for the "First World Citizen", the people of Berlin *were*. I recommitted myself to getting there.

I went to the German Consulate in New York and applied for a visa. After examining my World Passport, the Consul informed me that the German Federal Republic could not issue me a visa. I asked him to refer the matter to authorities in Bonn, but he refused.

"You haf not a national passport, Herr Davis," he informed me stiffly, "und so, dere is no question uf a visa."

Three days later, I was en route for Canada via Colbrooke, New Hampshire, fortified with a fresh birth certificate which I had procured from the Town Clerk at Bar Harbour, where I had been born thirty-six years before. "This here'n's the sixth you've asked fer in half a dozen years, Garry," our clerk Emery informed me, smiling, "Whatcha do with 'em, eat 'em?"

"Nope," I said, "jest naturally wear 'em out from the fingerin'."
There was no difficulty at the U.S.-Canadian border at Canaan. Only my driver's licence and the registration card of the motorcycle on which I was travelling were examined and noted by Canadian Immigration.

"What's your business, Mr. Davis?" an inspector asked me.

"Sightseeing," I informed him.

"Have a good time," he said.

"I sure will," I chirped, gunning the throttle.

The next day in Montreal I checked on sailings to Europe. Several cargo and passenger liners were leaving that week. Noting the freighters, I rode to the docks. There I spoke to several captains about working my way over. Each one of them told me I would have to belong to the Seafarer's International Union of North America before he could even consider it. I went to S.I.U.N.A. headquarters on St. James Street, and there I was told brusquely by the men checking cards at the door that membership was closed because thousands of their own men were out of work.

Sitting in a cafeteria that night watching the busy St. Catherine Street crowd, I pondered the situation. Should I stow away, then explain the situation to the captain and ask him to let me enter a European port on my own? There would be no point in returning me to Canada since I had arrived illegally anyway... or non-legally. I wondered what Canadian authorities would do should I be discovered? Could they legally deport me to the United States even though I had not existed legally in the United States when I "left"?

I forced my thoughts back to the travel situation. Since passports are checked both before boarding and before disembarking, two problems presented themselves: first, to get aboard without a passport inspection; second, to get off without a passport inspection. Damn passports anyway! I had learned from my S.S. *Liberté* experience that it was better to have the passage prepaid rather than to risk stowing away.

During the next days I met various people with whom I talked of world citizenship. A well-known Montreal priest, widely travelled throughout the world, became enthusiastic to the point where he agreed to give me the necessary passage fare to Bremerhaven. He had earned the money, he said as a speaker, on television. I left my motorcycle with him in exchange.

August 20th, 1957. I am released from jail in Hanover after being "convicted" of entering West Germany illegally.

My Frascati "mug shot".

Thinking out my course on a patch of Capri land donated by a friend between my two "visits" to Frascati.

On July 5th, I read that S.S. *Arosa Sun* was sailing on the 10th, stopping at Plymouth, England; Le Havre, France; and Bremerhaven, Germany. I went to the agency handling the line and made a tourist reservation for Bremerhaven.

The large ticket was in triplicate. "The first copy you keep for yourself," the young agent told me. "The yellow copy is for Immigration before boarding, and the blue is for the ship's purser. Now, may I see your passport, please?"

I searched around in my pocket. "I seem to have left it at the hotel," I told him.

"Oh, that's all right, Mr. Davis," he said. "Just a formality." He handed me the ticket. "Immigration will have a look at it before boarding."

I returned to my hotel and wrote a letter to West Germany's Chancellor, Dr. Adenauer, explaining the circumstances of my voyage. Then I wrote a press statement to be released when I was on board the *Arosa Sun* on the high seas. Making copies of both, I mailed them the next day to Alex Franke in Berlin, Peter Troost in Rotterdam, and Guy Marchand in Paris, instructing these friends of mine to release the statement on July 13th to the press in their respective countries. I held the original copy of the letter for mailing to Dr. Adenauer just prior to sailing.

The stevedores at the dock took the luggage marked for my stateroom. I walked casually to the second level from which the gangplank extended and to my dismay saw a small group of uniformed men suspiciously eyeing everyone who came toward the gangplank. A portable office with a counter was set up to the left of the gangplank and several passengers were there presenting tickets and passports to the Immigration officials standing behind. Paying no attention to anyone, I walked straight for the gangplank and started up, ignoring the policemen standing there. One of them stopped me. "Teeket, pleeze."

"Oh, pardon," I said. "Je suis un visiteur."

He gestured toward the counter and said that I should get a visitor's pass. "Thank you," I replied and went to the counter. "May I have a visitor's pass?" I asked. Without a glance, the official gave me what looked like a hat check. I presented it to the guard at the gangplank. "*Voilà!*" he said, and I went aboard.

In a half hour the boat horn sounded and a voice came from the loudspeaker requesting all visitors to go ashore. People were scurrying to and fro as white-coated stewards, white-uniformed stewardesses, waiters, crewmen, officers, were all engaged in that last-minute frenzy which marks the outset of a transatlantic crossing.

A boat sailing from Quebec takes two and a half days to clear land—that is, two days to clear the St. Lawrence and approximately twelve hours to clear Novia Scotia. Should I be discovered in that time, I speculated, it would be a simple matter to put me ashore. With my passage already paid, however, the possibility was minimized. In any case, I wanted to make myself scarce for at least half a day on the assumption that by the end of that time a kind of ship's routine would exist into which I could fit unobtrusively.

It wasn't until the fourth day out that the ship's officers learned of my presence. And then, almost miraculously, the purser asked me no questions about my World Passport but merely asked to see it and marked down the data he needed for his register.

On the seventh day out I was asked to lead a discussion on world citizenship during the daily current events hour. Many of the ship's officers, including the staff captain, attended. We arrived at Le Havre the next day. French Immigration, I learned, was not due until the following morning. A whole night to jump ship!

The porthole of my stateroom was just level with the dock, which was a scant five feet away. I noted the circumference of the porthole and decided that I could squeeze through if need be. But how to get across the five feet? I looked down. Fifteen feet below, the oily harbour water sloshed menacingly against the ship's hull. I went forward to the open deck. There the drop to the dock was a good twenty feet. I could make it, I thought, if I weren't seen, but I would run the risk of a sprained ankle. The gangplank was guarded by a sergeant-at-arms. I thought of going over the other side of the ship and swimming across to a breakwater, but then I wondered how I would explain wet clothes if caught. Logistics!

I had not been so close to France since the S.S. *Liberté* episode in 1956. The difference was that this time no one in France except my confidant, Guy Marchand, knew of my presence. I had eight hours to figure a way to get off the ship.

Back in my cabin, I packed my bags. Then I heard sounds of laughter and shouting. Looking out, I saw two couples from the ship making their way along the quay. I darted out the cabin and up the stairway. The gangplank was for the moment unguarded. Instinctively I rushed down it, shouting, "Hey, wait for me!" to my fellow passengers. They turned and I saw they were half drunk. All the better. I joined them and, locking arms, we all started into Le Havre together.

I left the group at the end of the long deserted dock where the road divided, a sign pointing to Rouen, 86 kilometres, and Paris, 226 kilometres away. I was going to get a taxi, I told them. After an hour of fast walking, I was a good five miles from the dock. At each passing car, I dived into the brush along the side of the road, often finding myself face down in the wet grass or in a ditch with brambles cutting my hands. But nothing could have dampened my spirits then! I was in Europe and back in my beloved France for the first time in seven years.

Begging, borrowing and, I confess without apology, even stealing, I made my way to Paris and on through France toward the German border. An old friend in Strasbourg gave me a pair of rubber boots, a small backpack, a flashlight, a compass, and a map indicating the most deserted point on the frontier for me to cross into Germany. Having "jumped ship" in France, I was about to "crash" the German border.

I reached the crossing point—an old route of the French underground—at midnight. Following a dirt road for several miles, I came to a stop and continued along a narrow path, almost invisible and overhung with heavy foliage. Then the path came to an end! My heart was pounding. I didn't know whether this frontier was patrolled or not. In fact, I did not know exactly where the frontier was. Could I be lost? I asked myself, horror-stricken. Risking a brief flash of my light, I checked my map and compass. As far as I could tell, I had come in the right direction. I sat down, exhausted, the black silence enfolding me like a blanket. My throbbing pulse soon returned to normal and then, wondrously, as I listened I heard the gurgle of water. I beat my way through the brush in the direction of the sound. All at once, the brush gave way and I was standing on the bank of the great river Rhine. It looked cold, black and ominous.

I struggled with myself for a full half hour before gaining the courage to dip one leg into that wet blackness. Wallet, papers and flashlight had been transferred to my beret. When I stepped in, the river proved, to my great relief, to be only waist deep, and just about twenty yards wide! At midstream, however, the current was swift, nearly upsetting me. Finally I clambered up the far side and lay down for a moment, then took off my boots and socks, pouring water from them. Soon I struck out again and immediately found a narrow dirt road running east. Both the road and the trees, rising like silent sentinels on either side of it, were so straight, I thought with a chuckle, I must now be in Germany! A small sign about a half mile farther marking a crossroad confirmed my belief. It was in German.

At 4:00 a.m. I came to a tiny village, my boots sounding loud on the ancient cobbles. Several dogs barked from behind shuttered windows, and as I heard one open, I moved swiftly to the shadows. By 8:30, after three hectic rides on the backs of motor-cycles piloted by leather-jacketed young men going to work, I was in Baden-Baden, where I thought one of the original German World Citizens lived, Joachim Müller. Tired, hungry, and with only a few Deutschmarks given to me by my friend in Strasbourg, I needed assistance. The paradox of my situation was that if I had made myself known at the nearest newspaper office, my physical predicament would have changed in moments. But I could not risk detection at this point.

Posing as a free-lance journalist, I found in a bookshop a salesgirl who had heard of the World Citizenship Movement and thought Herr Müller had moved to Cologne several years ago. Coffee, cheese dips and bits of this and that in the various food departments of a German 5-and-10 cent store assuaged my hunger. After a few hours' sleep in a large Victorian armchair in the corner of the lobby of a small hotel, I started off for the nearest autobahn, hoping to hitch a ride to Frankfurt and thence to Cologne.

Within the hour I was riding in a large van going north, the driver a lean-faced Westphalian with a penchant for frequent beer stops—to all of which I was invited. At around ten o'clock, my head spinning and my throat hoarse from trying to keep the driver company by singing German folk songs, we approached the great Frankfurt-am-Main Airport with the adjacent U.S. Army Air Force base. As I stared at the tall, brightly lit control tower, the gleaming rows of transports and bombers, an idea struck me.

"*Ich will hier . . . davonkommen,*" I said over the noise of the engine. The driver ground to a halt. We shook hands and I climbed out.

At the main gate to the air base there were both U.S. Army M.P.s and German civil police. I walked briskly up to a young corporal, pulling out my ancient Adjutant General Officer's card which identified me as a first lieutenant in the U.S. Air Corps. Holding the card with my thumb over the part punched *Inactive*, I asked the way to the Bachelor Officers' Quarters. The corporal saluted me, gave directions and I passed through.

After a delightful night's rest at the B.O.Q. and a bacon and egg breakfast at the canteen, paid for out of my remaining marks which a kind captain had exchanged for Occupation money, I went to Operations and asked the desk sergeant the chances of getting a ride on one of the daily flights to Berlin.

"Are you on active duty?" he asked.

"No."

"Sorry, no dice."

I hitched a ride into Wiesbaden instead, and went directly to the plush Hotel Von Steuben. In the lobby I sat down next to a man reading the Paris *Tribune*. Soon we were talking as "foreigners" do in a "foreign" country and he asked me to join him for dinner. The conversation turned to philosophy and he revealed an enthusiastic knowledge of Eastern theosophical writings. I spoke of my studies with Guru Natarajan. We discussed the theory of reincarnation during the meat course and the problems of man-made war during dessert. The subject of world government followed.

"Say, you're not *the* Garry Davis, are you?" he asked.

It was as good a time as any to tell him a bit more of the story, I thought. ". . . So you see," I wound up, "I've got to arrange it so I can remain here in Germany and particularly in Berlin if I can."

"But what do you do for money, Davis?"

"I don't worry about it," I replied.

"Don't worry about it! But how do you eat?"

"I'm eating now, aren't I?" I said as I finished the last piece of apple strudel. His eyes narrowed.

"What do you do, go bumming off people all the time?"

"You've been kind enough to offer me dinner without even knowing me," I replied. "Would you do any less now that you do know who I am?"

He looked puzzled and shook his head. "You're nuts," he said, "but I don't know why. Come on." He called for the bill, paid it, and we got up.

Moments later, he shoved two hundred marks into my hand. "Here," he said gruffly, "here's a contribution to . . . whatever the hell you're doing. At least I'll know you're eating."

The next morning, July 24th, a map of Germany revealed to me that I was less than 75 miles from the East Zone, Helmstedt being the nearest East-West Zone control point to Berlin. The nearest large town to Helmstedt was Braunschweig, near Hanover. A train took me to Braunschweig that evening. There, the road due east led through Wolfsburg to the small village of Velpke, then six kilometres farther to the town of Obisfelder in the Soviet Zone of East Germany. Somewhere between Velpke and Obisfelder was the frontier. Somewhere between these two German towns, the world was divided artificially. It was only a country road on the map. Surely soldiers were not staked out every twenty yards, I thought. No doubt there were patrols, but I thought that they could be avoided simply because neither side would be expecting anyone to cross from west to east over open territory.

I hitched a ride to Wolfsburg. At the outskirts of town I took a bus to Velpke. There I rented a bicycle and early the next morning pedalled my way east through the predawn mist.

The sun was just below the horizon when I sighted a church spire of Obisfelder in the distance. The East Zone! But where was the control point? Maybe there was none along this road. I rounded a bend and there, not forty yards away, were four West German Passkontrolle policemen walking toward me! I continued on toward them nonchalantly, my heart beating a tattoo. As we came within speaking distance, one said in surprise, "*Wohin gehen Sie?*"

"I'm sorry," I said smiling, "my German is somewhat rusty. Do you speak English?"

"Yes, I speak," he said.

"Ah, good. Well, I seem to be lost. Please, where am I?"

"Where are you? You go fast into the Russian Zone," he said pointing. "That is where you are."

"Good Lord!" I said. "I *am* lost!" I was turning around. "Not this trip across, I'm afraid." I was pedalling away.

"*Vielen Dank,*" I called behind me as my feet bore down on the pedals.

"*Auf Wiedersehen*," he called after me.

I rounded the bend and continued for a hundred yards, searching desperately for a road or a pathway to right or left. Ah, there it was, a single-lane dirt road to the left running south, parallel to the frontier. I turned down it, pedalling furiously. The sun was rising, a magnificent red ball in the east. Suddenly I spied far down the road another patrol coming toward me. A dirt path between two cornfields was at my left. I turned down it and leaped off the bicycle. The path led straight toward the frontier. I hurried along, half wheeling, half dragging the bicycle in the mud. Finally I abandoned it at the end of the field. I looked back and could see no police. I looked ahead and drew a sharp breath. Not ten yards in front of me was a wide strip of ploughed ground running as far as I could see from north to south. On either side were fences of thickly entwined barbed wire. The frontier! For years I had been opposing the ideological frontier of East-West with the ideology of one world. But here was the naked physical evidence, the barbaric folly of men exposed to my eyes, dead ahead.

I moved forward and found a place where I could crawl under the wire. Shoving my pack ahead of me, I inched my way through on my stomach. Halfway across the ploughed ground, I heard a sharp "*Achtung!*"

It came from in front of me. I looked up. Standing slightly to my right and behind the wire were two grim-looking Volkspolizei in grey uniforms, their sawed-off machine guns pointing directly at me. Gathering my wits, I smiled broadly and waved to them. A flicker of surprise and annoyance crossed their faces. As I came forward and emerged on the Soviet side of the barbed wire, they separated automatically, both covering me with their weapons.

"*Wohin gehen Sie?*" the first barked.

"Berlin," I replied brightly. "*Ich bin ein Weltbürger*" (World Citizen).

"*Welt... Was? Haben Sie einen Pass?*"

"*Ja. Hier ist mein Pass.*" I shoved the World Passport at him. He stepped back, giving his comrade a quick glance. The latter tightened on his weapon. Then the first soldier put down his gun and examined the passport. Obviously he couldn't read either English or Esperanto. Handing it back impatiently, he motioned for me to come with them.

As we fell into step, the first soldier marched alongside me, his comrade about ten paces to the right and five to the rear. I chattered like a magpie. Neither guard paid any attention to me, but on the other hand, I was pleased to note, neither took a shot at me. Eventually we came to a small and gloomy town. My captors were known and greeted monosyllabically by the early risers as we passed. Certainly no town I had seen in West Germany seemed as poor as this one. Streets were in disrepair, houses looked bleak and the clothes on all the people I saw were threadbare. I couldn't help but recall the "proles" of Orwell's *1984*.

I was taken to the local headquarters, a long, barrack-like building with soldiers going in and out. The officer-in-charge had the World Passport in his hand. "But, you have no pass for Berlin," he told me in German. I tried to explain that as a *"Weltbürger"* I did not need one.

"Ach so, ein Weltbürger," he said with a tight smile. He barked an order and I was escorted to a large room with a library on one side. The windows were open with no bars across them. I was left alone. I walked slowly to the window and looked out. I could see no one about. An eight-foot wall faced me but the village road was plainly visible beyond. Escape would have been a simple matter. Too simple. I remembered the sawed-off burp guns.

After fifteen minutes a policeman came in carrying a tray with a large cup of coffee and a full platter of sandwiches of various meats. *"Bitte,"* he said, putting it on the low table. I fell to eagerly.

After an hour of waiting, the door opened and two guards came in. *"Kommen Sie,"* one of them said. I picked up my backpack and we went out. Outside in the yard, they mounted bicycles, motioning for me to do the same. We started down the road together, me in the middle.

The Obisfelder railway station, our destination, was just south of the town. There I was closeted in a small room in the guardhouse. At noon, a train chugged into the station and I was put aboard. The guards did not follow me. This is strange, I puzzled. Are they allowing me to go to Berlin alone? The train started. It was going in the wrong direction. Then it dawned on me: I was being shipped back to West Germany!

15

"I think maybe you should read this," I said to the officer at the Hanover station who asked to see my papers. I gave him a copy of my letter to Chancellor Adenauer. I was hustled to the Passkontrolle office on one of the platforms. The small room was crowded with young men going to work in their dark blue uniforms. They changed clothes, checked over papers, laughed and chatted, and finally filed out, leaving me alone with an English-speaking guard. The door of a small inner office opened and the Chief came out to have a look at me. He and my guard talked a bit and then both retired to his office, closing the door. I tiptoed to the other door, opened it stealthily and slipped out. Then, racing down the platform stairs, down a long corridor past the ticket punchers' booths, and vaulting over a low iron railing, I escaped from the station in seconds.

In fifteen minutes I was seated in the modern downtown office of the editor of DENA, the news agency which services all of Germany. I wrote out a brief statement which the editor put on the wire immediately. Then I left.

I intended to remain out of sight for at least twenty-four hours, but it was only by the most remote coincidence that my plan failed. I took a bus from the outskirts of town. Then someone sat down beside me. It was the very Passkontrolle chief from whom I had just escaped! He was no less amazed than I. He was going home to have lunch, he told me *sotto voce*, and he asked if I would consent to accompany him.

"Some other time perhaps," I replied, getting off at the first stop. But he was right behind me. I started out, walking briskly. He picked up his pace. I began to trot and he did likewise. Finally I turned on the steam. As the Chief was slightly stout, I thought I could outrun him, but I didn't reckon with my own fatigue and his allies. After dashing madly up and down several blocks, during which the Chief called ahead to civilians to stop *"Der Ausreisser,"* I was cornered, corralled, and captured by three patrolmen who had joined the chase.

Back at the station, once more seated in the outer office of the Passkontrolle police but now in the custody of two officers, I awaited events. It wasn't long before the Chief came out of his office and approached me hesitantly.

"Do you consent to a radio interview with *Nordwest Deutscher Rundfunk?* They have now called four times. Also, the *Hannoversche Allgemeine Zeitung* wants to speak with you."

"But I am not a free man, am I, sir? Do you allow my words and voice to go free when you keep my poor body here?"

"That is not up to me whether you go free or not. We have our regulations. You have entered Germany illegally. I just do my duty."

"But is it not absurd to imprison the least part of a man—that is, his body—while you permit his spirit and his ideas to roam the world at will?"

Confused, the poor man retreated behind his door. Ten minutes later, the outer door opened and two young men with tape-recording equipment trailing a long wire entered.

"Mr. Davis?" one asked politely.

"Yes."

"We didn't quite understand whether you consented to be interviewed or not, so we came along anyway. Would you mind answering a few questions for us?"

The situation was so incongruous, I burst out laughing. Obviously, the Chief, under pressure, had said it was all right with him. I was reminded of the tremendous power of public opinion spearheaded by a persistent press. It opened locked doors and battered down iron walls. If the public really wanted to know something, no government or private force could hold out for long against its thirst for information.

I gave the newsmen an interview saying I was delighted to be in West Germany after so many years of refusal. When asked of my plans, I told them that, as long as I was in the custody of the Passkontrolle police, I could not afford the luxury of plans. I had several other interviews that day including one with DENA and one with the *Hannoversche Presse* but always with my two "escorts" at my side. That evening I was taken to a temporary prison and locked up in a cell for the night. The next morning, I was brought to the Hanover city prison, given prison garb and a cell on the main block. Two days later I was transferred to a room in the prison hospital with a foam rubber mattress, a desk and a chair, and a large window overlooking the exercise yard.

On the third day I was taken before a judge.

There is something about being in prison for no other reason than being improperly identified that makes my blood boil. No amount of rationalization or idealistic thoughts about humanity or understanding of the innate goodness of Man could erase the brutal fact that I had been bounded by four walls and a door locked from the outside for three miserable days. I erupted with indignation and fury at the trial.

"Please tell His Honour," I said to the court translator, "that I do not consider myself in Germany. To me I am in, or on, if you prefer, the world. I had assumed that other men shared my view, especially those who continually advocate such human rights as freedom of travel." In translation, about one-quarter of my idea got through to the judge, and he only shook his head in bewilderment.

I learned the next day that I had been charged with illegal entry, convicted and sentenced to twenty days' imprisonment or fined five Deutschmarks per day. I decided to accept the sentence, since presumably I did not recognize the charge.

Along about the tenth day I was taken to a small office to meet three officials from the Hanover city government. Would I consent to receiving a Fremdenpass (foreigner's passport) from the City of Hanover? they asked. I stared at them in amazement.

"A Fremdenpass? You come to me while I am in a prison for entering Germany illegally and offer me a paper to be *in* Germany?"

"That is correct."

"But if I can have a paper, what am I doing in prison?"

"Well, you see, Mr. Davis, it is the federal government that charged you with entering illegally and it is the city government which offers you the passport."

I couldn't believe my ears. The city could issue a passport while the government could not. "Do you mean to tell me that every time I asked for a visa to enter Germany, I should have asked one of the German cities rather than the federal government?"

"No, for a visa it is the federal government, but once a foreigner is in Germany, it is the city which issues him a passport."

"In other words, for me to live in Germany I first have to enter illegally, since I cannot get a visa while outside, and then, once in, automatically I get a Fremdenpass from whatever city I happen to be in?"

"Well, it's something like that," one of the officials agreed, "that is, if there is no other country to which you can be sent."

I couldn't help asking, "Does the federal government know you're here?"

They smiled. "We have merely come to visit you."

"Well, if I had known how the system works, I would have been in Germany nine years ago. But why do I have to serve time for entering illegally if now you are willing to give me permission to remain?"

"We are not competent to discuss this with you, Mr. Davis, only the question of the Fremdenpass."

"Hmm. If you ask me whether I consent to such an illogical procedure, my answer is no but should you offer me a Fremdenpass, I will not refuse it. However, I have one condition."

"Yes?"

"I must be identified on the Fremdenpass as the Co-ordinator of World Government."

They took out pen and paper and asked me statistical questions needed for the document: full name, birth date, birthplace, permanent residence, occupation, etc. For permanent residence I said "Hanover". They took it all down, thanked me and left. The next day a photographer was allowed into the prison to take my photo for the passport.

On the day of my release, there was great excitement among the guards, and even the prison director himself came to visit me. The German newspapers had carried the news of my incarceration, and an impromptu press conference was organized directly outside the prison with mobile TV trucks to catch the event for the nightly news telecast. The story later found its way around the world to such diverse publications as *Time*, the *Deccan Herald* of Bangalore, India, the South Carolina *Post* and scores of others.

A Hanover citizen, Mr. Wilfred Hildebrand, offered me hospitality. He had been one of the original World Citizens in Hanover, he told me as we drove briskly through the city streets.

"I have invited a few friends over tomorrow night to meet you," Herr Hildebrand said in good English. "They are very much interested in hearing your views. I hope that is all right with you."

"Yes, perfectly, except that I will not be able to speak to them in German."

"Oh, that's quite all right. As a matter of fact, most of these men speak English quite well. There will be several lawyers, a senator from the Hanover senate, several industrialists—one who owns our biggest paper factory—a teacher from the Technische Hochschule, a few writers, but there in a private capacity, and I think Helmut Hagedorn. You know Helmut Hagedorn, don't you?"

"No, I don't think so."

"Ah, he was a very active World Citizen in 1949 and '50. You will meet him."

Not only was I to meet Helmut Hagedorn, but I was to stay at his beautiful modern apartment for four days and delight in his exuberant friendship and wonderful zest for living. As far as I could tell, he was an advertising magnate, his company handling general merchandising accounts of large firms including Dujardin, one of the giant wine and liquor businesses of Europe.

In Mr. Hildebrand's spacious living room the next evening we sat informally while I expounded on the philosophy of world citizenship.

For over an hour I talked about a direct approach to life, seeing things as they are, wholly, and practising principles daily.

"Surely we all agree with you, in principle," the paper factory owner said, "but when it comes to living it, practising it in the down-to-earth competitive society in which we live, how does it come out, eh? We are businessmen, lawyers, writers, teachers; we work for a living. It is nice to be idealistic, but this does not pay the rent or feed the children. So, Mr. Davis, how do you earn your living, *bitte*?"

I shrugged. "When I need money, I make it."

"*Ach so*, I thought so. And in what way? Do you sell articles? Have you a craft?"

"No, you don't understand me. I just make money."

"Yes, yes, of course. But how?"

"Well, give me a piece of paper and I'll show you."

Someone handed me a piece of paper and I folded it in the shape of a U.S. dollar, creased the edges and tore off the excess. At the top, I wrote in large letters ONE WORLD CREDIT, and under it, EIN WELT KREDIT. In brackets underneath, I wrote, *One World Credit equals five Deutschmarks*. In the centre I drew the world citizen emblem, on the right-hand side the number "000001", and directly beneath this inscribed my signature and the title "Co-ordinator, World Government". On the left-hand side, I wrote *One Value, One World, One Mankind*, and underneath *Ein Wert, Eine Welt, Eine Menschheit*. Under the emblem, I wrote, *World Government Bank*, marking the German translation below. At the lower left, *Hanover, August*, 1957, and in the four corners, the large numeral 1.

Holding it up, I said, "Here it is—money; in fact, the first world money."

There was general laughter.

"That's all very well, Herr Davis," said the paper factory man, "but what is behind your so-called money? Who will recognize it?"

"I am behind it," I replied, "and as to who will recognize it, I'll let you have second recognition, since I recognized it first. You see, I've pegged it at five marks, officially, so you may exchange it for five of your marks. If you do, then of course your own five marks will be backing it. And you have my word that should you wish to change it back, I will honour your request, minus a minimal charge, say 1 per cent, for the exchange service."

They were amused as he reached into his pocket.

"Well, I know you have no money, and I would be happy to make a contribution."

I held up my hand. "Oh no, I do have money, although it is not your kind. You're doing me no favour by exchanging this first World Credit for your five marks and if you think you are, I'll just raffle it to the highest bidder in this room. Since it is the first, it has a certain historical value besides the five marks. I'm quite sure it would bring far more than its mere par value."

He had the money in his hand. "Yes, yes, I quite understand. Here are the five marks."

"The reason this is world currency," I said, making the exchange, "is that it is negotiable for any national currency. In fact, I will guarantee that you may exchange this note for any currency throughout the world through me. Of course, the service charge will be slightly higher if you should wish Afghanistan puls."

"But of course," he said, carefully putting the new bill into his wallet.

"You have just engaged yourself in one of the most positive acts of peace in our times," I told him with a smile. "Without money, war cannot be waged, and since wars are waged by nations it is, of course, national currency which pays for wars. More specifically, it is from tax money that national leaders collect the funds to wage war with each other. But the only government able to tax the World Credit is the World Government. And the World Government uses taxes only for the welfare of mankind. You might say, World Government has just taxed you five Deutschmarks and given you its receipt in the form of its own currency. Your marks will be used only for peaceful purposes, and, better yet, the Bonn Government cannot possibly tax your receipt without at the same time recognizing its issuing agency or World Government. So you see, a valid act of peace has just been inaugurated here in Herr Hildebrand's living room."

Several of the group then asked me to write World Credit notes for which they would each pay me five marks. Not wishing to turn my host's living room into the "World Government Bank," I declined politely.

The five of us, including the possessor of the first World Credit, repaired to a local inn—Der Tausend Schnapps—to quench our thirst. I was delighted as well as amazed with the evening's experiment and as we drank our tall steins of dark lager, flushed with success, I decided to put the first round on the World Government expense account.

"I'll take the first round," I said to the group.

Protests came from all sides.

"Oh no, you only have five marks."

"No, you are our guest; we couldn't think of it."

I called the waiter and asked for the check. Happily enough, it came to four Deutschmarks, seventy Pfennigs. That left thirty Pfennigs for a tip! With the waiter there, the rest of the group remained silent. I asked for a blank piece of paper. Our waiter tore out a blank check from the back of his order form. I wrote out another World Credit, numbering it "000002", and signed my name as before. All watched in mute consternation. I put the World Credit on top of the bill and handed the small tray to the waiter. He took four steps, examined the bill, looked at us, hesitated, then motioned to the manager. The manager came over. He looked at the note, muttered something, looked up at us, smiled benignly, then signed the check and went off, leaving the perplexed waiter holding a World Credit in his hands.

"Mr. Davis, when you are ready to print your world money," said the owner of the paper factory, taking out his handkerchief and mopping his forehead, "please, I will offer you first-grade rag paper."

"Yes, and I know a fine engraver who will make you a design," another said.

"And I have a girl friend who will spend it for you," a third added and we all laughed.

The waiter returned several moments later to put down on the table three Deutschmarks. He explained, pointing to another table where a portly gentleman was waving the World Credit in his hand and smiling. My friends burst into laughter.

"Already the money is circulating," Mr. Hildebrand said. "Here are three more marks for you, Garry. The waiter has been busy."

"But why only three?" I asked.

"*Ach*, the waiter is not as good a financier as you," he replied. "He devalued the World Credit by two marks!"

On their way out the portly gentleman and his friend stopped at our table and his friend said to me, "Herr Davis, I am from Zurich and we have heard much about your ideas there. Would you be good enough to give me a World Credit also?" I looked around at the table. Everyone was looking at me smilingly, now thoroughly convinced that I was a veritable moneymaker.

"I'd be glad to, except that I don't have any more," I said.

"Please," he said and handed me his pen. I went about the business of making money on the back of a blank check donated by the management. It was "No. 000003". As I handed it over, I was given a crisp five-mark note.

"Many thanks, Mr. Davis," he said, carefully putting it into his billfold. "I shall will this to my children."

I now had thirteen Deutschmarks for the night's work. What I did not know at the time was that, on the German autograph market, my signature was worth seven marks!

During the next days, I made a design, found a printer and set him to work. The first issue of World Credits came off the press on September 17th—1,000 crisp new bills valued at 5,000 German marks.

The printer, however, insisted on being paid in coin of the realm!

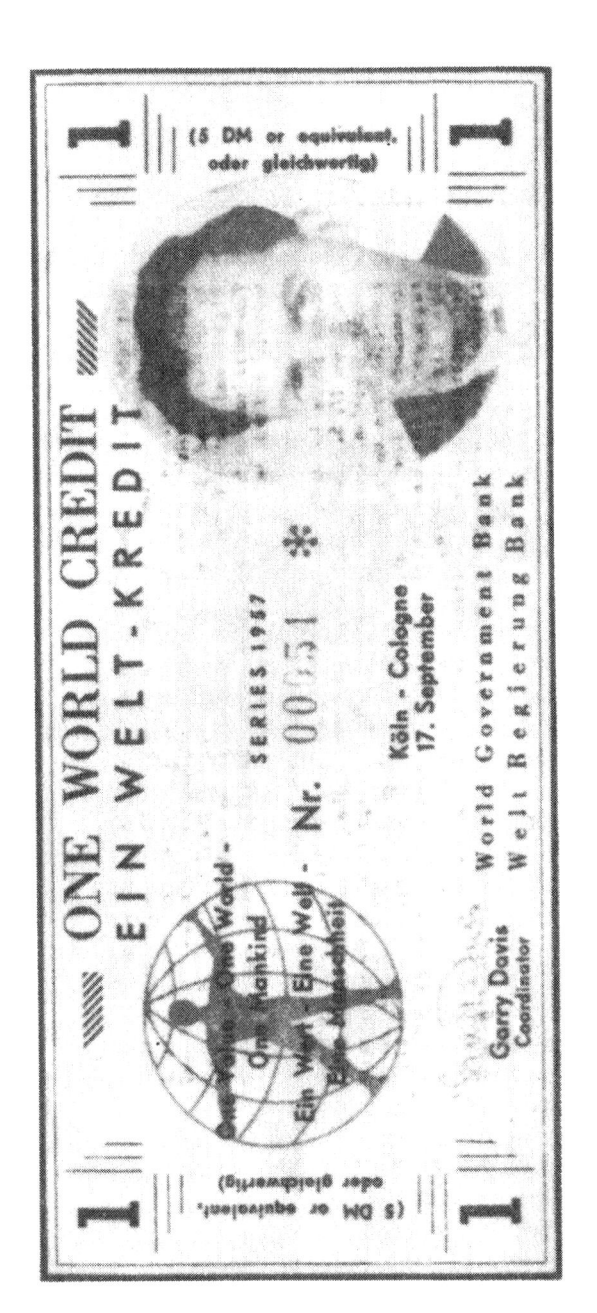

The World Credit.

NOTICE

This note is authorized for issuance publicly as world legal tender by WORLD GOVERNMENT according to World Authorization Order No. 2 of 17. September, 1957. Issuing agency, the World Government Bank, is a governmental fiscal division under the supervision of the WORLD SERVICE AUTHORITY. This note is sanctioned by Articles 2 and 23, Section 3 of the Universal Declaration of Human Rights and Section V, Part 2 of the Memorandum on World Government. Par value subject to revision without notice. Speculation and/or exploitation is unlawful and will be punishable by heavy penalty.

BEKANNTMACHUNG

Dieser Schein ist durch die WELT-REGIERUNG gemäß Welt-Ermächtigungs-Order Nr. 2 vom 17. September 1957 zur öffentlichen Ausgabe als Weltzahlungsmittel ermächtigt worden. Der Herausgeber, die Welt-Regierungs-Bank, ist die Regierungs-Finanzabteilung unter Aufsicht der WORLD SERVICE AUTHORITY. Dieser Schein ist sanktioniert durch die Artikel 2 und 23, Abschnitt 3, der Allgemeinen Erklärung der Menschenrechte und Abschnitt V, Artikel 2, des Memorandums über die Weltregierung.
Der augenblickliche Wert unterliegt einer Revision ohne vorherige Bekanntgabe. Spekulation und oder Ausbeutung ist ungesetzlich und unterliegt strenger Bestrafung.

The World Credit.

16

Toward the end of September, I decided to put aside for the present my efforts to get to Berlin. As it turned out I was putting them aside for good, but I wanted to visit Paris. Many things influenced this decision—among them an invitation from Camus and also the prospect of meeting my old friends in Paris, with many of whom I had been corresponding steadily. Finally, I felt a kind of sentimentality, I suppose, at the thought of returning to the city which had become my birthplace as a world citizen and which I had learned to love so dearly in the days just after the war.

I left Germany much as I had entered it, in a clandestine fashion. Using a Belgian identity card loaned to me by a friend, I registered at a small hotel in the Montparnasse section of Paris. There I was "safe", and for the first few days of my visit I enjoyed the perfectly lavish hospitality of my old friends, many of whom I greeted with tears in my eyes. Still, however, I was intensely uneasy about my illegal status in France. Then I had an inspiration.

Just at this time, France was in the midst of one of its governmental furors. The premiership of Bourgès-Maunoury hung on a vote of confidence regarding his controversial Algerian policy. It appeared as though there was about to be a shuffle in the government and this might mean that for a short space of time there would be no Minister of the Interior. It would be an opportune time for me to make my move, I thought.

I decided to commit a crime that would come under the civil code. Then I would make sure that I got caught. I would be arrested and charged with a violation of the civil code as a man before the law, and at the same time charged as a stateless person who had entered France illegally. In theory the two charges should cancel each other out, thus leaving me free to do as I pleased in Paris.

Having decided to follow this course, I was immediately faced with the problem of what crime to commit. Stealing seemed obvious. But what should I steal? Well, I mused, it ought to be small enough to fit in my pocket, or into a small bag. Also, the object must have no political significance whatsoever. Most important, however, it should be an object which, along with the theft itself, would attract the immediate attention of the Paris public. Experience had taught me the tremendous value of publicity. It ought to be, in short, a "gimmick", but a gimmick with a moral.

Walking slowly down Boulevard Montparnasse, pondering this matter, my gaze turned idly toward the shop windows I was passing. There were small firearms and ammunition—no good at all! Stationery, food, magazines, a bicycle, clothing, lingerie— I stopped, staring at the latest in female underpinnings. Lingerie! Of course. In Geneva, certainly watches might have been appropriate; in Venice, crystal glasses; and in Munich, beer steins. But for Paris, the perfect foil was certainly *lingerie!*

The next morning, with a small zippered bag in my hand, I walked confidently into the Galeries Lafayette, one of Paris's largest department stores. Lingerie was on the first floor. All the counters were surrounded by what appeared to be sharp-eyed women. Yet in half an hour my little zippered bag was heaped full of delicate ruffles, frilly laces, and filmy nylons. No one had tapped me on the shoulder. No one, to my knowledge, looked at me twice, least of all the busy salesgirls. I made more room in the bag and continued. After a bit, it became a challenge. Could I fill the bag? I wondered. Could I take a slip from a rack? Could I take a peignoir from a dummy? Could I be *selective?* I began to check prices, examine stitching, note quality and then steal only the very best and in the most straightforwardly brazen manner. Still, I could not seem to get myself caught, try as I might.

Looking as furtive as possible, I slunk out of the store by a back door and remained standing on the sidewalk in the hope that I would be arrested in the street. Nothing happened except that I got jostled to and fro by the pedestrian traffic. The sun shone; the bustling throngs hurried past. I was becoming quite provoked with Galeries Lafayette's security system.

Across the street was Le Printemps, a French five-cents-to-a-dollar store. I wandered in. Facing me was a nightgown counter, the merchandise wrapped in crinkly—and noisy—cellophane. *Bon!* Zipping down the side of my bag, I cast a glance around, noted the two salesgirls doing nothing near by, eased a cellophane wrapped nightie into my bag, got it stuck halfway in, gave it an impatient shove, zipped up the bag brusquely and walked along the counter nonchalantly, smiling at the salesgirls as I passed. Leaving the store I again stood on the corner watching the traffic go by.

"Monsieur?"

I turned at the voice. She was formidable all right, a determined, middle-aged woman built like a wrestler.

"May I see the sales slip for that article, please?" she said in French, pointing to my bag.

I made it! I thought to myself, but tried to play it straight, asking, "And who are you?"

"An inspector. Do not try to run as I have a companion watching us who will blow a whistle for the police if you make a move."

"I have made my move," I said smiling. "Now it is your turn."

She took a crushing hold on my arm and commanded: "Let us go."

We came to a small office just off the street. I handed the bag over to her and she in turn handed it to one of the men, who took it into an inner office. She motioned for me to follow him. He began emptying the contents. As each garment came out, he grew angrier. The inspectress looked upon me with pity. Several other women had come crowding in upon hearing the news. As the garments came into view in a seemingly never-ending stream, cries of "*Cochon!*" "*Salaud!*" and other expletives were directed at me. I sat wondering at this strange reaction. When however a young man came toward me, fists upraised, I thought to myself, there's more to national pride than saluting a flag and going to war! I could somehow visualize the staid Swiss undergoing the same emotional metamorphosis if Movados, Girard-Perrégauxs, Breitlings and other proud watches came clandestinely pouring out of a small zippered bag apprehended in Geneva.

"But why don't you call the police?" I pleaded.

The young man flashed a *sécurité publique* badge at me. "*Moi, je suis la police!*"

"Then please follow the law," I implored. Finally someone thought to call the local commissariat and within moments a policeman arrived. Shortly thereafter I was shown to a large cell where sat three disconsolate men. I took stock of my situation. Something was wrong. Though everything had gone according to plan, I sensed that I had neglected an important detail. Suddenly I knew. The statement! There was no press statement out. I started to sweat, fighting down an emotional panic. The news would be simply DAVIS STEALS LADIES' LINGERIE! I began to imagine what the world press would make of that! The over-all plan fled from my mind and I desperately wanted to escape from the whole thing.

"Mr. Davis, would you like something to eat?" asked the sergeant at the desk. I mumbled yes and handed him 300 francs. In a few moments he returned with a ham sandwich and a bottle of beer and told me I could eat in the main office. I came out numbly. He was alone, reading a paper. Someone called from inside. He got up and went inside. I was alone. Without thinking, I crossed rapidly to the door and bolted down the steps three at a time.

Halfway down the long block, I heard behind me, "*Il s'évade!*" but I rounded the corner, crossed the street, followed another side street, turned right at the end, entered a small gallery opposite Galeries Lafayette, and ran into the basement of the very store of my recent "crime" where I knew there was a subway. I bought a ticket and scurried breathlessly on to the first train to arrive. Transferring several times, I ended up at Neuilly. Now I've really botched it, I thought to myself, as I sat in a bistro over a coffee.

The next morning, I contacted my sister, then living in Paris. She volunteered to return to the police station to retrieve my trench coat and papers which had been taken from me there. When she arrived, however, she was told that only I could reclaim my possessions. No news either of the theft or of the arrest appeared in the papers or on the radio, and relieved by this, besides now having regained my composure and initial resolve, I decided to go through with the original plan.

The police were surprised to see me again, politely and confidently booked me for theft and ushered me into a cell for the night. The next morning I was taken to court.

"Now, Mr. Davis, do you know why you are here?" the Commissioner asked, looking over his papers.

"No, sir," I replied.

He looked up. "But you are a thief, sir! Do you not know it?"

"That depends, sir, on your definition," I said, searching for the right words.

"What? Definition? A thief is a thief and you have stolen ... let's see ... certain articles of clothing from some of our department stores. Do you deny it?"

"No, I don't deny it, and I expect to be charged as a thief. But in that case, what is my status in France?"

"Your status? You are a common thief."

"That I know, but if I have to suffer punishment from the law which says I'm a thief, I also ask protection from that same law."

"Protection? But you have protection. We protect you in prison, eh?"

"Well, is it not under the law for citizens that I am being prosecuted?"

"That is correct."

"Then according to this code, I must have the status of a citizen and if I have a legal status, I must have a *carte d'identité*, the right to work, travel freely——"

"*Mais non*, Monsieur Davis, you are a foreigner, and I note here that there is a charge against you for having entered France illegally."

I took a deep breath. "How is it that I can be a foreigner, charged as such for entering the country illegally, and at the same time considered as a person before the civil code, charged with a civil crime?"

He looked at me and opened his mouth. Nothing came out. He closed it, then opened it again. The clerk was looking at him with concern.

"But you are a thief," he said finally.

"Then am I also a foreigner?" I asked, feeling for the first time some confidence returning.

He sat back in his chair. "Mr. Davis, why do you bother us here in France? Why don't you go to Russia? We have done nothing to you."

"Yes, sir, indeed you have," I returned firmly. "You have committed a grave injustice against me. For seven years you have denied me the right of free entry into your country."

"Ah ha!" he exclaimed with a glint in his eye. "Now I believe

I understand your so-called theft. It is merely a pretext, is it not?"

"Of course. Did you really think I was a common thief?"

"Hmm. I had wondered about that," he mused. "Well now, Mr. Davis, if you were in my place, what would you do?"

I laughed. "Free me, naturally. If you prosecute one issue, you will have to drop the other. Frankly, my object here is to be as free in practice as I am in principle."

"We can take no time for your theories, Mr. Davis," he returned testily. "However, I can see no point in your coming to trial ... at least for this time. So I am freeing you ... provisionally, that is, in case we want to follow up your case. You may go."

I thanked him and as I turned to go out, he called after me, "Don't leave Paris. That's a court order."

The walking distance between court and the Bureau des Etrangers was a matter of three minutes. This monstrosity of a building, with its wooden corridors and partitioned offices, was by now extremely familiar to me. From here in 1948 I had received my first *refus de séjour*.

"You will wait in here, Mr. Davis," said the policeman leading me into a small room across from the "Chef de Bureau" office. After several hours, a brisk young man entered and escorted me to the same office from which my original *refus de séjour* was issued. A clerk was making out another, same name, same reason, new date.

"Now, Monsieur Davis, you have forty-eight hours to leave France."

"One moment," I said. "I was just ordered by the Commissioner to remain in Paris."

"Ah, but that is the department of justice; this is the department for foreigners. We have nothing to do with them!"

"But if I obey your orders, I'll disobey his," I protested. "On the other hand, if I obey his, I'm disobeying yours."

He shrugged as he handed me the paper. "If you return at the end of forty-eight hours, perhaps we can give you an extension of another forty-eight hours."

My theory had worked! Taking advantage of the duality of the state, I committed myself to two legal negatives in areas mutually exclusive, thus neutralizing them both. Unfortunately, however, because of my tactical blunder of not preparing a statement beforehand, I had unwittingly created an entirely false impression in the public mind and "scandalized" the world citizenship movement. Friends showed me press clippings from all of the Paris dailies as well as the *Herald Tribune* with such headlines as SURPRISED IN THE MIDST OF STEALING FEMININE LINGERIE IN A DEPARTMENT STORE, GARRY DAVIS ESCAPES; or in *Le Monde*, GARRY DAVIS, THE FIRST WORLD CITIZEN, IS ARRESTED IN PARIS FOR THEFT. The *Kölnische Rundschau* of Cologne quipped, NOW REALLY, MR. WORLD CITIZEN NO. 1: LINGERIE! And the Miami *Herald* told its readers: GLOBAL CITIZEN STEALS PANTIES.

At the headquarters of the International Registry of World Citizens on rue Lacépède, I issued a statement of clarification. Then, with money donated by an amused American in Paris, I hired a conference room in the swank Palais Royal near the Gare des Invalides for a press conference. But although I announced the conference through *Agence-France-Presse*, which flashed it out on teletype to all of the dailies, only three correspondents showed up. I knew enough by this time about the workings of the press to realize sadly that my answer would never really catch up with the scandal. He who lives by the press, I reflected despondently, must fall by the press. I was deeply gratified by the loyalty of two old friends, George Altman, editor of *Franc-Tireur*, who printed my full statement, and Edgar Gevaert, editor of *Parlement*, published in Belgium, who wrote, "One must be courageous to come before the view of the whole world as a mean thief, this only to serve the truth and the high weal of human unity which alone will save our generation."

But so far as the general public was concerned, at least for the moment, I remained a not-so-common pantie thief.

The next morning, I was awakened by a knock on my door at the Hôtel Quai Voltaire at seven o'clock.

"*Qui est-ce?*" I called out sleepily.

"*La police!*"

They told me I was wanted at headquarters. I hastily dressed and went with them. They bought me a coffee and croissant at the tiny station cafeteria while we waited for the offices to open. Finally I was issued an "Expulsion Arrest", an order to leave France in two days. Failure to do so would subject me to from six months' to three years' imprisonment.

With the bitter taste of defeat and humiliation in my mouth, I resolved not to fight the order. I decided to try Italy. The next day I had my things packed and boarded the Paris-Rome Express. Italian Customs, however, would not accept the World Passport, and I was put off the train, winding up, of all places, in Monte Carlo. There, friends helped me purchase a one-man inflatable rubber boat, complete with pump and two oars. Our plan was for me to embark just after midnight on a moonless night and row my way about three kilometres past the Italian frontier, land and then make my way up to the road where these friends would meet me with my luggage in a car.

According to plan I inflated the boat on the end of a narrow causeway and slipped out to sea just after the stroke of twelve. The water was calm and looked like black glass. I rowed silently but quickly, giving a wide berth to a rotating beacon light. Slowly I came opposite the French Custom house just beyond Menton about three hundred yards from my path across the dark water. The barely perceptible gurgle of the whirlpool caused by my oars was the only sound in the still night. I even tried to hush my breathing. In a half hour I was past the Italian post. I was in Italy! Technically, I was entering Italy not from France, but from the sea. There would be no proof that I had not rowed out three miles from the coast into international waters and then turned back into Italy. Nevertheless I was entering Italy illegally. I was breaking a national law by rowing over that political fiction so strenuously maintained, called a "frontier". But I was not concerned with such technicalities just now. First I had to contend with an altogether clifflike coastline.

I looked ahead and could dimly make out a promontory reaching down to the sea edge a quarter of a mile away. As I approached, the water became turbulent as it swirled around the jutting rocks. One tiny scratch in my "freedom boat" would deflate it, putting me in the drink. My clothes might pull me under and, what's more, I had heard that large hammerhead sharks came in close to these shores at night.

I proceeded cautiously, letting the breeze carry me toward shore and using my oars as an outrigger stabilizer. But suddenly a large wave swept over me, soaking me to the skin and swamping the small boat. I had no choice but to ditch. Luckily an underwater rock, slimy but flat, was beneath my foot. Another jutting rock formation was directly to my left. I managed to beach the boat on it. Then, with a small flashlight as guide, I made my way by a circuitous underwater rock path to the shore. There I deflated the boat, wrapped it up, stuffed it into its canvas bag and started up the gradual incline, the sodden boat wrapped like a giant sausage over one shoulder. The area was desolate and, as far as I could tell, unpatrolled. Coming at last to a path which ran parallel to the road high above, I took it in the direction of the frontier in the hope that another path would soon turn off to the road. As I made my way, the cliff to my right grew steeper. Eventually there was only the narrow path before me, a sheer drop of two hundred feet at my left, and an almost forty-five-degree shale slope stretching interminably up at my right. I squinted ahead. If I continued along the path, it might eventually bring me back to the Italian Custom house where I had absolutely no desire to be!

The boat was getting heavy on my shoulder. I looked down at my shoes. Fortunately I had had the foresight to buy a pair with corrugated rubber soles. Should I chance an ascent on that loose shale? I reached up and grabbed a small handful of grass which grew in patches through the shale. It was tough and wiry and, I thought, might hold my weight if my feet also had some support. Not wishing to retrace my steps in case I had been seen and was being followed, and not wanting to go farther back toward the frontier, I started slowly up the steep incline, seeking precarious hand and foot holds in the loose rock formations. Determined to hold on to my boat, which permitted me only one free hand, I inched and panted, digging my way up the tortuous route. Halfway up, I grabbed for a rock above me. It came loose in my hand. I started slipping, my hand digging frantically for a hold, a cold sweat breaking out on my face. I knew a fall would take me five hundred feet below into the Mediterranean. But my feet, slipping backward, breaking the loose shale so that it cascaded down in tiny avalanches to the rocks far below, somehow found a tiny niche which miraculously held me. I lay panting, trembling, my right hand bleeding and raw, my left still clutching the rubber boat down by my side. There is one consolation to all this, I thought to myself grimly: If I'm being followed, it's not by a governmental agent, but by a damn fool!

Slowly I crept on. After an eternity, I dimly perceived a light, directly ahead and slightly above me. I realized it was a road light. Only five yards to go! Gathering my last reserves of strength, I crunched forward and, reaching the road at last, sobbed out my relief and offered a humble prayer of thanks.

After allowing myself only a ten-minute rest, I hid the boat in the brush and started down the road toward the frontier, thinking I would go as close as possible in case my friends had parked along the road in that direction. I was late and the hour of our prearranged rendezvous had passed. I entertained little hope that we would make contact. Within sight of the Italian Customs post, I turned and walked the two kilometres back to the rubber boat, retrieved it and continued on to Ventimiglia, ten kilometres distant. I stopped to wash my muddy and bloodstained hands at a small moss-lined spring at the side of the road. The water was clear and refreshing—but I dared not linger and got up quickly to hurry on.

The road twisted and turned, the majestic Mediterranean, always serene and beautiful in the starlight, to my right. I would hitch a ride to San Remo, I thought to myself as I strode along, then take a train to Rome, and from there, with the help of friends maybe, go on to Naples or Capri. The lights of Ventimiglia loomed ever closer as I came on to a long, straight stretch of road just outside of town. Suddenly a car approached. Should I hide or let the headlights fall upon me? I wondered in a moment of panic. I was a disreputable sight and certainly a suspicious-looking customer, what with the front of my raincoat mud-smeared, my hair untidy, and a rubber boat slung over my shoulder at 2:30 in the morning. If this were a frontier patrol approaching, I was surely in trouble. On the other hand, suppose it was my friend?

The headlights bore down on me. I stood still, numb and rooted to the spot. The car roared past. There was a screech of brakes. I winced, then looked around. It was my friend! I rushed to the car, pulled open the door, and together we started laughing, shouting, slapping each other on the back, and exclaiming, "We made it! We made it! We made it!"

17

A curious sense of well-being pervaded me as I struck out for the delightful and picturesque Isle of Capri, where I planned to stay with friends for a rest.

On Sunday, January 17th, I had visited Vatican City, attending one of the rare public appearances given by Pope Pius XII. His Holiness was brought in on a thronelike chair carried by twelve men dressed in bright red velvet. Lining the aisles were the picturesque Swiss Guards, their pikes at attention. As His Holiness came down the aisle, the people on either side broke into applause and began to cry out "Papa! Papa!" their faces wreathed in smiles, many ecstatic, the nuns near me becoming almost hysterical. Everyone was waving his rosary frantically in the air, and Pius XII again and again made the sign of his blessing. I held up the World Passport as he passed, and His Holiness made the sign of the cross.

Now, as I headed south, my rebuffs in Germany, the blunder in France, the harrowing experience of crossing the Franco-Italian border, all seemed well behind me—a closed book, a nightmare from which I had been mercifully awakened when I landed. Possibly it was the exhilaration I felt on confronting Pius XII, a great humanitarian and a one-worlder in his own realm, or may be it was the sun-drenched Bay of Naples with the Isle of Capri resting like a precious jewel in its centre, which lived up to all of my expectations—but somehow, for the first time in many months, I was ebullient and filled with the joy of living.

I was soon to be awakened brutally to the fact that Capri's peaceful natural environment did not correspond, at least for me, with its legal environment. After registering at a local inn, I was summarily arrested by the authorities and taken to Naples for "questioning".

The questioning was conducted first by the Commissioner of Police in Naples and then by a court magistrate. I told both officials the whole truth—that I had come to Italy on January 15th from the sea in a small rubber boat, that I claimed asylum in Italy and that I wished to be left alone on Capri where I had been staying with friends.

In due course I was informed that I was to be sent to Frascati for "an indeterminate period".

"What is this 'Frascati'?" I asked my interpreter.

He shrugged. "A little camp not far from Rome. Do not worry. It is only temporary." Something in his attitude, an attempt at deliberate casualness perhaps, alarmed me.

At eleven o'clock that very night, accompanied by four officers, I was driven to the main Naples station where a milk train stood waiting. I had nothing with me but my toothbrush and toothpaste, not even a change of clothes. The five of us crowded into a tiny compartment and the train lurched forward, jerking to a stop at every tiny station along the route. Four and a half hours later we stepped off the train and I was turned over to several military-looking men dressed in the rough grey uniforms of the Interior Ministry. In the company of my new guards, I was driven away from the station along a highway toward Alatri. A few miles after passing this ancient town, we turned off the highway and followed a winding dirt road for about a mile until, in a small valley between towering mountains, I saw Frascati. I stared, unable to believe my eyes. It was a walled concentration camp!

There were armed soldiers everywhere. The car stopped and we got out.

"This way, Davis," one of the guards said, indicating a squat two-storied building just ahead. My mind was in a turmoil. Horror-stricken, I could only think of the ghastly purpose for which Hitler had designed such edifices. I looked at the hulking, twelve-foot-tall walls about to engulf me. There would be no escape from here. My mind flashed back to the moment I stood before Pope Pius XII in St. Peter's. "Papa, Papa," I murmured as the guards pushed me forward.

I became No. 9184.

Pierre M., a French collaborator with the Nazis during the war, had a bed next to mine on my first night in the camp hospital.

"The walls do not answer back," he said quietly after I had sat on my bunk for five minutes, staring vacantly into space.

Small-eyed, with a tiny black moustache, thinning grey hair, sunken cheeks, and a small, petulant mouth, Pierre introduced himself as a chemist by trade, specializing in perfumery. He gave me the "low-down" on Frascati. The camp enjoyed no legal status but was under the arbitrary rule of the greatly feared Signor Tambroni, the Minister of the Interior, who held the power of life or death over all inmates. A former concentration camp where Communists and enemy aliens had been detained during the war, Frascati was now used to harbour Italy's lost international riffraff to whom the authorities refused, for one reason or another, social integration. There were only two ways to leave Frascati, Pierre informed me: immigration to another country, which was impossible without papers, or marriage to an Italian citizen, which was highly unlikely for a denizen of a concentration camp.

"Our fingerprints are now on file with Interpol at Paris," Pierre told me. "If you should happen to escape, a general alarm goes out throughout Italy. You may succeed in escaping detection for weeks, months or even years, but sooner or later, especially without valid papers, or forged ones, you will come up against the police of one country or another. They will take your prints, send them to Interpol, and a cable will be returned immediately marking you as an escapee from Frascati. One poor fellow tried it four times. The last time he was brought back, he slashed his wrists. Some poor beggars have been here since the end of the war."

Two beds away from Pierre was a mountain of a man, with a thick black beard, black eyes and unruly hair. He introduced himself as Dr. T. from Geneva, the head of a Buddhist society in Switzerland. He was paralysed from the waist down. When I mentioned that I had recently been in south India and studied with a spiritual leader there, he told me that he was familiar with the teachings of the East and that he himself had a guru.

"The only guru he had," Pierre told me later, "was money. He was a petty munitions dealer during the war, buying up French cannons and selling them to the Germans. Finally, it became too hot for him even in Switzerland and now he is glad to be in Frascati."

I was given two blankets, two sheets, a pillow, a towel and a mattress from the warehouse outside the camp and told I could take any bed I found available in the big dormitory-like buildings. There were five of these structures each divided into two sections with about thirty beds in each, the toilet and washing facilities in a separate area. A sixth building contained about thirty private rooms and represented the "Park Avenue" of the camp. A seventh building contained a small library and a television room. The only heating facility was a pot-bellied stove in the centre of each barracks section, around which huddled the international pariahs for whom human rights, justice, freedom and equality were searing mockeries.

Gradually I learned who my fellow inmates were. There were many refugees from Communist countries including Russia, some of whom had been in Frascati for years with no chance of immigration further west; some petty criminals to whom the Italian authorities refused to give residence rights, preferring to consider them as undesirable aliens; a few deserters from both the French and Spanish Foreign Legions; a number of war veterans from Italian Somaliland who had fought with the Italians during the war but refused to go back to their native land and had, in turn, been refused citizenship in Italy; Albanians, Yugoslavs, Hungarians and Bulgarians who had escaped one Communist regime or another in the hope of finding freedom; and even one horn-rimmed-spectacled Communist who wanted me to write a letter to Khrushchev explaining my situation and asking asylum in the Soviet Union!

The second day I went to the tiny library, having been told there was a small selection of English books there. Imagine my surprise on finding a copy of Wendell Willkie's *One World*! My laughter might have cracked those solemn grey walls!

At around 9:00 P.M. on my third night at Frascati, as we grouped around the stove listening for the hundredth time to each other's miserable tales, I happened to mention my World Passport. Although the police at Naples had kept the original, I had several duplicate passports which I showed around. At once anxious questions assailed me.

How did one get them? Who issued them? How much did one cost? Were they recognized? By whom?

To men with no papers in a world where to be paperless is to be sub-human, a passport is as good as gold.

Their eagerness to have the passports was a welcome and yet a pathetic sight. It was an eagerness born of absolute desperation, a clutching at any straw. I realized at once that displaying my passports could have a cruel effect—like passing a sizzling steak under the nose of a starving man—and so I explained with great care all of the anguish the World Passport had caused me.

"So you see," I concluded, "the World Passport is no easy ticket to freedom. It is rather a pledge of allegiance to humanity and to a frontierless world one carries that may very well cause you more hardship and misery than you are suffering even now."

At this, most of the men around me got up and moved away —to bed or out into the yard to wander aimlessly, their eyes averting the ugly walls of the camp where hope died each night. But a few of my listeners were kindled with excitement. They pleaded with me for the passports in my hand. I looked at them. There was one for each. I could not resist these eyes which had seen so much. Silently, I handed out the World Passports, got up and went to bed.

Word of my issuing the World Passports must have reached the concentration camp authorities and caused concern. For, on the seventh day of my imprisonment, I was informed that I would be released to the care of my friends back on the Isle of Capri. I was elated! Until this time I had practically become resigned to spending the rest of my days in Frascati. Oddly enough, I was told that I was being released not for good but only for a period of twenty days. Presumably, the authorities in Rome were hoping—perhaps, after the passport incident, praying—that I would seize this opportunity to "escape" Italy and trouble them no longer. This strategy was pretty good, I had to admit. Who in his right mind, once let out of Frascati, would wait around idly to be reinterned!

But I fooled them. Twenty days later, I presented myself to the Naples police and asked to be returned to this international cesspool. The police looked at me with astonishment, but could not turn me down. I was under orders.

"Am I out of my mind?" I asked myself as the milk train jerked along toward Alatri. Perhaps—was the answer. And yet I knew in the depth of my soul that I would never be able to face myself again, that I would shudder every time I saw one of those posters asking for clothes for refugees, and that I would somehow compromise whatever freedom I might ever achieve for myself, if I did not go back to that pitiful junkpile of humanity and finish the work I had started.

The next morning, back in my now-familiar barracks, I pulled a table beside my bunk and set up the "Frascati World Passport Issuing Office". I had a good supply of blank documents with me and had sent back to the States for my dry seal for affixing photographs.

The following days at *Il Campo Refuggio* stamped in my mind one of the indelible memories of my adventures as a world citizen. The mixture of fear and hope on the faces of the inmates as they received their passports was unforgettable. Frascati became more than a miserable concentration camp for me, indeed for all of us. If I and my fellow refugees had been rejected by nations, here together we found a common vitality, hope, born of a common anguish and the dawn of a new reality. Living in Frascati—sealed off from the outside world as in a tomb—it was as if we were the sole survivors of World War II starting out afresh. Here was a true microcosm of a world community, even if warped and disfigured. Here, as preposterous insults to the nationalist myth, we humans lived together, talked and laughed together, we former Russians, former Americans, former French, Swiss, Germans, Ethiopians, Spanish, Albanians and Croats. Here brotherhood was real, immediate and obvious.

Having issued some fifty World Passports to the inmates of Frascati, I decided that it was time for me to move on. Of course, leaving a concentration camp was not merely a matter of tipping the bellboy and checking out. It was not quite that simple. One had to escape.

It set me to thinking: there were those huge, forbidding walls; the men in the grey uniforms with their high-calibre rifles; maybe even bloodhounds and only the Lord knew what else. But I had gotten out once before and I felt strangely confident that I could do it again.

One of the guards had come to me when I was alone and asked for a World Passport. He was young with good eyes. I issued him one and said nothing. Now I approached him. Would he help me? Yes! Over a period of three days he smuggled my belongings, piece by piece, out of the camp and left them at a restaurant in Alatri. Then, late one evening when he was on duty at the gate, he allowed me to slip by and glide into the dark, nonchalantly distracting the other guards. By eight o'clock the next morning, I stumbled my way into Alatri. There I picked up my luggage—a suitcase, typewriter and large briefcase—skirted the main square where the Frascati guards usually loitered on their time off, and struck out for the main road to Frosinone where I caught a bus to Rome.

Two and a half hours later, I was entering the Eternal City and reflecting that here was once the seat of Caesar's "world government".

From the bus station I made my way to fashionable Via Vittorio Veneto where the present United States Embassy is housed.

At approximately 11:30 A.M., March 25th, I "left" Italy. A second later, by stepping into the Embassy, I "entered" the sovereign territory of the mythical United States of America. But my asylum was short-lived. I asked that the Consul prepare papers for me for a return to the U.S.A. Impossible. I would have to make such a request at the Consulate General's office in Naples.

By this time I was sure that the alarm had gone out from Frascati, so, rather than risk hitch-hiking to Naples along the highway where I might be spotted by a patrol car, I spent some of my last lira on bus fare. As soon as I arrived in Naples—now wearing dark glasses and with my beret far down over my face—I repaired to the U.S. Consul and asked the young officer in charge, William Bradford, to prepare my papers. He said he would be glad to oblige, but that it would take a few days.

Fine kettle of spaghetti, I thought to myself as I walked out of the office, and a fine kettle of spaghetti it turned out to be. Two days later I was arrested by a policeman saying, "I know you. You have escaped from Frascati! You will go back for good now!"

The Commissioner at Naples was determined to return me to the camp immediately.

"Please get Mr. Bradford of the U.S. Consulate General's office on the phone," I asked. "He will assume responsibility for me." Young Mr. Bradford came over immediately and assured the Commissioner that I had indeed requested papers to enter the U.S.A. I was needed in Naples, he said, for a medical examination, mental test, signature, and other details of my application.

"I cannot take the responsibility," the Commissioner replied emphatically. "Rome wants him back at Frascati pronto." He waved a telegram in the air.

"I refuse to return," I said. "I will resist. I shouldn't have been there in the first place."

Bradford looked from the Commissioner to me. "Under what conditions will you allow Mr. Davis to remain in Naples?" he asked.

The Commissioner thought for a moment. "All right," he said, "Mr. Davis must report here twice a day, morning and night. Also, no statements to the press. Those are my conditions. Oh, and we will choose the *pensione* where he will stay."

I looked at Bradford. He fidgeted. "Better go along."

I accepted the conditions.

"Do you guarantee his word?" the police chief asked Bradford.

"Of course," Bradford snapped.

Naples was beautiful under the morning sun as I made my way along the sea front to the Consulate General's office after reporting to the police the next morning. There I was directed to a small room to fill out the standard visa application form for immigrants.

"What's this?" I asked the clerk.

"Immigration form," he replied matter-of-factly. "That's what they told me to give you, Mr. Davis."

Directly after the word *Name* was a blank for *Home Address*. Here I entered: 101 *Central Park West, New York* 20, *New York*, my last address in the States, not realizing what consternation this would cause later on. Then I proceeded to fill out the rest of the complicated form—which required among other things information on whether the applicant is insane, epileptic, or intends to practise prostitution in the United States, and finally, a statement that the applicant does not believe in overthrowing the Government by violence, which meant, as far as I could tell, that the applicant denounced the United States Declaration of Independence as Communist-inspired and went on record as calling George Washington, Tom Paine and Thomas Jefferson traitors. I signed and handed the form to the clerk. He glanced through it briefly, nodded with satisfaction, and was about to file it when suddenly his glance fixed on the top of the form.

"Uh, Mr. Davis, your home address . . ."

"Yes?"

"Well . . . er . . . you have here '101 Central Park West, New York 20, New York.' "

"Yes, that's right."

"But . . . this is an immigrant application."

"Yes?"

"Well, you understand of course you can't immigrate to your own home. I mean it just doesn't make sense."

"I didn't ask to immigrate," I told him. "I simply asked for the proper papers to return to the United States. My home address happens to be 101 Central Park West, New York 20, New York. You don't want me to make a false statement, do you?"

"Oh no. No, of course not. But I don't see how you can immigrate to your own home." He scratched his head.

Here, I saw at once, was a new wrinkle. According to Webster's Dictionary, "to immigrate" means "to come into a country of which one is not a native, for permanent residence". Should I be issued a visa on the basis of the information contained on that application form, I reasoned, the State Department would be in effect denying the fact that I was born in the United States. On the other hand, if the State Department refused me an immigrant's visa on the basis that my native home was indeed the United States, I could not be prevented from re-entering my homeland, papers or no papers.

The clerk was still puzzling this as I rose quietly to leave. It was a paradox created by the State Department and, I decided, one which I would leave in their—in this case unwilling—hands. As one might expect, the matter was never resolved.

Nevertheless, by April 12th, all was in readiness. The cabled confirmation from Immigration had come through, my steamship ticket had been bought, my bags packed. I was about to become the first native immigrant in the history of the United States.

The police arrived bright and early April 12th, the morning of the sailing, and "escorted" me to the pier. The Commissioner of Naples himself was on hand to bid me *bon voyage* . . . and to make certain no doubt that the boat and I sailed on schedule.

As I approached the gangplank, followed by the Commissioner and his "honour guard", I dug into my pocket for my World Guard Badge and flashed it at the two officers standing guard on either side as I strode by. They came to attention and saluted smartly.

18

Once aboard ship, I was relieved of my obligations to the Police Commissioner and could finally meet the press. The Fourth Estate was present in full regalia, pencils poised, newsreel and TV cameras focused, teletype and cable wires open and ready. On the upper sun deck of the S.S. *Constitution*, I read aloud my final statement:

> Out of respect for the opinions of the public and in the interests of general understanding, I want to issue this final communiqué as the *symbolic* "First World Citizen".
>
> For ten years as of May 25th, I will have personally served the ideal of one world before the bar of world opinion, sometimes fitfully, sometimes confidently, but always, I believe, honestly and with good will. Though there is much of a practical nature still to be accomplished, yet the seeds of world unity are well sown and many buds promising rich fruit are sprouting in our community of which national leaders are becoming increasingly aware.
>
> Nine years after my original declaration, I have the happy satisfaction of witnessing the advent of the Space Age where man-made satellites are forcing practical reconsideration of the concept of absolute national sovereignty. Such reconsiderations inevitably lead men of reason and good will to the united world whose path I have helped to light during these years.
>
> With these considerations in mind, there is vital need now for wise and practical leadership, and the symbols, useful up to a point, must now give way to the men qualified for such leadership. As simply one individual conscious of the totality of war and the fundamental interdependency of the world community, I have tried to apply universal and unitive principles directly in actual worldly circumstances facing me personally, outside the national framework.
>
> The results I have observed, both in myself and in the world community in which I worked, allow me to conclude with ten years of empirical proof that the ordinary human being, naturally endowed with wisdom and conscience, is entirely willing and capable of accepting responsibilities and operating on the world level, that is, to be a law-abiding citizen of the world as well as a national and local

citizen. Based on natural and civic rights and duties, such a citizenship relates one's normal inclinations to peace and co-operativeness with one's fellow man as his national citizenship does not and cannot.

In short, I have, at least to my own complete satisfaction, "proven" that a world legality grounded in reasoned freedom and justice is both theoretically and actually feasible from the individual's viewpoint.

I feel my task, therefore, as the *symbolic* "First World Citizen" is finished, other than the final recording of it. I wish to make clear that my original renunciation of nationality was in no way an act of disloyalty to or disaffection for America. On the contrary, I consider my espousal of the one-world cause the highest act of loyalty I could perform both as an American and as a conscientious human being. In its negative aspects, my gesture was a personal protest to the exclusiveness of the *institution* of nationalism itself, which encloses all countries today and which has been, in fact, rendered obsolete by actual world conditions.

Further evidence of this loyalty is that I have never sought citizenship in any other country and have suffered imprisonment many times due to my stateless circumstances. Further, I have never been associated with any exclusive ideology or organization except by its opposition to my open one-world stand. As a testament to my personal disinterest, I have, as a matter of principle, refused all moneys, profits, and material benefits resulting from my activities, investing all income, sometimes at great personal sacrifice, into the work itself.

To my many friends and supporters throughout the world, I extend my heartfelt thanks for their generous help, both moral and physical, throughout these years. Without them, my task could not have been accomplished. To my spiritual preceptors and guides, both in India and America, I offer my humble gratitude; to the many world citizenship and world government organizations born during my representations, I bequeath the results of my experiments and all profits therefrom to be used to continue the humanitarian work begun; to the great world press and photographic service, I pay my grateful respects.

Finally to the world public, whose spokesmen are daily growing in power and numbers, I say this: "The real sovereign on this our planet earth is we, the human race. In us as a whole all power ultimately resides. No dictator, no tyrant, no untruth can stand for long against us in our unity, for in that unity are embodied the principles of brotherhood and understanding; but any dictator, any tyrant, any untruth finds an easy prey when we, in these basic principles, divide ourselves."

The great blast of the ship's horn sounded at precisely twelve o'clock noon. Then the rumble of the giant engines commenced and slowly, inching along at first, the ship began to move. When we had cleared the bay, I reached into my bag for my treasured copy of Thomas Paine's *The Rights of Man*, left my cabin and climbed up to the top deck and the open sky. The cool, clear air greeted my lungs refreshingly. Looking out at the gracefully dipping sea gulls following our wake, the propellers churning a great white swath for a quarter mile behind us, the sun high in the heavens, the wind fresh and the day full of promise, I opened *The Rights of Man*, and as we steamed westward my eyes fell upon the words: *Independence is my happiness and I view things as they are, without regard to place or person; my country is the world.* . . .

APPENDIX

The purpose of the material in this Appendix is to illustrate with actual documents some of the events and decisions described in *My Country is the World*. The selection does not pretend to be a definitive documentary history of my involvement in these years. The exchange of letters with Dr. Evatt, for instance, illustrates the first official U.N. recognition of the world citizenship movement. The July 24, 1949, press statement may offer some insight into why, at the time, I felt it necessary to leave the International Registry of World Citizens. These are merely documents of some of the events which were important to me and to what I was doing.

Oath of Renunciation

I hereby swear that I desire to make a formal renunciation of my American nationality, and pursuant thereto hereby absolutely and entirely renounce my nationality in the United States and all rights and privileges thereunto and abjure all allegiance and fidelity to the United States of America.

Statement of Renunciation (May 25, 1948)

In the absence of an international government, our world, politically, is now a naked anarchy. Two global wars have shown that as long as two or more powerful sovereign nation-states regard their own national law as supreme and sufficient to handle affairs between nations, there can be no order on a planetary level. This international anarchy is moving swiftly toward a final war.

I no longer find it compatible with my inner convictions to contribute to this anarchy, and thus be a party to the inevitable annihilation of our civilization, by remaining solely loyal to one of these sovereign nation-states.

I must extend the little sovereignty I possess, as a member of the world community, to the whole community, and to the international vacuum of its government—a vacuum into which the rest of the world must be drawn if it is to survive, for therein lies the only alternative to this final war.

I should like to consider myself a citizen of the world.

Oran Declaration (November 22, 1948)

Mr. Chairman and Delegates:

I interrupt you in the name of the people of the world not represented here. Though my words may be unheeded, our common need for world law and order can no longer be disregarded.

We, the people, want the peace which only a world government can give.

The sovereign states you represent divide us and lead us to the abyss of Total War.

I call upon you no longer to deceive us by this illusion of political authority.

I call upon you to convene forthwith a World Constituent Assembly to raise the standard around which all men can gather, the standard of true peace, of One Government for One World.

And if you fail us in this . . . stand aside, for a People's World Assembly will arise from our own ranks to create such a government.

We can be served by nothing less.

Letter to Dr. Evatt (November 23, 1948)

HOTEL DES ETATS-UNIS
135 BLVD. MONTPARNASSE
PARIS 6ME, FRANCE

RT. HON. H. V. EVATT
PRESIDENT OF THE THIRD GENERAL ASSEMBLY
UNITED NATIONS
PALAIS DE CHAILLOT
PARIS 16E, FRANCE

DEAR DR. EVATT:

May I explain my motives in interrupting the proceedings of the General Assembly last Friday? I must apologise, sir, not for the substance of my plea for a world constitutional convention, but for the manner in which I was obliged to present it. Although it was irregular, and likely to be called the work of an "exhibitionist" or "crackpot", I was firmly convinced that a dramatic appeal for world government as a route to lasting peace had to be made. Our world of troubled half-peace—the world of atom bombs, the Berlin impasse, of starving children and homeless men and women, of unreconstructed ruins and uncontrolled inflation, of the Great Arms Race and cold and lukewarm wars—is fast moving toward the nightmare of Total War III.

I shall continue to work for the calling of a revisional conference under the provisions of Article 109 of the Charter, with the hope of getting at least a limited world federal government through the orderly processes of the United Nations. Failing the achievement of this end, I shall join many others in working for the calling of an unofficial but heavily mandated People's Constitutional Assembly which will take an initiative which is not without precedent in history, although it has never been tried on a continental or world scale. The history of the forming of the American and Australian federal systems provides interesting evidence in support of the quasi-legal and extra-diplomatic roads toward governmental changes not achievable through conventional political means. (I naturally am not pointing up any exact parallels, but many of us believe that such an eventuality as an unofficial constitutional convention could succeed even in the face of strong and mature national sovereignties if the demand from the people is overwhelmingly manifest.)

You yourself have expressed concern over the structural weaknesses of the U.N., as have many other leaders today. In my opinion the problem is so complex, and the changes so revolutionary, that our statesmen will not sincerely begin to try to effect a transferal of national sovereignty to a world authority until the demand from the people for this action is deafening, and can no longer be ignored. Whether or not I am a fanatic, Dr. Evatt, is for you to judge, but in the light of present-day headlines (WESTERN DEFENCE LINE WILL BE ALONG THE RHINE . . . PLANS FOR "M-DAY" IN THE U.S. . . . THREE HUNDRED RUSSIAN SUBMARINES, etc.) is my action so strange? We have fought as individuals; we shall die as individuals. May we not speak out positively for peace as individuals?

Please accept my assurance, your Excellency, that my future plans include no more "out-of-order" demonstrations within the chambers of the U.N. But I shall continue to do my level best to mobilize public opinion everywhere else so that our statesmen may see that the people want them to take the "calculated risk" of world federal government. We must end anarchy among nations before it is too late.

This letter, sir, is not intended as a publicity release, and I shall not issue it to the press. It is sincerely directed to you, to explain my position. Although my statement (Friday) was reported in the French press with little distortion, the *Daily Mail* (Continental Edition) published a completely fabricated account of what I said, apparently intended to make me out a Communist. I should like to mention, moreover, that the number of my friends and supporters in the audience Friday numbered exactly twenty-four, and even *they* were not instructed to act as a "claque". The audible support which astonished me as much as anyone else, was honestly spontaneous.

With the warmest personal regard for your own courageous efforts toward peace in the face of almost impossible obstacles, I remain, sir,

Yours sincerely,
GARRY DAVIS

Dr. Evatt's Reply

UNITED NATIONS
LAKE SUCCESS, N.Y.
Office of the President of the General Assembly

NATIONS UNIS

PARIS, 24TH NOVEMBER, 1948

DEAR MR. DAVIS:

I am much obliged to you for your letter of yesterday referring to the interruption of the proceedings of the General Assembly on Friday last.

I thank you for your explanations and at once accept your assurances as to your motives and objects.

I am extremely interested in your comments on the Charter of the United Nations, and any written communication that you care to address to me elaborating your opinions I shall certainly communicate to all the delegates of the Assembly.

Finally, I should like to thank you for your reference to my own work, and I hope that on some occasion you will pay a call upon the Secretary-General and myself.

Yours sincerely,
H. V. EVATT
President of the General Assembly

MR. GARRY DAVIS
HOTEL DES ETATS-UNIS
135 BLVD. MONTPARNASSE

Telegram of Greeting from Albert Einstein to the Meeting at the Salle Pleyel, Paris (December 3, 1948)

I AM EAGER TO EXPRESS TO THE YOUNG WAR VETERAN DAVIS MY RECOGNITION OF THE SACRIFICE HE HAS MADE FOR THE WELL-BEING OF HUMANITY. IN VOLUNTARILY GIVING UP HIS CITIZENSHIP-RIGHTS HE HAS MADE OUT OF HIMSELF A "DISPLACED PERSON" IN ORDER TO FIGHT FOR THE NATURAL RIGHTS OF THOSE WHO ARE THE MUTE EVIDENCES OF THE LOW MORAL LEVEL OF OUR TIME. THE WORST KIND OF SLAVERY WHICH BURDENS THE PEOPLE OF OUR TIME IS THE MILITARIZATION OF THE PEOPLE, BUT THIS MILITARIZATION RESULTS FROM THE FEAR OF NEW MASS-DESTRUCTION IN THREATENING WORLD-WAR. THE WELL-INTENDED EFFORT TO MASTER THIS SITUATION BY THE CREATION OF THE UNITED NATIONS HAS SHOWN ITSELF REGRETTABLY INSUFFICIENT. A SUPRA-NATIONAL INSTITUTION MUST HAVE ENOUGH POWERS AND INDEPENDENCE IF IT SHALL BE ABLE TO SOLVE THE PROBLEMS OF INTERNATIONAL SECURITY. NEITHER CAN ONE NOR HAS ONE THE RIGHT TO LEAVE THE TAKING OF SUCH A DECISIVE STEP ENTIRELY TO THE INITIATIVE OF THE GOVERNMENTS.

ONLY THE UNBENDABLE WILL OF THE PEOPLE CAN FREE THE FORCES WHICH ARE NECESSARY FOR SUCH A RADICAL BREAK WITH THE OLD AND OUTLIVED TRADITIONS IN POLITICS. I GREET THIS ASSEMBLY AS A SERIOUS EFFORT TO SERVE A MOST IMPORTANT MISSION OF OUR GENERATION.

A. EINSTEIN

Statement to the Press, by Garry Davis (July 24, 1949)

In a letter to Robert Sarrazac, Secretary General of the International Registry of World Citizens, I attempted to explain as simply and honestly as I could the reasons why, after a year and two months of activity, I now find it necessary to enter a period of study and meditation. I feel that for me personally a phase of activity is over which might be considered the birth of world citizenship. The next phase will be more exacting and demand a higher degree of wisdom and moral courage than I have hitherto displayed. I shall now prepare for this phase.

I consider the work of world citizenship too important in our world of cynicism and easy disillusionment to be mishandled, and therefore deceived, by one not fully conscious of its responsibilities. I feel, by recognizing the need for this period of study and meditation, that I am just beginning to realize these responsibilities. When I first started working for world peace, I had unbounded optimism, but confess I was naïve to the point of childishness. This was apparent to everyone but me. My optimism is still great but it is now grounded on concrete observations, rather than on impractical dreams.

The task is of course longer than I first thought. It is a mountain to be climbed, not a foothill. Had I known this before I started, no doubt I should have prepared myself more adequately. However, the first ledge has been reached. World Citizenship has spread to the far corners of the earth. I confess in all sincerity this first ascent for me was often difficult. I was in a strange country. The language barrier was immense. The rôle was new. And I was to a large degree mentally and morally unprepared. But on the whole I must say the results were extremely gratifying and have increased my faith enormously that world peace is not only possible but is nearer than most of us think. Two main facts substantiate this viewpoint: first, the rapidity with which the idea of world citizenship and news in general is spread throughout the world; and secondly, the receptiveness of people everywhere to a proposal for a better world.

So now that the first ledge is reached, I find that personally I must stop, and make further and more careful survey so as to choose the best path for the next ascent. This is in no way abandoning the climb. Rather it is recognizing its exacting requirements and preparing for them. The summit is there to be reached. But it will be reached only by careful planning, resolute determination, and moral fortitude.

I have not given a time limit to this period of study and meditation, for at present I have no way of knowing at what moment I shall be ready to resume the steep climb. But because I do feel the weight of responsibility and the pressure of time, I should presume that a period of two to three months should suffice.

I have often said, and I hereby say again, that it is not my intention to head a movement, or to become a president of an organization. In all honesty and sincerity, I must define the limit of my abilities as being a witness to the principle of world unity, defending to the limit of my ability the Oneness of man and his immense possibilities on our planet Earth, and fighting the fears and hatreds created artificially to perpetuate narrow and obsolete divisions which lead and have always led to armed conflict.

I need hardly mention that I have no monopoly on world citizenship. It is each man's to claim. And during my absence the International and National Registries will function, receiving registrations and sending out the World Citizens card. Despite military pacts of Great Powers, despite sincere but futile attempts of the world's collected diplomats to deal with our problems of peace and food, despite the unrest, the misery, the starvation of huge masses of people, indications that we are witnessing the dawn of world civilization are unmistakable. Tiring of stupidity and oppression, men in the mass are not-so-slowly finding their unity. But until enough of us declare ourselves above the fear of our petty differences and recognize the common ground on which all men stand, thereby creating a common authority to attend our needs, my task will not be over and I shall not be able to return to the life and work which I personally desire.

I am a Government.
(Excerpts from a speech delivered by Garry Davis at the City Hall, Ellsworth, Maine, Sept. 4, 1953)

... Here in this City Hall of Ellsworth, Maine, in the sovereign United States of America, I, a world citizen, exist in a world anarchy.

... By the authority vested in me as a world sovereign, it is my duty and my responsibility to myself and to my humanity to hereby proclaim for myself a World Government with full legal powers and prerogatives based on the 3 Prime Laws of one God, One World, and One Mankind. This government for the moment exists only in my person, but since all men are world citizens with full world sovereignty based on a full recognition of the 3 Prime Laws if they but affirm them, the proclamation of world government is everyman's right, privilege, and responsibility.

... A world government is here born and if there be wiser and better men, let them come forward, challenged by its obvious failings and helplessness ... Let the spiritual leaders and Gurus, the World Teachers, come from their ashrams, their meditative retreats and monastic centres in this grave hour of our common need, and give us their moral council and guidance. Let them breathe into this newly born government... the spiritual substance it must have if it is to prosper and serve men wisely.

... To solve the problem of managing our common (world community) for the mutual benefit of all, the most able scientists, technicians, managers, and administrators must come forward to give us their services.

... One for all and all for one must be the prime basis of a World Citizen's economy.

... The World Government here proclaimed and open to all, will undertake to initiate ... a World Citizen's Corporation as its proper corollary on the physical or economic level of human activity.

... Then we call to the common citizenry from which we have come, to our brothers in the world community. We call them in all corners of the globe, in every market-place, in every secluded retreat, and from all walks of life. We call to the reason and conscience which we know to be a part of each man. In the name of Humanity of which he is an integral and valuable unit, we ask him to identify himself, not only as a citizen of his own hearth, his local community, his region, and his nation, but also as a citizen of the entire world as his natural and fundamental right as well as duty.

... And in Humanity's name ... I, a World Sovereign, hereby claim the territory of the entire earth as the proper home and the rightful possession of all mankind. As an actual symbol of that ownership, and for the now existent World Government, I here claim in the soil of my birth, the dot of land on which I now stand, as World Territory. Let it be henceforth known as World Citizen's Point, and marked only as 68° 25' 30" Longitude, 44° 32' 30" Latitude.

Let all World Citizens accept this point as the territorial symbol of the highest allegiance, whereas this World Citizen claims it as the only legal territory within the continental limits of the United States whereon he can reside.

... As a world sovereign, existing only legally in a worldly sense, I am able to give this point a legal existence in a worldly sense based on the three Prime Laws of Mankind. So be it. Now every national citizen throughout the world is able to make a valid extension of his loyalty to the world community through his legal world territory without at the same time renouncing any humanitarian local or national responsibilities which are a part of the Whole.

... At this moment, this is the only neutral but inclusive government in existence. It has no foreign policy, no political parties, indeed no politics even, no army, navy or air force ... Its door is open to all and will be closed to none.

... The completing of mankind, so long talked-about by philosophers and spiritual leaders, so long dreamed of by the persecuted down the ages, is at hand. It is started here tonight. A World Government exists ... if only in one common man and having but one dot of territory. No longer need we collectively hesitate. No longer need we argue about the principle, or about how long it will take, or whether the neighbour will come in. This neighbour *is* in, and it but remains for everyone to recognize and apply his own in-ness, or oneness.

... The main job is over, that of completing the microcosm. Each microcosm completed brings the macrocosm that much nearer completion ... This work is unprecedented in these modern terms. Thus we are all youths in this task. But experience can only be gained by living our goal from the outset, by *being* members of the world community. And if we stumble, falter, even fall, there are others to carry on, for the reality of Man's unity is a truth that cannot die.

I am a world sovereign ... a forefather of the Human Race. Its government is here proclaimed.

Brothers and sisters, fellow World Citizens, join me in this glorious destiny.

SEPTEMBER 15, 1956

TO THE AMBASSADORS AND/OR REPRESENTATIVES OF STATES
ALL EMBASSIES AND/OR CONSULATES, NEW DELHI
TO THE PRIME MINISTER OF INDIA, NEW DELHI

YOUR EXCELLENCY:

This is to advise your Government that as of 5th October, 1956, World Government, founded 4th September, 1953, at Ellsworth, Me., U.S.A., will be declared *de juris*.

From that date all human beings will be represented as World Citizens by World Government according to the principles of *jus soli* and *jus sanguinis* which prescribe the legal bases for one world and one human race, two of the three unitive principles of foundation of World Government, the third being One Absolute Value (Truth, God, Ideal, etc.).

From that date also, due to the termination of the "Alien" status temporarily imposed on us personally under the Indian Foreigners' Act, we shall be represented legally only by World Government, our status as a Sovereign Citizen of the World allowing us thereby to represent legitimately the General Good and the Good of all.

From the 5th October, 1956, therefore, as a Sovereign World Citizen and founder-head of World Government, we invite official representation from your national Government. Your Government will be informed on 4th October as to the precise location of our temporary sovereign headquarters in New Delhi.

Given under our hand and seal
In the name of humanity,
(*Signed*) GARRY DAVIS

Pledge of Allegiance

I, the undersigned, do hereby, willingly and consciously, declare myself to be a Citizen of the World. As a World Citizen, I pledge my prime and sovereign allegiance to the World Government, founded on the three unitive principles of One Absolute Value, One World, and One Mankind which constitute the basis of Common World Law. As a World Citizen I acknowledge my world government as having the right and duty to represent me in all that concerns the General Good and the Good of All.

As a Citizen of World Government, I affirm my awareness of my inherent responsibilities and rights as a member of the total world community of all men, women, and children, and will endeavour to fulfil and practise these whenever and wherever the opportunity presents itself.

As a Citizen of World Government, I recognize and reaffirm citizenship loyalties and responsibilities within the communal, state, and/or national groupings consistent with the principles of unity above which constitute now my prime and sovereign allegiance.

Made in the USA
San Bernardino, CA
06 December 2016